Managing Performance

MANAGING PERFORMANCE

A Comprehensive Guide
to Effective Supervision

Marion E. Haynes

Lifetime Learning Publications
Belmont, California
A division of Wadsworth, Inc.

London, Singapore, Sydney, Toronto, Mexico City

Designer: Nancy Benedict
Copy Editor: Rich Osborne
Illustrator: John Foster
Composition: Bi-Comp, Inc.

Printed in the United States of America

1 2 3 4 5 6 7 8 9 10—86 85 84 83

Library of Congress Cataloging in Publication Data

Haynes, Marion E.
  Managing performance.

  Bibliography: p.
  Includes index.
    1. Supervision of employees.   2. Perfor-
mance.
I. Title.
HF5549.H3669   1983   658.3'02
83-17527
ISBN 0-534-02723-7

This book is dedicated to my brothers
Mel, Ray, Les, and Ken.

Contents

Preface

This book will help you become a better supervisor. As a result of reading it you will know both what to do and how to do it in order to be successful. As you proceed through the book responding to the exercises, completing the questionnaires, and studying the examples, the full scope of a supervisor's job will become clear to you. Checklists are provided throughout to serve as quick references and reminders for you after you complete your study of each chapter; you will find them particularly helpful as you face the daily challenge of supervision.

You will find very little theory in this book. Instead, you will discover practical, detailed guidance on how to plan, organize, lead, and control the performance of your work group. Chapter 1 seeks to analyze where you are as a supervisor in terms of leadership style. Chapter 2 shows you how to become acquainted with the members of your group so that you may fully utilize their abilities, skills, and interests. The next nine chapters show you how to handle the following critical steps in successfully managing performance:

- Developing Performance Expectations
- Monitoring Performance Progress
- Evaluating Individual Performance
- Providing Feedback on Performance
- Making Administrative Decisions
- Developing Performance Improvement Plans

- Delegating Responsibility and Authority
- Managing Performance Problems
- Managing Group Performance

The book closes with a case study in Chapter 12 showing how the recommended system would actually be applied.

The job of supervisor is potentially the most satisfying assignment available in today's world of work. Because, as a supervisor, you are able to increase your range of influence and accomplishment beyond your own capacity to produce, you multiply your individual capacity by the number of employees in your unit. In the process of expanding your range of influence to include others, you are tapping a further source of personal satisfaction—the opportunity to work with others in a unique way and share in the joy of their successes.

This human dimension, unique to supervision, can also be a source of frustration and disappointment if not properly handled. I am convinced that reading this book and diligently practicing its lessons will help you realize the full potential of satisfaction and joy inherent in a supervisory assignment, thus avoiding the frustration and disappointment experienced by those who attempt the job without a clear understanding of how to carry it out.

There are several people to whom I owe a special thanks for their part in helping this book become a reality. First, Mr. Louis Koudelik, now retired from the University of Houston, is due a thank you for recommending me to Lifetime Learning Publications as a potential author. Without his initial recommendation the project would never have been undertaken. Second, the staff at Lifetime Learning Publications is due a special thanks for their support and guidance in bringing this project to completion. In particular, I acknowledge the contributions of Stephen C. Keeble, Laurel Cook, Richard Mason, Bernie Scheier, and Rich Osborne. Finally, I express a special thanks to my colleagues and associates for their support in granting me the privilege of sharing with others beyond our own organization the ideas I have developed during the past fifteen years.

Marion E. Haynes
Houston, Texas

Managing
Performance

Overview

The core of this book is the Performance Management System—a six-step program that provides an orderly method for effectively managing your employees. Knowing yourself as a supervisor and knowing your employees as individual members of your workgroup are essential prerequisites to making practical use of this six-step system designed to assist you in fulfilling your responsibilities as a supervisor. For that reason, getting to know yourself and getting to know your staff are the subjects of chapters 1 and 2, which, together, create the foundation for the six steps covered sequentially in chapters 3 through 8.

As you will see, each step in the Performance Management System serves as preparation for the following step. Establishing performance expectations with your employees is the first step you must take as a supervisor. Without shared expectations regarding job definitions and duties, the quality and quantity of work to be accomplished, the methods or procedures to be followed, and appropriate on-the-job behavior, you may find yourselves at odds with each other and, more importantly, the results for which you are held accountable may not be produced. Obviously, step 1 is critical and deserves careful consideration.

Once performance expectations have been established, the next step is to monitor progress, focussing on results achieved rather than specific activities your employees engage in or procedures they follow. (Monitoring activities and procedures becomes necessary largely when there is deterioration, or shortfall, in the results you had expected to attain.)

The third step, evaluating performance results, is a natural outcome of monitoring performance against expectations. Any evaluative decision is arrived at by a process of comparison. In terms of performance, your employees will either exceed, equal, or fall short of agreed upon expectations. (In comparing performance of different employees or the same employee at different times, it is critical that you use the same base of comparison.) Remember, performance evaluation is never an end in itself: it is the "homework" you do as a basis for giving your employees feedback, for making appropriate administrative recommendations, and for determining where and when performance improvement is required.

Step 4, providing performance feedback, is vital. Not only are employees interested in how their performance is viewed by management, but specific feedback, constructively offered, is a powerfully motivating force for future performance. Obviously, there are different types of feedback you will be required to give, and how to handle each effectively is one of the main concerns of chapter 6.

Making administrative decisions affecting members of your workgroup—decisions about whether or not to continue someone's employment, who should be promoted, who should receive a salary increase, and who should be transferred or reassigned—appears in the model as step 5. This function is expected of any manager and good decision making in this area relies on your effective evaluation of employee performance. In addition, administrative decisions can be a source of performance feedback to employees. The relationship between administrative decision making and performance management is the subject of chapter 7.

The final step, step 6, discusses how to develop improvement plans for employees whose performance does not measure up to expectations. If your performance evaluation has been properly carried out, it will give you the "diagnostic tool" you need to pinpoint the cause of poor performance and to identify what specific remedies are in order. As in establishing performance expectations, the most effective approach to developing an improvement plan is to get the collaboration of your employee in working it out.

With the conclusion of the sixth and final step in the Performance Management System, it is time to take a closer look at three broad management issues: the delegation of responsibility, the management of performance problems, and the management of group performance. How to handle these managerial functions using the concepts and methods of the Performance Management System is presented in chapters 9, 10, and 11, respectively. Finally, in chapter 12, you will find a case study illustrating how the system actually operates.

You should know that throughout the book I have drawn upon the work of many experts in the field of management and management theory. Rather than burden the text with footnotes, I have included their names in a REFERENCES section at the end of each chapter.

THE PERFORMANCE MANAGEMENT SYSTEM

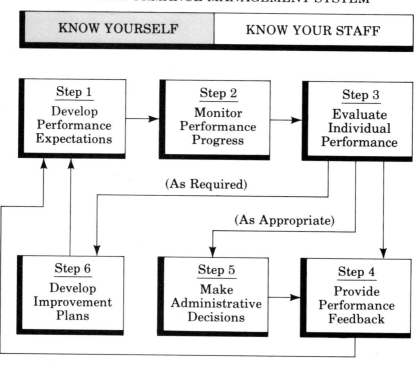

CHAPTER 1

Knowing Yourself As a Supervisor

As a result of reading this chapter, you will know

- Who you are and what you do as supervisor
- What *results* mean in the game of supervising
- What it means to "manage"
- How researchers regard what you do and how you do it
- What goes into leadership style
- How to vary your style according to employee needs

The book's title, MANAGING PERFORMANCE, deliberately omits *whose* performance is being managed; for even though it is clear that your function is to manage others, the skill with which you do that job depends on how well you know yourself as supervisor—in other words, how well you manage *your* performance.

The Job of Supervising

As one who supervises others, you are at the focal point of your organization. You have continuous contact with employees and you are expected to carry out the decisions, implement the policies, and attain the goals of higher management. How you go about your job can either close off or unlock the productive potential of the workgroup you're responsible for. If you are unsure of yourself as a supervisor, you tend to provide little guidance or direction, hoping that no one will notice. Alternatively, if you are certain of your own capabilities for doing the work you supervise, you may not trust anyone else to "do it right" and, as a result, you're likely to specify exactly *what* must be done and *how* to do it. On the other hand, you may be one of the few who, confident of yourself and the members of your group, simply specify outside boundaries and then give group members substantial freedom for carrying out their assignments.

Using the Performance Management System presented in this book, you will discover ways to free up the potential of your employees and direct it productively. In this system, the supervisor-employee relationship is viewed as a partnership in which you and your staff share common goals and interests. As such, it encourages both sides to participate actively in determining *what* should be done and *how* it should be done. Before discussing the six steps that form the core of the system, we need to look at what it means to manage, what is meant by "leadership style," and what researchers are able to tell us about supervisors as a group and the choices we make when it comes to managing others.

Results—The Name of Your Game

Your primary responsibility is to achieve results, whether in the form of a product or service. It is the delivery of a product or service that provides focus, direction, and purpose to the company and to each workgroup within it. This kind of result is generally obvious to everyone. As a supervisor, however, you must not only work to generate your company's product or service, you must be alert to how your staff members feel about the work they do and the conditions under which it is done. Their *morale,* or satisfaction, is every bit as important as the product or service they generate. In the short term, certainly, production output can be increased regardless of whether employees are satisfied in their work. Today, however, most employees do not tolerate an oppressive work environment—that is, one that gives them little or no opportunity to influence the decisions that directly affect them, to use their full range of talents, or to satisfy personal needs and interests. An unsatisfied, uncommitted employee will, sooner or later, leave the company and, in the long run, the constant turnover will seriously affect productivity. In other words, for those who manage others, *results* mean more than just the output generated.

What It Means to Manage

Results do not simply happen—you make them happen. As a supervisor, you achieve results by skillfully managing the resources available to you—people as well as money, facilities, and time. In this book the focus is on managing people, your human resources. How well you carry out your managerial responsibilities depends both on how well you perform the four basic management skills—*planning, organizing, leading,* and *controlling,* and on the leadership style you adopt.

Planning.   The planning function looks to the future. For management, it involves forecasting, establishing objectives, and developing plans and budgets to reach those objectives. It also includes establishing policies and procedures—two activities that are generally not regarded as part of the planning function but should be since they have an impact on future practices.

Organizing.   The organizing function establishes order between the work to be done and the people available to do it. It includes the activities of identifying and grouping work, delegating responsibilities and accountabilities, and determining working relationships among people.

Leading.   The leading function includes all activities whose purpose is to influence the workgroup to achieve its goals. You do that by selecting people to fill positions in the group, developing them in the positions they hold, and motivating them to contribute at appropriate levels. Communicating and decision making are also *leading* activities.

Controlling.   The final function, controlling, includes three basic activities—setting standards of performance, evaluating performance against established standards, and taking corrective action as required.

Who Does the Managing?

Even though the four functions just described are presented as "managerial" functions, it's not necessary that they remain exclusively in the hands of management. There's a wide range of choice in the degree to which these activities are shared with your staff. How much you hold on to or let go of the managerial reins generally has to do with where your preferences fall along the continuum from the *traditional* to the *contemporary* view of good management.

Traditional View.   The traditional view of management is that managers and supervisors *manage* and workers do the *work* of the group. The term "workers" here means any nonmanagement employee—whether engineer, salesperson, secretary, accountant, laboratory assistant, file clerk, mechanic, operator, or unskilled laborer. In this traditional view, the supervisor would "call all the shots" in the workgroup, deciding not only *what* is to be done but *how* it is to be done. Traditional supervisors usually lack confidence in the ability of their staff. Employees managed in this fashion are completely dependent upon their supervisor. In the absence of direction, they wait for orders. They generally do not offer suggestions or ideas on how to improve operations, and they are certainly not rewarded if they do so. Those who stay for any significant length of time generally fall into a pattern of doing only what they are told to do.

Diagrammed, the traditional view might look like that in Figure 1.1.

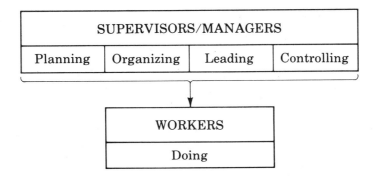

Figure 1.1 The traditional view of management

Contemporary View. The contemporary view of management takes the position that every employee should be delegated an area of responsibility, be instructed in the skills to carry it out successfully, and then be allowed the opportunity to manage it. Supervisors holding this view demonstrate considerable confidence in members of their workgroup. While they are likely to be quite involved in deciding *what* is to be done, they give their employees a lot of latitude to determine *how* to do it. Managing in this fashion serves to tap the range of talents, skills, and interests represented in the workgroup. Workers are treated as mature adults, capable of handling their own areas of responsibility appropriately. They are not dependent on the supervisor to solve problems, make decisions, or give explicit directions. In fact, when operating as it should, this view of management permits work to progress effectively whether or not the supervisor is present.

Diagrammed, the contemporary view might look like that in Figure 1.2.

Direction, Participation, Delegation

As a supervisor, you have a range of choice between the two extremes—the traditional, which is essentially directive, and the contemporary, which is essentially delegative. In actual management situations, most of us adopt a style that is somewhere along the continuum from totally directive to totally dele-

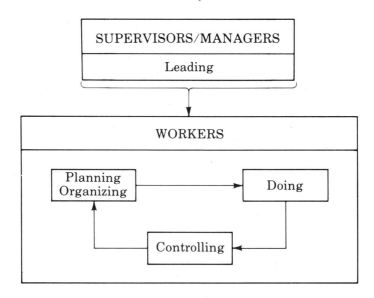

Figure 1.2 The contemporary view of management

gative; that is, we participate with our employees to more or less of a degree in making decisions about the specific tasks and projects they are to complete. As illustrated in Figure 1.3, you are able to move from being 100% directive with an employee through varying degrees of participation, or working together, until you are able, ideally, to delegate most or all of the decisions about how agreed upon work will be carried out.

You may know right now that you are essentially traditional or contemporary in your approach to supervising. You may even recognize, as you begin to consider it, that you vary your style depending on the employee or on the assignment. The

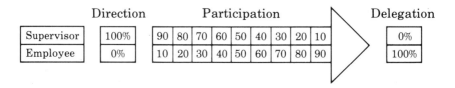

Figure 1.3 Sharing the power to decide how work will be done

matter of *style* is an important one, having much to do with the cooperation you can expect from your employees, their sense of satisfaction in the work they do, and their level of productivity. So important is the concept of management style that researchers have investigated it for a number of years. Some of what they have uncovered about managerial behavior is useful to know, for it provides a framework for looking at our own ideas, beliefs, and biases.

When we speak of management style, we are generally referring to your approach to managing the members of your workgroup, but the term also includes *leadership style*—the way you consistently go about influencing others to achieve common goals. Your style of leadership has a direct, major impact on the morale of your group members, and their morale, in turn, has much to do with their productivity. So let's look at how we came to adopt the leadership style we now have.

What Goes into Leadership Style

We all influence each other in our daily lives and actions and, aware of it or not, we each have an approach to influence that has developed as a result of our life experiences. The following are some of the most common contributors to the development of leadership style.

Values

The values and attitudes we hold shape our leadership style to a great extent. For some, authoritarian, or directive, behavior shows strength, and participative behavior shows weakness. Attitudes toward workers, which clearly have to do with leadership styles, have been studied by many. Of interest is Douglas McGregor's Theory X-Theory Y assumptions about workers. Although he acknowledges that these positions are extremes that no one person is likely to hold, McGregor's claim is that everyone has a tendency toward one or the other theory.

- *Theory X Assumptions:* People generally dislike work and will avoid it if they can. Because of this, most people must be directed, controlled, and threatened to get them to work toward organizational goals. The average person prefers to be directed, does not want responsibility, and has little ambition.

- *Theory Y Assumptions:* People prefer to be busy and involved in goal-directed behavior. People will exercise self-direction and self-control in pursuit of objectives to which they are committed. The average person learns, under proper conditions, to both seek and accept responsibility. The capacity to exercise imagination, ingenuity, and creativity in the solution of organizational problems is widely distributed in the population.

If you would like to know where you fit in the Theory X-Theory Y construct, fill out the attitudinal survey on pages 14–15 and then score yourself as directed at the end.

Personality

Obviously, people vary in personality: some are outgoing, others are reserved; some have high self-confidence whereas others are low in self-esteem. Some are generally optimistic and others are pessimistic. All of these qualities are reflected in a person's leadership style and have much to do with whether one is directive or more willing to interact with subordinates. As the word suggests, *interactive* supervisors shape group activity through discussion, in contrast to a directive supervisor who is apt to rely on established rules and procedures.

Organizational Preferences

Many organizations have clear preferences for certain leadership styles and select for advancement only those persons who demonstrate the behavior they value. Under such organizational influence, employees aspiring to positions of leadership will model the behavior they see rewarded. Also, in such firms senior members of the organization often coach new members on the "right" way to behave with subordinates.

Situational Variables

At one time or another, situational variables are bound to intrude and temporarily dictate leadership style. For example, a supervisor may prefer a participative style but find him or herself in an emergency situation where only directive, forceful leadership will remedy the immediate problem. Other examples of situational variables have to do with shifting interests of the workgroup who might want to contribute to one decision but not another. Or one may find that the leadership style so effective at the first level of management does not get good results when supervising managers or other supervisors. Finally, a leadership style that was effective in an unstructured research environment may not work at all in a structured production environment.

Chance

Just as chance plays a key role in our lives generally, so it does in the development of leadership style. We learn through trial and error what works for us, and we continually observe others for cues and as role models. Behavior that seems to work for *them* is tried out and that which doesn't work is avoided. These chance contacts with people, especially those in leadership positions, shape our own style.

The Four Leadership Styles

Early research into supervisory behavior singled out two "types" of supervisors: those who focussed on the job to be done, and those who focussed on the employee.

- *Job-centered behavior* involves organizing and defining the roles of group members—explaining what jobs each is to do and when, where, and how they are to be done.
- *Employee-centered behavior* involves developing personal relationships with employees and welding the group into a cohesive team by providing support, recognition, and reinforcement to both the group and its members.

EXERCISE 1.1

ATTITUDES TOWARD WORKERS

INSTRUCTIONS: Below are 15 scales reflecting attitudes commonly held about workers. Please indicate on each the extent to which you agree with the statement on the left end or right end of the scale. In marking your choices, think of workers in general, not a specific person.

| | Strongly Agree | Agree | Undecided | Agree | Strongly Agree | |

1. People are naturally lazy, they prefer to do nothing.
   — People are naturally active, they prefer to be striving.

2. People work mostly for money and status.
   — People work for many reasons — pride, challenge, friendships.

3. The main force keeping people working is fear of being fired.
   — The main force keeping people working is desire to achieve personal goals.

4. People are naturally dependent on their leaders.
   — People aspire to independence, self-fulfillment, and responsibility.

5. People expect and depend on direction from others.
   — People see and feel what is needed and can direct themselves.

6. People need to be shown and trained in proper work methods.
   — People who understand and care can develop their own methods.

7. People need close supervision — praise for good work and reprimand for errors.
   — People need respect as capable of assuming responsibility and correcting own errors.

8. People have little concern beyond own immediate material interests.
   — People seek to giving meaning to their lives.

Exercise 1.1   *(continued)*

	Strongly Agree	Agree	Undecided	Agree	Strongly Agree	

9. People need specific instructions on what to do and how to do it.

People need an overall understanding of their work and how it fits in.

10. People appreciate being treated with courtesy.

People crave genuine respect from their fellow men.

11. Work demands are entirely different from leisure activities.

People prefer leisure because of the better quality of work they can do during leisure time activities.

12. People naturally resist change. They prefer the same old rut.

People tire of monotonous routine and enjoy new experiences.

13. People should be selected and fitted to jobs.

Jobs should be designed and fitted to people.

14. People are formed by heredity and early experiences. As adults they do not change.

People consistantly grow. It is never too late to learn.

15. People need to be "inspired", pushed, or driven.

People need to be released, encouraged, and assisted.

SCORING: Assign the values 1, 2, 3, 4, and 5 to each of the points on the scale. Total your score for the 15 scales and write on the line below.

Score: _____

Less than 30	— Theory "X"
30 — 44	— Tending to Theory "X"
45 — 60	— Tending to Theory "Y"
61 — 75	— Theory "Y"

Based on: *The Human Side of Enterprise,* by Douglas M. McGregor (New York: McGraw-Hill, 1960).

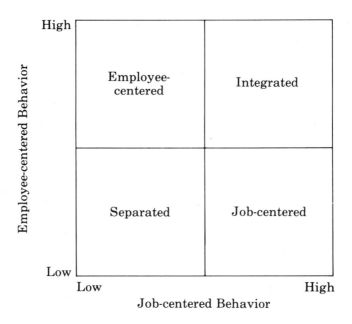

Figure 1.4 The four styles of leadership

It was thought that supervisors emphasized one of these behaviors over the other—that they focussed either on the job to be done or on the people doing it, but not both. More recent studies, however, revealed that supervisors demonstrate considerable variation in this respect; that is, while some do emphasize employee relationships over jobs and vice versa, many place equal emphasis on both, and others seem to place little emphasis on either. From these observations, a two-dimensional model was developed to describe four leadership styles reflecting different combinations of employee-centered and job-centered behavior. Figure 1.4 shows this model. Where there is an integration of both behaviors, the supervisor was said to have an "integrated" leadership style, and where neither alternative was evident, the supervisor was described as having a "separated" style.

Job-centered Leadership Style.   A job-centered leadership style is *high* in *job*-centered behavior and *low* in *employee*-centered behavior. Job-centered leaders tend to structure and direct the work of others by telling them what, where, and how things are to be done. They also prefer to define and solve problems on their own, operating from the position that they know best how to get things done. They tend to deal with staff members one by one, making each person directly accountable to them for a specific set of responsibilities. Supervisors who follow this style of leadership see themselves as influencing others through their own dedication to hard work. In other words, they believe that it is their personal example of competence and their careful use of power that maintains productivity in the workgroup.

Employee-centered Leadership Style.   Employee-centered leadership is *high* in employee-centered behavior and *low* in *job*-centered behavior. Employee-centered leaders provide little structure. They identify with their workgroup and strive for a collaborative work atmosphere that encourages self-expression and personal freedom. They use their relationships and recognition of others rather than their authority as a means of influencing. Because employee-centered leaders see their role as primarily supporting and encouraging their employees, they tend to be good listeners. They generally present a trusting and positive attitude, and prefer a participative approach to decision making.

Integrated Leadership Style.   An integrated leadership style is high in both job-centered and employee-centered behavior. These supervisors try to structure work by involving others in the cooperative achievement of goals. They include their employees in decision making, and they influence employee performance by stressing accountability and then providing feedback on results. They usually set high standards for performance and production and explain what they are doing to the workgroup. In their view, conflict is best resolved through open discussion. Such supervisors are seen by their employees as being personally interested in their development.

Separated Leadership Style.   Separated leadership is low in both job-centered and employee-centered behavior. These supervisors frequently delegate and usually in broad, general terms. Although regarded as being fair and objective about people and events, they rarely become emotionally involved. They enjoy monitoring goals, output, or activities of others. They tend to spend little time developing people or pushing for output. They spend most of their time keeping informed and analyzing data.

To find out how your own leadership style would be classified in this four-dimensional model, complete the Leadership Style Questionnaire on pages 22–25.

The Contingency Approach to Leadership

The next evolution in leadership theory was the recognition that each of the four styles identified could be appropriately or inappropriately applied. One of the currently most popular contingency theories maintains that the maturity level of the individual employee, or group, determines what leadership style is appropriate. Maturity is defined as the ability to set high but attainable goals, the willingness and ability to take responsibility, and the necessary experience and training for the work to be performed. In this sense, we have two dimensions—*job* maturity and *personal* maturity.

Job Maturity. Job maturity is the *ability* to do a job according to acceptable standards. In assessing job maturity, the experience and training for the current job assignment must be considered. Does the employee know the job? Has the employee been trained in how to perform at an acceptable level? Has the employee done the job at an acceptable level in the past?

Personal Maturity. Personal maturity is the *willingness* to do a job at an acceptable level of performance. In assessing personal maturity, interest and motivation, willingness to take responsibility, and self-confidence must be evaluated. Does the employee stay with a job until it is finished? Is the employee a self-starter? Can the employee prioritize the work to be done? Are necessary steps taken early enough to assure work being completed on schedule?

Once you have assessed your employee's maturity level on these two dimensions, you can combine them to determine the appropriate leadership style to follow with that individual. It works this way:

- An employee low in *both* maturity dimensions—that is, unwilling and unable to perform—is best supervised with a *job-centered* style. (Obviously, we don't keep many of these employees on the payroll for very long.)
- An employee high in personal maturity but low in job maturity (typical of a new employee) is best supervised with an *integrated* style.
- An employee high in job maturity but low in personal maturity (usually out of lack of confidence) needs encouragement to take on more responsibility. This task is best accomplished with an *employee-centered* style.
- An employee high in both maturity dimensions—that is, willing and able to perform to acceptable standards, should be delegated an area of responsibility and given the freedom to perform. In other words, as supervisor you can follow a separated style of leadership.

Figure 1.5 shows how the contingency model works.

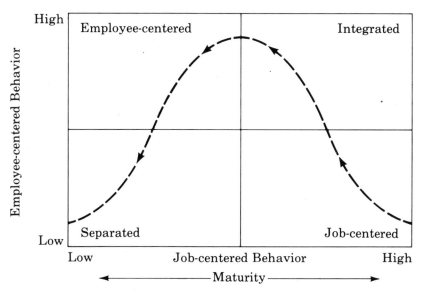

Figure 1.5 Leadership style as a function of employee maturity. Adapted from Hessey and Blanchard. Used with permission.

If we read the figure from right to left following the path of the arrows, we see that low maturity correlates with high job-centered behavior that becomes increasingly integrated with employee-centered behavior as the employee's level of maturity increases. For those employees who reach a high level of job/personal maturity, the supervisor backs off on both job- and employee-centered behavior and falls into a "separated" style of leadership. Most employees will cluster in the midrange (moderately mature) and continue to require a considerable degree of integration of employee and job-centered behavior. Your goal as a supervisor is to develop your staff to the point of high maturity so they can handle their day-to-day responsibilities without your direct involvement (separated style). This accomplished, your time is freed up to do the work of your department that only you can do—long-range planning, representing your department to higher management, coordinating activities with other departments, and improving the operation of your department.

Using What You Know Effectively

It should be clear now that you need not be locked into any one style—in fact, it should be clear that different employees require different treatment if you are to obtain their highest level of performance. It's up to you to know your employees well enough to determine which approach to take with each of them.

Let's test the theoretical ideas we've just presented. Assume that Merle, Fran, Terry, Leslie, and Bill are members of your workgroup, and take a few minutes to look at their hypothetical performance records and how they would be evaluated in a contingency model of supervision:

Merle. Merle is an experienced employee who is interested in his job and seems motivated to do well. Merle has a good understanding of his responsibilities, plans well, and sets appropriate priorities for his work. What kind of supervision is best for Merle?

> Merle is high in both job and personal maturity. Therefore, he should receive minimum supervision. He should be given his own area of responsibility and the freedom to perform—that is, a *separated* leadership style should be used.

Fran. Fran is new to your workgroup and has recently completed a two-week orientation program for new employees. This is her first real assignment. She seems interested in her work and committed to doing a good job. What kind of supervision is best for Fran?

> As a newcomer to the group, Fran is low in job maturity and too new to be fully assessed on personal maturity. Given that she does not yet know her job, she needs your guidance and direction. For the present time, then, she should receive *job-centered* supervision.

Terry. Terry has been a member of your group for three years. He knows his job and usually does it well. Occasionally, he seems to need some acknowledgment of his contribution in order to maintain his level of productivity. What kind of supervision is best for Terry?

> Terry is high in job maturity but only moderate in personal maturity as indicated by his occasional need for recognition. He needs the support and reinforcement characteristic of an *employee-centered* style of leadership.

Leslie. Leslie has been a member of your group for two months. During this time she has shown interest in her work and has responded well to your training. You normally spend six months training new group members. Leslie is on schedule in her development. What kind of supervision is best for Leslie?

> Leslie is moderate in both job and personal maturity at this time. You can involve her in determining both what needs to be done and how to do it. Participative involvement is characteristic of the *integrated* style of leadership, which is appropriate for Leslie at this stage.

Bill. Bill has been a member of your group for seven years. He knows his job but seems to lack interest in getting it done. Recently he was skipped over for promotion and subsequently the quality of his performance has slipped. What kind of supervision is best for Bill?

> Bill needs to talk about his problem and develop a positive approach to the future. He is clearly capable but chooses to withhold performance in response to what he sees as an unfair act by management. In other words, he can be regarded as high in job maturity but, presently, he is demonstrating low personal maturity. You can break down this negative cycle by using an *employee-centered* approach.

EXERCISE 1.2

Leadership Style Questionnaire

The following items reflect different behaviors by supervisors. Respond to each item according to the way you would most likely act as the leader of a workgroup. Circle whether you would most likely behave in the described way: always (A), frequently (F), occasionally (O), seldom (S), or never (N).

A F O S N   1. I would personally inspect all output of the group.

A F O S N   2. I would encourage overtime work.

A F O S N   3. I would allow members complete freedom in their work.

A F O S N   4. I would encourage the use of uniform procedures.

A F O S N   5. I would permit members to use their own judgment in solving problems.

A F O S N   6. I would stress being ahead of competing groups.

A F O S N   7. I would engage group members in friendly conversation.

A F O S N   8. I would speak as a representative of the group when visitors were present.

A F O S N   9. I would prod members for greater effort.

A F O S N   10. I would try out my ideas in the group.

A F O S N   11. I would let group members do their work the way they think best.

A F O S N   12. I would be working hard for a promotion.

A F O S N   13. I would encourage group members to take on greater responsibilities.

A F O S N   14. I would tolerate postponement and uncertainty.

A F O S N   15. I would organize the group to achieve greater efficiency.

A F O S N   16. I would keep the work moving at a rapid pace.

A F O S N   17. I would turn group members loose on a job and let them go to it.

A F O S N   18. I would settle conflicts when they occur in the group.

A F O S N   19. I would listen attentively to the problems and concerns of group members.

A F O S N   20. I probably would get swamped by details.

A F O S N   21. I would represent the group at outside meetings.

A F O S N   22. I would be reluctant to allow group members any freedom of action.

A F O S N   23. I would decide what should be done and how it should be done.

A F O S N   24. I would facilitate group discussion and problem solving.

A F O S N   25. I would push for increased production.

A F O S N   26. I would let some members have authority that I *could* keep for myself.

A F O S N   27. Things would usually turn out as I had predicted.

A F O S N   28. I would allow the group a high degree of initiative.

A F O S N   29. I would provide frequent feedback on the quality of group performance.

A F O S N   30. I would assign group members to particular tasks.

A F O S N   31. I would be willing to consider changes recommended by group members.

A F O S N   32. I would ask group members to work harder.

A F O S N   33. I would trust group members to exercise good judgment.

A F O S N   34. I would schedule the work to be done.

A F O S N   35. I would refuse to explain my actions to the group.

A F O S N   36. I would persuade others that my ideas are to their advantage.

A F O S N   37. I would permit the group to set its own pace.

A F O S N   38. I would urge the group to beat its previous record.

A F O S N   39. I would act without consulting the group.

A F O S N   40. I would ask group members to follow standard rules and regulations.

Scoring

1. Circle item numbers 3, 5, 11, 14, 17, 21, 26, 28, 33, 35, and 39.
2. Write an (X) in front of *circled* items you answered (S) seldom or (N) never.
3. Write an (X) in front of *uncircled* items you answered (A) always or (F) frequently.
4. Circle the Xs in front of items numbered: 3, 5, 7, 9, 11, 13, 17, 19, 21, 22, 24, 26, 28, 29, 31, 33, 35, 37, 39, and 40.
5. Count the *circled* Xs. This is your Employee-centered score. Write it in the blank following the letter E.
6. Count the *uncircled* Xs. This is your Job-centered score. Write it in the blank following the letter J.
7. Using these two sources, complete your Leadership Style Profile on the leadership profile sheet that follows.

E _____   J _____

LEADERSHIP STYLE PROFILE SHEET

To determine your style of leadership, mark your Job-centered behavior score (J) on the horizontal axis below and draw a line up from that point. Next, move to the vertical axis and mark your Employee-centered behavior score (E) and draw a line across from that point. The quadrant in which the two lines cross indicates your style of leadership.

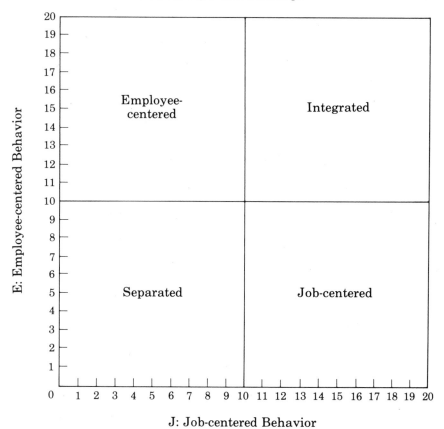

Adapted from J. William Pfeiffer and John E. Jones, Eds., *A Handbook of Structured Experiences for Human Relations Training,* Vol. I (San Diego, CA: University Associates, Inc., 1974). Used with permission. The original questionnaire was adapted from Sergiovanni, Metzcus, and Bruden's revision of the Leadership Behavior Description Questionnaire, *American Educational Research Journal,* Vol. 6 (1969), pp. 62–79.

The points discussed in this chapter are summarized graphically in Figure 1.6.

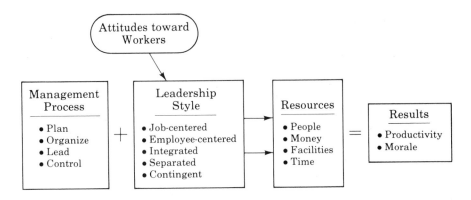

Figure 1.6 The effective manager's success formula

Your Action Guide

Through supervisors, the decisions, goals, and directives of higher management are translated from ideas into products or services. Supervisors must take the resources provided and integrate them in a way that best gets a job done. Effective management involves four basic functions: planning, organizing, leading, and controlling. To achieve results—high productivity and high morale—you need to be skilled in performing the basic management functions, but you also need skill in varying your leadership style to suit your individual employees.

Four basic leadership styles have been identified: *job-centered, employee-centered, integrated,* and *separated.* The "contingency" approach to management views each of the four styles as being appropriate depending on the employee's level of job and personal maturity. As maturity levels change, your stylistic approach should change.

- Encourage staff participation in decisions of what to do and how to do it. Work toward full delegation to staff.

• Make full use of all four leadership styles by applying each style appropriately to different employees and situations.

References

Louis A. Allen, *The Profession of Management* (New York: McGraw-Hill, 1964).

Robert R. Blake and Jane S. Mouton, *The Managerial Grid* (Houston: Gulf Publishing Co., 1964).

Paul Hersey and Kenneth H. Blanchard, *Management of Organizational Behavior,* 3rd edition (Englewood Cliffs: Prentice-Hall, 1978).

Rensis Likert, *New Patterns of Management* (New York: McGraw-Hill, 1964).

Douglas M. McGregor, *The Human Side of Enterprise* (New York: McGraw-Hill, 1960).

Scott M. Meyers, *Every Employee a Manager* (New York: McGraw-Hill, 1970).

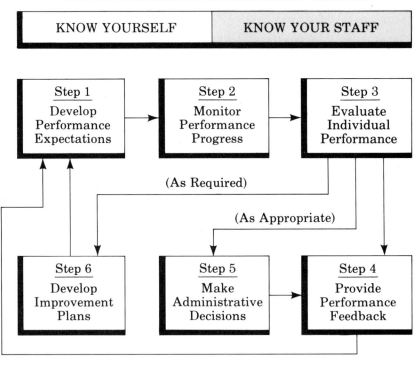

THE PERFORMANCE MANAGEMENT SYSTEM

KNOW YOURSELF	KNOW YOUR STAFF

Step 1
Develop
Performance
Expectations

Step 2
Monitor
Performance
Progress

Step 3
Evaluate
Individual
Performance

(As Required)

(As Appropriate)

Step 6
Develop
Improvement
Plans

Step 5
Make
Administrative
Decisions

Step 4
Provide
Performance
Feedback

DELEGATE RESPONSIBILITY AND AUTHORITY	MANAGE PERFORMANCE PROBLEMS	MANAGE GROUP PERFORMANCE

CHAPTER 2

Getting Acquainted with Your Staff

As a result of reading this chapter you will

- Understand why it is important to get acquainted with your staff
- Know what it means to be really acquainted with someone
- Know how to hold a conversation designed to become acquainted with the person you're talking with
- Know some of the ethical limitations on becoming acquainted with staff members

Knowing the people who work for you is an important prerequisite for each of the six steps in the Performance Management System. Your knowledge of your employees becomes the basis for many of the decisions you will consider, procedures you will implement, and evaluations you will make. You may be asking "Why should I spend valuable time just getting to know my staff? I see them every day. We talk. What should I learn that I don't already know? And just how do I go about it?" In this chapter we'll answer those questions.

Getting acquainted with each employee begins when you first meet, and continues throughout the time you work together. In the process you should become familiar with the talents, skills, and interests of each person and develop working relationships that encourage employees to willingly contribute their best effort.

Why Get Involved?

Specifically, there are five generally accepted reasons why you should take the time to become acquainted with those who work for you:

1. So you can match personal interests with jobs
2. So you can predict employee responses to planned change
3. So you can increase the flow of employees' suggestions
4. So you'll have a basis for influencing group members
5. So you'll have a basis for personal counseling

Matching Interests and Assignments

People do best the things they like to do. It's estimated that 80 to 90 percent of all performance problems are a direct result of a mismatch between employees' interests, skills, and talents and the jobs they are assigned. Therefore, to the extent you can match the interests of your staff with the work to be done, you increase the odds in favor of good performance. Consider the following examples.

- *John.* Upon graduating from college, John was hired as a trainee in the purchasing department of a large company. After about a year in purchasing, he decided he'd rather be in sales. John discussed his interests with his supervisor, who arranged for him to talk to personnel. Interviews were arranged, a transfer resulted, and today, 20 years later, John is a sales manager for the same company.

- *Mary.* Mary was hired as a computer programmer by a large company after her graduation from college with a degree in chemical engineering. She soon found that this job wasn't utilizing her full ability. Mary was a trained engineer, but she was not doing engineering work. After several conversations with her supervisor, Mary was reassigned within the department to an engineering position. She performed well, received several promotions and reassignments, and today, 15 years later, she is manager of a large laboratory for the same company.

- *Bill.* Bill was hired as a production operator by a large company when he was discharged from the army. He worked in the same department for seven years, advancing to a lead operator position. During this time he completed a college degree in engineering at night school. When he graduated, Bill requested a transfer to an engineering position. After three months without a response, Bill again asked about the transfer and was told he would be better off taking a foreman's position that was opening up soon. Today, Bill is an engineer with another firm.

By knowing your staff, you'll be aware of mismatched interests and jobs and be able to resolve them. For instance, rather than hire people from outside your department or company to fill new or vacant positions, first offer the job to current interested and qualified employees. When you can't accommodate an individual's interests or desire for change within your own department, consider letting the employee transfer to another department. The alternative frequently is that the person will quit, becoming a loss to both your department and the company.

John, Mary, and Bill each took the initiative to resolve their mismatch. Unfortunately, employees often don't express their dissatisfaction or attempt to resolve it within their current organization. They simply seek opportunity elsewhere or become increasingly apathetic in their job. Don't wait for your employees to initiate conversations regarding their interests and their jobs—bring up the subject yourself.

Simply knowing your employees' talents, skills, and interests isn't enough to resolve mismatches with the jobs. To solve these problems you must be able to *change* current arrangements. And this isn't always possible. Your company may not need the type of contribution a staff member is interested in and qualified to make. Don't expect to be able to resolve all of these problems, but do get involved in those you can handle.

Predicting Responses to Planned Changes

Would you be able to accurately predict your employees' reaction to the following situations?

- *Change in pay procedures.* The payroll department calls and says it is considering changing its practice of mailing paychecks to employees' homes in order to save several thousands of dollars a year in postage. How do you think your staff would react to having their paychecks distributed by you in sealed envelopes on payday?
- *Safety program.* The safety department calls. It is considering a safety award program to recognize individual employees for every 2,000 hours worked without an injury. How do you think your staff will react to the proposed program?
- *Attitudes toward unionization.* At a staff meeting, your manager reports that a union-organizing attempt is under way at a neighboring plant similar to yours. He asks you and other supervisors how you think your employees would react to such a campaign at your plant. Would employees support unionization?

These are typical examples of the kinds of questions supervisors are asked every day. The only valid basis you have for responding to them is your personal knowledge of your group—their interests, needs, attitudes, and values. The better acquainted you are with them, the better you can predict their reactions.

Increasing the Flow of Suggestions

Employees who are actually doing a particular job are often a valuable source of information on how that job might be done better and more safely. One of the best ways of gaining access to their ideas is to create and nurture a climate of free-flowing communication and cooperation.

Communication within the group is necessary but, by itself, not sufficient to maintain a flow of suggestions. *You* must take time to listen to employee's suggestions. Evaluate each idea that's offered and report the results of your evaluation to the person who made the suggestion. Implement ideas that are feasible and be sure to give appropriate credit and recognition to their originators.

Influencing Individual Behavior

As a supervisor, you constantly deal with members of your staff in situations that require you to influence what they do. The situations range from getting employees to improve their work quality to getting them to come to work on time to motivating them to prepare for a promotion and more responsibility.

You'll find yourself more effective at influencing employees if you are well acquainted with the person you are attempting to influence. First, the very process of getting acquainted establishes a relationship in which members of your staff are more open to your influence. Second, by being acquainted, you'll know what's important to each of them in terms of values and needs and can relate to each in regard to these. See how personal familiarity helps resolve the problems below.

- *Professional pride.* The quality of work on a particular project is marginally adequate. You know the employee working on the project usually has a high degree of pride in his or her work. You point out that this work does not measure up to the professional standards typical of past performance and offer to help solve whatever problem is causing the decline in performance.

- *Taking turns.* A particular task that no one enjoys doing comes up periodically, and, everyone takes turns doing it.

One employee is reluctant to take her turn. You point out that everyone has a duty to do this job and it is only fair to take turns. Because you know this person places a high value on duty and fair play, you're effective in seeing that the job gets done.

- *A matter of choice.* You are asked to have one of your staff make a presentation on the operation of your department to a local high school class. You know that some staff members enjoy this sort of thing while others don't. You offer the opportunity to someone you know will enjoy doing it.

Counseling Staff Members

From time to time members of your staff may face personal situations such as financial problems, family difficulties, or career guidance, that may affect work performance. It may help if they could talk with someone. When you're well acquainted with your staff, they'll feel more comfortable in bringing these to you.

In the area of personal counseling you must be sure to define the limits in which you're comfortable. For example, you might be willing to help someone make better arrangements for getting to work, but not want to discuss personal financial problems. That's okay, help people when and how you can and refer them to other, qualified counselors, either within or outside your organization, when you're unable to help.

How Well Should You Get to Know Your Employees?

Some people you "click" with right away. Other people you can be acquainted with for years without ever really getting to know. Just how well should you know your staff? Or more accurately how well can you *expect* to get to know them?

In his book *Talking,* Dr. Bugental discusses seven levels of knowing a person. In the workplace you should never expect to know anyone deeper than the third level, with an occasional glimpse into the fourth level.

"Sunday Best."   The first level is called the "Sunday best." In presenting your "Sunday best" you "put your best foot forward" in order to appear at your most favorable. Particular attention is paid to dress, grooming, language, and manners. People usually put on their "Sunday best" for those who have the power to give them what they want—employment interviewers, supervisors, etc.

Everyday.   This level reveals how you usually present yourself to everyday acquaintances. You're sensitive to social convention and group norms but aren't trying to impress anyone. It's unrealistic to expect to penetrate beneath this layer with *everyone* you meet. But, unfortunately, some supervisors never develop a relationship deeper than this layer with members of their staff.

Relaxed.   Here, people aren't concerned with conforming to social convention or group norms. They simply relax and say what they truly think and feel. This is the level you must reach with each person on your staff in order to have access to the information you'll need to effectively work with them.

Comfortable.   The comfortable level is characterized by projection into the future and disclosure of hopes, dreams, fears, expectations, and goals. It's unrealistic to expect to be *completely* exposed to this level of a staff member. However, you should discuss goals and expectations that properly relate to the working relationship.

What You Can Expect to Learn About an Individual

When you penetrate the surface and get down to the second and third levels, several aspects of an individual open up to you.

- *Biographical data.* This is personal history. It includes where a person grew up, schools attended, honors received, marriage, children, military, and so forth. Also included are reactions to experiences, such as the most exciting times and greatest disappointments.

- *Employment history*. This would include types of jobs, duration of employment, and reactions to these experiences.

- *Interests*. This includes both on the job and off the job activities, interests, hobbies, and pastimes.

- *Self-image*. How does the staff member view himself or herself? Everyone has a self-image, which basically is how they value themselves compared to others. It includes a combination of ego, pride, ambition, and tradition.

- *Needs*. Unfulfilled needs drive people to action—to do something. You should know your staff well enough to determine which of their needs provide motivation and fulfillment, and when unfulfilled, which are sources of frustration.

- *Values*. Values—the ideals, or principles, that a person's heritage, education, and environment establish as worthwhile—are usually held dear. Values represent boundaries, or limitations, on a person's range of acceptable decision alternatives.

- *Expectations*. When people enter into any activity, or relationship, they expect certain outcomes or results. Their satisfaction with an experience depends on how well their expectations were fulfilled. Understanding what your staff members expect from their work experience will help you better understand their satisfactions and disappointments.

- *Standards*. Everyone has a set of personal standards that generally controls the quality of their work, as well as forms the basis of their judgment of others' work.

- *Goals*. Goals, aspirations, and dreams provide direction in a person's life. You should spend some time trying to understand where each staff member sees himself or herself going.

- *Perceptions*. Different people often have different perceptions of the same things. Getting acquainted with your staff will give you a better understanding of their perceptions.

You might keep a file or list of personal information on each individual. Exhibit 2.1 offers a format for organizing the information.

EXHIBIT 2.1   Personal Data Summary

I. Identification Data

Name: _____ Birthdate: _____

Job assignment: _____

Employment date: _____ Assignment date: _____

II. Family Data

Spouse's name: _____ Marriage date: _____

Spouse's employer: _____ Occupation: _____

Children's names and dates of birth:

1. _____   4. _____

2. _____   5. _____

3. _____   6. _____

III. Education and Training Summary

	School	Date completed	Degree/certificate
1.	_____	_____	_____
2.	_____	_____	_____
3.	_____	_____	_____
4.	_____	_____	_____
5.	_____	_____	_____
6.	_____	_____	_____

IV. Work Experience Summary (Include Military Service)

	Organization	Inclusive dates	Job
1.	_____	_____	_____
2.	_____	_____	_____

Exhibit 2.1   _(continued)_

3. _____   _____   _____

4. _____   _____   _____

5. _____   _____   _____

6. _____   _____   _____

7. _____   _____   _____

8. _____   _____   _____

9. _____   _____   _____

10. _____   _____   _____

V. Hobbies and/or Special Interests

_____

_____

_____

_____

VI. Short-term (3 to 5 years) and Long-term Goals

_____

_____

_____

_____

_____

VII. Career Limitations or Restrictions (e.g., travel or reloca-
tion)

_____

_____

_____

_____

Exhibit 2.1   *(continued)*

VIII. Motivational Forces (e.g., recognition, security, power, acceptance)

_____

_____

_____

_____

IX. Attitude Toward Present Assignment

☐ Enjoys it and feels challenged   ☐ Is bored by it

☐ Likes it   ☐ Hates it

☐ Tolerates it

X. Estimated Maturity Levels

1. Job maturity   2. Personal maturity

_____ High   _____ High

_____ Moderately high   _____ Moderately high

_____ Moderately low   _____ Moderately low

_____ Low   _____ Low

Developing the Right Climate for Knowing Your Staff

Understanding why you should get to know your staff is one thing, actually getting acquainted with them is quite another. If you expect staff members to tell you their goals, interests, and concerns, you must have a climate in your workgroup that supports this degree of personal disclosure. Then you can use conversations as a means of learning about them.

Three ingredients are necessary for an open, supportive climate:

1. Acceptance
2. Support
3. Trust

Acceptance

People generally want acceptance from those who play a significant role in their lives. People respond to others based on their perceptions of acceptance versus rejection. (See Figure 2.1.) Both acceptance and rejection usually evoke strong feelings. Acceptance leads to cooperation, while rejection leads to alienation.

If you convey that you accept your staff as people, they'll generally have strong positive feelings and be more open with you and more willing to cooperate. When you remain neutral toward an individual, he or she typically feels apathetic. If you convey rejection, you invite alienation. Either of these condi-

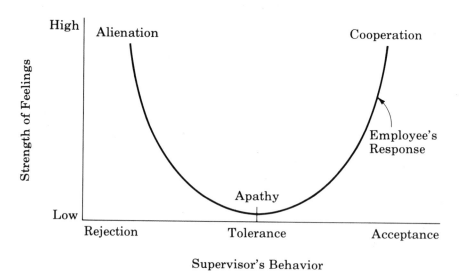

Figure 2.1 Employee's response to acceptance
or rejection from supervisor

tions, apathy or alienation, will severely restrict the flow of information. (Remember, however, that accepting an employee as a *person* does not mean that you must also accept all of the employee's work, regardless of whether it is well done.)

You communicate your acceptance by your words, your tone of voice, and your actions. Below are some additional suggestions.

- Be available when needed rather than be inaccessible
- Respond rather than ignore
- Help solve problems rather than blame or punish
- Accept the ideas of others rather than argue, debate, or criticize
- Share ideas, feelings, and information rather than withhold
- Show a genuine interest in others rather than appear indifferent
- Listen for understanding rather than to criticize or judge
- Speak in a soft tone of voice rather than a hard one
- Display a smiling, interested expression rather than frown or remain poker-faced
- Have a relaxed, forward posture rather than a tense or withdrawn one
- Maintain a close physical distance rather than withdraw
- Maintain appropriate eye contact rather than avoid it
- Use open, smooth gestures rather than closed, guarded ones

Support

By making your workers feel you support them, you'll create a climate in which they'll feel comfortable disclosing to you their goals, aspirations, and interests. In fact, the willingness of an individual to open up can be directly related to the amount of your support. Figure 2.2 is a diagram of this relationship. As shown by the curved line, as your support increases, so does an employee's willingness to be open with you.

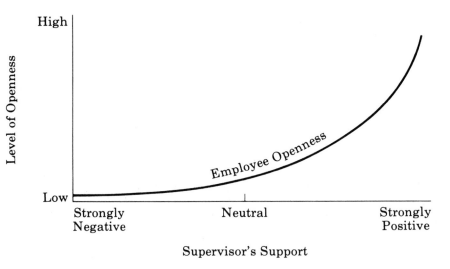

Figure 2.2 Relationship between employee's openness and
supervisor's support

If employees disclose ideas to you and encounter a lack of
support, they'll be reluctant to discuss similar ideas in the future. On the other hand, if they experience support, they'll be
more open to future disclosures and sharing.

A prerequisite to supporting someone is confidence in the
individual—confidence that the person will make decisions that
in the long run will turn out for the best, and confidence that the

Supportive	Defensive
1. Description	1. Evaluation
2. Problem Solving	2. Control
3. Spontaneity	3. Strategy
4. Empathy	4. Neutrality
5. Equality	5. Superiority
6. Provisionality	6. Certainty

Figure 2.3 Supportive versus defensive reactions
Adapted from Gibbs, "Defensive
Communication," *Journal of Communications.*

person will temper plans with reality and be willing to modify them as required by circumstances.

Occasionally, you'll find it difficult to support a staff member's plans or interests. When faced with these situations, make a clear distinction between what you would want for yourself and what you can support for someone else. You needn't necessarily want something yourself in order to support someone else's wanting it.

There are six issues that make a difference in the level of support experienced in a conversation. Try hard to avoid a defensive reaction. Instead, in your conversations, focus on the supportive alternatives to defensiveness. See Figure 2.3.

- *Evaluation–Description.* People tend to evaluate what others say and do. This often leads to defensiveness. You can improve your conversations by minimizing your evaluation of what is said and instead concentrate on describing the action or ideas under discussion and the effect you see them having on you and others.

- *Control–Problem solving.* When you tell someone that he or she should or should not do something, it can easily be seen as an attempt to control. This type of approach tends to question the person's own ability to choose an appropriate course of action. It leads to defensiveness. A better way to handle a conversation is to describe the situation as you see it, neutrally without judgment, then involve the other person in exploring alternatives together.

- *Strategy–Spontaneity.* The more you go into a conversation with a strategy to accomplish a particular outcome the more you ignore the other person's part in the conversation. Be spontaneous. Be open to ideas presented by the other person—react in a relaxed, natural way rather than a controlled, calculated way. Be flexible and responsive to the other person.

- *Neutrality–Empathy.* Empathy is when you identify with what someone else is feeling. To be able to say "I really understand how you feel" contributes to a supportive climate and an open conversation. On the other hand, remaining neutral to or apart from the other person demonstrates a lack of concern. A lack of empathy is often viewed as an insult: the other person has taken a risk in sharing and was not respected nor understood.

- *Superiority–Equality.* Differences in position within a company may lead some supervisors to feel superior to their staff. An attitude of equality will lead to more open discussions.

- *Certainty–Provisionalism.* If you take a very strong position in a conversation you may come across as being dogmatic and closed minded. If the other person sees things differently, you'll have a negative impact on the conversation. Your certainty discounts the other's point of view and often leads to frustration. Encourage conversation by recognizing that others may honestly see things differently.

Trust

The last ingredient for a comfortable climate that encourages communication and cooperation is trust. Your employees must feel you can be trusted before they'll be open with you. Trust covers a range from complete trust on one end to complete lack of trust on the other end. You can't expect total trust, but you should be moving in that direction. The relationship between how much your employees trust you and how open they are is shown by the curved line in Figure 2.4.

What does it mean to trust someone in the context of becoming acquainted? Basically, trust is the belief that being open and honest is okay, that anything disclosed in confidence will be properly handled and won't be used to embarrass, ridicule, or manipulate. No retaliatory action will be taken for having made the disclosure. For example, if a staff member tells you that he plans to move in a few months and will be resigning, he's trusting that you won't terminate him early. Trust also means having confidence that information disclosed will not be passed on to other people inappropriately and that it won't become the basis of gossip or idle conversation. Finally, trust means believing that you won't think less of the person for having revealed something.

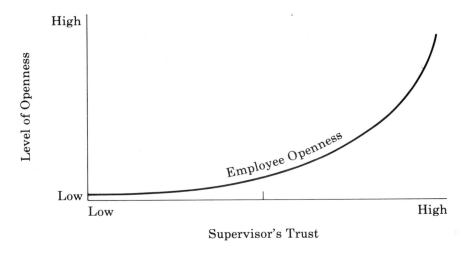

Figure 2.4 Relationship between employee's openness and
supervisor's trust

Establishing trust is a relatively simple process when handled properly. It involves three elements—*time, behavior,* and
openness. It takes time to build a trusting relationship. Don't
take shortcuts. To build trust you must behave in a trustworthy
manner. As your staff realizes that you can be trusted, they'll
become more open themselves. Share something of yourself;
others tend to be guarded when they don't know you. This is true
even if your record is clear—that is, even if you have never
violated someone's trust. You'll encourage others to trust *you* if
you demonstrate a trust in *them* by being open yourself.

Developing Your Conversational Skills

Conversational skills can be one of your most important
tools as a supervisor. If you were to tune in to a conversation,
you'd observe four basic elements.

1. The extent to which both people are talking about the
   same subject
2. The extent to which subject matter is dealt with in either generalities or specifics

3. The extent to which factual data are emphasized or feelings and reactions are emphasized

4. The extent to which each is listening

Each element is related to a conversational skill that you can develop and refine in order to help you get the most out of talks with members of your staff.

Controlling the Topic of Conversation

Unless everyone is talking about the same thing, there's little chance for a meaningful conversation. In many conversations people simply take turns talking about different subjects.

The skill and patience to stay with a topic long enough to fully understand the other person is very important. Staying with a subject allows the participants in the conversation to become comfortably immersed in their discussion, thereby breaking down some of the barriers to disclosure.

You can manage the content of a conversation in four ways—each uses techniques that increase your control.

1. Maintaining   In maintaining the topic of conversation you actually exercise *no* control over its content. Whatever the other person brings up, you discuss. You are simply there listening, supporting, acknowledging, and confirming what the other person says.

2. Expanding   By expanding the topic of conversation you exercise a minimal amount of direction and control. You do this by asking questions and encouraging conversation. Some examples of expanding are when you ask "How did you feel about that?" or when you say "Tell me more about that." Expanding allows you to stay with a topic and explore it in depth. Your result is a better understanding of the subject discussed and of the person you talked with.

3. Steering   Steering the conversation increases your control. It allows you to move to other topics without breaking the other person's immersion in the conversation. You steer a conversation by first addressing the subject introduced by the other person in adequate detail and then asking a question about a related topic. Thus you maintain the conversation but gently direct the subject.

4. Changing   You change the subject of a conversation by ignoring the topic introduced by the other person and interjecting your own. This breaks immersion and occasionally generates hostility if you don't adequately permit the other person his or her own topic of interest.

Moving from Generalities to Specifics

You can discuss a topic very generally, very specifically, or somewhere in between these two extremes. Talking about something in generalities is usually less threatening than talking about it in specifics. Therefore, introduce a topic in general terms and then, as the conversation develops, narrow it down to specifics.

Emphasizing Feelings and Reactions

As you attempt to become acquainted with your employees, you'll need to discuss not just their experiences but also their feelings and reactions. Many opportunities to know someone better are missed if you fail to ask questions about feelings relating to experiences. All too often, people assume that others must feel the same way they would under similar circumstances.

Listening

In all of your conversations, don't forget to *listen*. It does little good to develop conversation skills and create a climate supporting openness unless you listen to what your staff members say. Effective listening is not just a matter of remaining silent. It is an engaging, active process.

Appropriate Silence.   Sit back and allow the other person the opportunity to talk. Don't jump in and take over the conversation. You are there to become acquainted with the other person, not to tell him or her about yourself. Silence begins to become *inappropriate* when the other person doesn't know what to say or has decided not to respond on a topic. When this happens, get involved and relieve the stress.

Bridging.   By demonstrating your attention and interest you encourage the other person to talk. Bridging typically includes eye contact, nodding your head, and words that add no content to the conversation, such as "yeah," "okay," "uh-huh," and "I see."

Restating.   Select the last significant word or two that were spoken by the other person and say them back. You have to listen closely to be able to do this, but it encourages further elaboration on the point.

Summarizing.   Occasional summarizing during a conversation serves two major purposes. It demonstrates that you've been listening and understand what was said, and it permits you to verify your understanding.

Conducting a Conversation

Conversations specifically intended for you to become better acquainted are frequently held upon your initial contact—when either you or the staff member is first assigned to the department. Subsequent conversations might be triggered by specific events or be held periodically, say monthly or quarterly. Whenever these conversations occur, try to make them as positive as you possibly can for both of you.

Choose a Convenient Time

Select a time when both of you can devote proper attention to the conversation. These conversations need time to develop immersion and depth. You must be sensitive and considerate of what your staff member is doing. If he or she is facing a critical work deadline, it will be difficult to relax and get involved in this conversation. Show your employee the simple courtesy of asking "Do you have time to talk now, or would another time soon be more convenient?"

Choose an Appropriate Setting

Physical environment can either support or detract from a conversation. For effective communication, you need both privacy and comfort. Select a setting that's free from intrusion and distraction. It could be your office, your staff member's office, a conference room, or even a restaurant, if it's quiet and private. When meeting in offices be sure to either turn off the telephone or have it answered by someone else. Seating should be arranged to minimize distraction from activity in the area. Sit close enough to be easily heard and try not to have anything, such as a desk or table, between yourself and the other person.

Appear Relaxed

When you are relaxed, open, and responsive, others will be more at ease. Consider such things as facial expression, posture, freedom of movement—particularly hand gestures—how communicative you are, and how loudly or softly you speak. To encourage conversation, facial expressions should reflect the mood of the conversation. In the absence of contrary indications, a warm friendly smile almost unfailingly reflects acceptance and support. Posture should be comfortable and relaxed. Gestures should be smooth and open. Speak freely and openly, but be careful of taking over the conversation or leading it off course. Speak softly, but loudly enough to be heard.

Finally, suggest through your actions that there is adequate time for the conversation. Don't appear anxious to end it by continually checking the time, looking at the door, fidgeting, or starting to get up. Sometimes you may have a time limitation. If so, deal with it openly, then give the other person your full attention during the time available.

Stay with a Topic

To gain depth in a conversation you must stay with a topic. Wandering from one topic to another is probably the most common reason for not getting to know someone through a conversation. First, you must dedicate sufficient time to the conversation in order to allow immersion to develop. Second, you must stay with a topic long enough that you really get to know the other person's viewpoint.

One way to look at the process of getting acquainted is by comparing it to exploring a cave. If you really want to know what's at the end of the cave, you have to stay with your exploration. Sometimes you'll run into side passages that lead nowhere. Sometimes you'll discover a good reason to turn around and go back. But to really find out what's at the bottom, you must stay with it and press on. In the end, you'll look back and marvel at what was found, the experience of finding it, and the satisfaction of attaining a worthwhile goal.

Get Beneath the Surface

Staying with a topic leads to immersion, which allows you to move from a discussion of objective facts to a discussion of feelings and reactions. When you move to the feelings side of a topic you begin to penetrate the various levels of a person. A four-step procedure is involved.

1. Ask general questions that emphasize feelings and reactions.
2. Listen to the responses including how things are said as well as what is said.
3. Draw inferences from what you hear.
4. Check out your inferences either by summarizing them for verification or seeking confirming information from other sources.

Some questions you might ask the employee are:

- Describe your most satisfying work experience. Why did you feel that way about it?

- Describe your most dissatisfying work experience. Why did you feel that way about it?
- Describe the best supervisor you ever had. What qualities caused you to feel that way about him or her?
- Describe the worst supervisor you ever worked for. Why do you consider this person to be the worst?
- What do you look forward to? What is your goal for the next five years? What do you see as the next significant event on your life's horizon?
- What concerns do you have for the future? Why do these things concern you?
- What type of workgroup do you prefer to be a part of?
- What has been the major influence in your life that accounts for where you are today?

Avoid Contamination

When you ask a question in a way that reveals your own attitude, you contaminate the question. Faced with *your* attitudes, the other person must choose to agree with you, differ with you, or brush the topic aside with a noncommittal response. How would you feel about responding to the examples below if you were an employee?

- **Example 1.** *Poor:* "What do you think of all these crazy kids entering the workforce today? All they want to do is work as little as possible and draw a paycheck." *Better:* "What's your assessment of the new generation of employees we are seeing in the workforce?"
- **Example 2.** *Poor:* "You don't have any limitations or restrictions on traveling, do you?" *Better:* "Do you see any limitations or restrictions on your traveling?"

Avoid Making Value Judgments

As your employee discloses various experiences, reactions, and plans, avoid expressing your value judgments of them. By criticizing what someone tells you, you risk cutting yourself off from future disclosures. People simply don't like to be judged negatively, so they'll avoid talking about things that might incur it. This doesn't mean you have to agree with everything you're told. Feel free to express your own honest feelings, but without judging the other person. For example, if a staff member tells you of some plans that you think are really "out in left field," rather than criticize the plans, consider saying something like: "While I can't see myself doing anything like that, I can see it really makes you happy. If your plans eventually materialize, I wish you lots of luck and success."

Don't Make Assumptions

You should never make assumptions about people. *Don't assume anything.* While this may be an overstatement for the sake of emphasis, one of the major interferences with effective communication is created by assuming rather than asking. It is a common practice that you must overcome. There are three ways to avoid this.

1. Clarify your understanding of what someone tells you by asking such questions or making such statements as: "What do you mean by that?" "I don't understand." "Could you give me an example of that?" "Is this what you mean?"
2. Verify the other person's understanding of what you have told him or her by such questions as: "What is your understanding of what we have been discussing?" "What has each of us agreed to do as a result of this discussion?"
3. Add sufficient context to your communications to ensure understanding. The meaning of words comes from individual understanding of them and from the context in which they are used. Ease the burden on your listener by choosing readily understood words and by adding background and explanation to your discussion.

✔ Checklist of Conversational Techniques

- Control the conversation by
  - maintaining it

- expanding it
- steering it
- changing it
- Explore feelings and reactions
- Actively listen by
  - bridging
  - restating
  - summarizing
- Choose an appropriate setting
- Appear relaxed
- Stay with a topic
- Get beneath the surface
- Avoid contaminating the conversation
- Avoid making value judgments
- Don't make assumptions

Your Ethical Limitations and Responsibilities

Getting acquainted with members of your staff has limitations. It *is* possible for you to get *too* well acquainted and become unable to maintain the supervisor–employee relationship. In this regard be especially watchful of

- expression of emotions
- inappropriate disclosure
- autonomy and freedom of choice

Expression of Emotions

Cultural constraints limit what we consider to be acceptable expression of strong feelings—happy, sad, angry, excited, hurt, and so on. Expression of strong feelings is often seen as evidence of inadequate self-control or as a character weakness. When an emotional outpouring occurs, the one who expressed the strong emotions may later feel embarrassed, vulnerable, or inadequate. The individual may be reluctant to face the other person again.

Be careful to avoid or minimize these highly emotional scenes in your talks with employees. If someone seems headed toward this depth of expression try to break the direction by emphasizing objective information rather than feelings, or change the subject.

Inappropriate Disclosure

Occasionally a conversation may progress to the point where an employee inappropriately discloses experiences, feelings, or attitudes that might best be left private. When the fine line between a working relationship and friendship is crossed, there is potential for embarrassment and dependency. Embarrassment results if the information isn't treated with confidence and respect. A person may also be embarrassed for having made disclosures that disconfirms his or her self-image. Dependency results if the information is used either openly or subtly to manipulate or exclude the person from opportunity. How would you handle these two cases of inappropriate disclosure?

- *Marital Problems.* "In a relaxed moment, he talked about his marital problems. I mentioned the only anonymous sexual experience I'd ever had. It didn't seem inappropriate at the time but halfway through the story I realized he was pulling back—looking embarrassed. I knew I'd gone too far, but it was too late."
- *Drug Use.* "I confided to my boss that I'd had a flashback, from a 60s LSD trip. At the time he was noncommittal, but later I found out he told his boss I was *having* flashbacks—not that I had had *one* a year ago!"

Responsible supervisors will be sensitive to these potential dangers. When disclosure begins to take on the appearance of going beyond what is appropriate, raise a concern. Ask the employee to decide whether or not to continue. If disclosure is made, treat the information with strict confidence. Never probe into inappropriate areas of an employee's life.

Autonomy and Freedom of Choice

As a responsible supervisor you must recognize the autonomy of others and not use your relationship and knowledge of your staff to influence them for solely self-serving reasons. Everyone has the right to make his or her own choices in life. Sometimes your interests will be in opposition to the best interests of a staff member. An example might be your interest in keeping a good employee and the employee's interest in leaving for a better opportunity at another company. It would be inappropriate for you to attempt to influence the individual against his or her best interests in this instance. However, you *can* create opportunities to discuss and explore alternatives with your staff and still allow them the freedom to decide what is best.

Your Action Guide

When you take time to talk with the members of your staff, you enhance your working relationships and become acquainted with information that allows you to work more effectively together. You can better match your employees' talents, interests, and skills with work assignments. You can predict your staff's responses to planned change. You can increase the flow of suggestions from your staff. And you can influence staff behavior, and counsel individuals on their personal problems.

Getting acquainted means discovering what makes an individual unique—what makes him tick. You begin to see how the person is motivated, what interests him, what he expects from his work experience, how the individual sees himself, what standards guide his performance, what he values, and where the person sees himself going in life.

It takes time to develop a relationship that will support this depth of disclosure. It also takes an interpersonal climate that says it is okay for people to reveal this much about themselves. Such a climate is characterized by acceptance, support, and trust. It requires skill on your part in conducting conversations with your staff.

There are potential dangers of going too far when you have a climate and the skills to get this well acquainted. A responsible supervisor will be sensitive to this possibility and never probe in inappropriate areas and will either caution or head off those who seem to be headed there on their own.

People are very complex. The "real" person is difficult to get to know. Often, people hide their inner thoughts and feelings because they believe revealing these thoughts and feelings would make themselves less acceptable to others. As a supervisor don't expect to become fully acquainted with your staff, but do try to move to a level of acquaintance that exposes you to true and honest personal information relevant to a successful working relationship.

- ✔ Set aside 5 to 15 minutes each week to talk privately with each staff member.

- ✔ Establish a climate of trust, first by being open with staff members, and second by not embarrassing or ridiculing them.

- ✔ Stay with a topic of conversation until you have a complete understanding of the other person's point of view— don't assume anything.

- ✔ Explore reactions to, and feelings about, experiences.

- ✔ Listen attentively—summarize and play back your understanding for verification.

References

James F. T. Bugental, *Talking* (In Press).

Jack R. Gibb, "Defensive Communication," *Journal of Communication,* September 1961.

Marion E. Haynes, "Communicating for Understanding," *Texas and Southwest Hotel–Motel Review,* December 1979.

Marion E. Haynes, "Becoming an Effective Listener," *Supervisory Management,* August 1979. (Reprinted in *Transactions on Professional Communication,* June 1980.)

Marion E. Haynes, "Communication Problems on the Job," *Health Services Manager,* March 1980.

Niki Scott, "Don't Tell the Boss More Than He Wants to Know," *Houston Chronicle,* October 3, 1980.

Ed Yager, "When New Hires Don't Make the Grade," *Personnel Journal,* May 1980.

THE PERFORMANCE MANAGEMENT SYSTEM

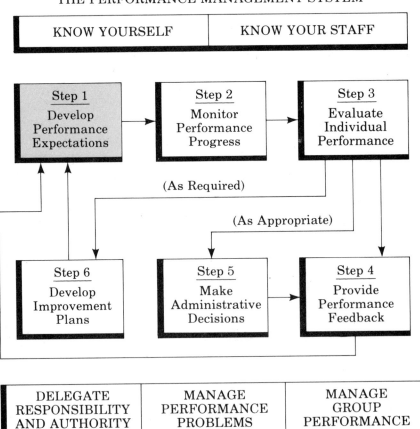

CHAPTER 3

Developing Performance Expectations

As a result of reading this chapter you will

- Understand the need for developing performance expectations
- Be able to write job descriptions for your staff
- Be able to develop results areas and performance indicators for your staff
- Understand the role of performance standards and be able to determine them for jobs under your supervision
- Be able to implement a managing by objectives system in your department
- Be able to establish performance expectations for each member of your staff

Step 1 in the Performance Management System is to *develop performance expectations* with your staff. Agreement between you and your staff about the work they are to do is fundamental to effective supervision. Your agreement should include descriptions of duties to be performed, results to be achieved, and priorities on your workers' use of their time. Such an agreement becomes the cornerstone of performance management and provides motivation and direction for your staff to carry out their work. And, it provides you a means of control and a basis for evaluating your staff and their effectiveness.

You and Your Staff May See Things Differently

Most employees, some authorities estimate as much as 95 percent of the workforce, want to do a good job. These people go about their work as they see it. But sometimes their results don't measure up to their supervisor's expectations. Frequently, this is because the supervisor and employee have different perceptions of the job. (See Figure 3.1.)

The lack of a clear understanding of performance expectations that are shared by both worker and supervisor has been demonstrated in a number of research studies. One such study was conducted in a semiprofessional, federal government agency. Among other things, it examined the priorities that

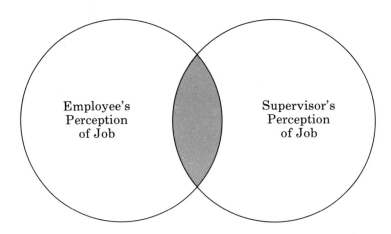

Figure 3.1 Differing perceptions of a job

	Priorities Set by:	
Duties	Supervisors	Managers
Monitor and control performance	1	1
Lead and motivate employees	7	2
Review and evaluate performance	2	3
Assign and distribute work	3	4
Provide technical assistance	5	5
Coordinate group operations	4	6
Train and develop employees	6	7
Communicate downward	9	8
Maintain good human relations	10	9
Handle administrative duties	8	10
Communicate upward	11	11

Figure 3.2 Comparison of priorities set by supervisors and
their managers on supervisory duties in a federal
government agency
From Hunt and Lichtman, "Role Clarity, Communication, and
Conflict," Management of Personnel Quarterly.

first-level supervisors and their managers placed on various specific duties. The results are shown in Figure 3.2.

Notice the difference in the priorities set by the supervisors and managers. Supervisors place higher priorities on monitoring technical performance—assigning and distributing work, monitoring and controlling performance, and reviewing and evaluating performance. They see their main role as "pushing the work through" by passing the expectations of management down to the worker level and assuring their fulfillment. Managers, on the other hand, place higher priority on leading and motivating employees.

Another study was conducted among the membership of a professional association. It examined the priorities that personnel administrators and the executives they report to placed on various duties and activities. Figure 3.3 shows the results.

Again, the differences in priorities are striking. While there tends to be *general* agreement about the first three items on the list, substantial disagreement occurs over the next three.

	Priorities Set by:	
Duties	Personnel Administrators	Executive Managers
Affirmative action	2	1
Recruiting	3	2
Wage and salary administration	1	3
Employee selection	27	4
Training and development	23	5 5 >tie
Human resource planning	12	

Figure 3.3 Comparison of priorities set by personnel administrators and their managers on administrative duties in a professional association
From White and Wolfe, "The Role Desired for Personnel Administration," Personnel Administrator, June 1980.

Executive management places much greater importance on planning, selection, training, and development than do personnel administrators. Regardless of which group is "right," there's obviously been a breakdown in communication between the two groups concerning the personnel department's role.

The lack of clear understanding of performance expectations not only concerns priorities but also duties to be performed and results to be achieved. Differences in perceptions in these critical areas are a major factor in many cases of substandard performance. The following pages present ideas for clearing up this ambiguity in job perceptions.

Clearing up Job Ambiguities

Essentially speaking, developing performance expectations is probably mostly a matter of defining and clarifying. There are four elements in a *systematic approach* to removing uncertainty and ambiguity from jobs. These are:

1. Job descriptions
2. Results areas with performance indicators

3. Performance standards

4. Objectives

Figure 3.4 illustrates these elements and how they interrelate.

The starting place for clearing up job ambiguity is a job description. At this point you and your staff reach an agreement on basic job content and scope. The next step is to identify areas in which staff members are expected to produce results—that is, areas where they spend their time and other resources. Within each "results area," performance indicators are identified that can be monitored to let both you and the employee know how progress is going. "Performance standards" should then be developed for each performance indicator, so that actual performance can be measured against each indicator. Objectives are set within various results areas for new opportunities for performance, as well as when actual performance compared to performance standards indicates a need for improvement.

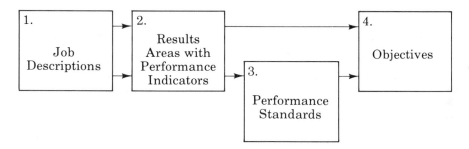

Figure 3.4 Elements of a systematic approach to establishing performance expectations

Some jobs do not lend themselves to this systematic approach. A *simplified approach,* in which a job description and performance standards are combined into *performance requirements,* is presented on pages 83–87.

Job Descriptions

Most modern personnel management specialists recommend job descriptions for all positions in an organization. Job descriptions definitely help clarify ambiguous performance expectations, but they also serve many additional functions as well. Some of these are described below.

- *Salary administration.* Job descriptions form the basis for comparing jobs within a company to ensure proper alignment of salary ranges and also for comparing jobs externally to ensure competitive community pay practices.

- *Personnel selection.* Job descriptions are a significant aid in recruiting, selecting, and placing employees. They serve as a resource for developing job specifications that list the qualifications applicants must have in order to be considered for a job.

- *Orientation.* Job descriptions can quickly and efficiently introduce employees to new job assignments.

- *Performance appraisal.* Job descriptions serve as one means of comparing how an employee fulfills an assigned job to how it *should* be fulfilled.

- *Training and Development.* Job descriptions permit an accurate analysis of training needs and the development of a logical sequence of promotional opportunities to aid in career development.

- *Organization clarification and planning.* The initial development of job descriptions shows where overlaps and gaps in responsibilities occur. Job descriptions clarify who is responsible for what in an organization. This can lead to a reallocation of duties and responsibilities to ensure complete coverage and a better balance in assignments.

- *Clarification of responsibilities.* Job descriptions help individuals understand the various duties and responsibilities assigned to them and provide a means for supervisors and staff to agree on job content, scope, and authorities.

Writing Job Descriptions

A well-prepared job description requires two basic ingredients—knowledge of the job being described and writing skills. Writing job descriptions should be reserved for a time when your department is in a fairly stable state of affairs. Descriptions written when operations are in a state of turmoil or change are often wasted because they soon become outmoded or hold little resemblance to the normal working conditions and actual work.

Most job descriptions are written either by the person actually doing the job or by a staff specialist from the personnel department. Frequently, the best approach is to have these two people work as a team.

Depending on your approach and on the complexity of the job, it may take from four to seven hours of staff time to finalize a job description. Here are the steps usually involved in the process.

1. *Information-gathering.* First, necessary information about a job is gathered. This can be handled by a staff specialist through observation, interview, or questionnaire. Ordinarily, it's simply a matter of the person actually doing the job listing all the duties or activities associated with it.

2. *Drafting.* Next, a first draft is written—usually by the staff specialist who collected the related information. This draft should follow any standard formatting desired by the company or individual department.

3. *Reviewing and approving.* The first draft now undergoes review and revision or approval by the appropriate people. Review and approval usually starts with the employee directly involved in the job, then proceeds to the supervisor in charge of the job, and may continue to include second-level management and the personnel department. At each step in this review and approval process, the draft is revised as necessary as different views of the job are reconciled.

4. *Finalizing.* Once the draft copy is finally approved, putting it in its final form should be fairly simple. This step is usually handled by a staff specialist in order to ensure uniformity of style and content.

5. *Updating.* It's unlikely that any job will stay the same for very long. Therefore, regularly reviewing job descrip-

tions, say once every one or two years, provides the opportunity to make whatever changes are required to reflect the current state of affairs. When updating a description, just follow the same steps taken in developing original job descriptions. Updating, however, usually takes substantially less time and effort.

What Goes into a Job Description?

The format and content of job descriptions vary between companies. You should check to see if your organization has a standardized approach already developed. If not, the format and content used as an example in Exhibit 3.1 and described on the following pages might work well for you.

- *Job identification.* At the top of the job description is information identifying the job being described. This includes department, location, salary grade or range, and overtime status under the Fair Labor Standards Act.

- *Basic function.* This opening section serves as a summary and general introduction to the job. It typically states the job's basic purpose, telling why it exists and what distinguishes it from others in the organization in brief, direct language.

- *Duties and responsibilities.* Next is a list of the principal duties and responsibilities that must be carried out in the job. These are usually presented in the order of their importance. Appropriate subheadings can be used to define related activities.

- *Delegation of authorities.* Financial and/or personnel authority related to the job is defined here. This section is optional and depends on the level of job being described.

- *Working relationships.* Relationships that are key to effectively carrying out the job are described. These are frequently grouped under the headings of internal and external relationships. The section should include staff members, other departments, customers, suppliers, government agencies, and so forth.

- *Working conditions.* This section describes the environment in which the job is performed, along with other appropriate conditions, such as safety hazards, work pace, and travel required.

- *Qualifications*. This is where the necessary experience, training, and other qualifications required to successfully fulfill the job are covered. You should be careful that actual talent, knowledge, and skills are described rather than artificial qualifications such as degrees and years of service.

Limitations of Job Descriptions

Job descriptions are an excellent starting place in developing performance expectations. However, two limitations, or concerns, must not be overlooked. First, job descriptions are *activities-oriented* rather than *results-oriented*. That is, they typically detail what an employee does rather than the results to be achieved. Second, employees may see the job description as defining the *limits* of their jobs and therefore refuse to do anything not specifically listed in the duties and responsibilities section. To circumvent this potential problem, the last item of the *duties* section on many job descriptions reads: "All other appropriate and reasonable duties that may be assigned." This usually allows sufficient flexibility for meeting changes that might occur between revisions of the job description.

EXHIBIT 3.1   Example of a Job Description

Instructor: Management and Supervisory Skills

Department: Employee Relations   Date: July 1, 1981
Division: Management Development   Salary Grade: 10-12
Location: Head Office   FLSA Status: Exempt
                                                             (Prof.)

I. Basic Function

Instructors in management and supervisory skills design and present training seminars and workshops to increase

Exhibit 3.1   (*continued*)

the effectiveness of the company's managers and supervisors. They are expected to utilize effective instructional techniques in order to maximize the learning experience. Program designs vary in length from two hours to a full week or more depending upon the nature of material to be covered.

II. Duties and Responsibilities

1. Present training material in a classroom setting in lecture/discussion format supplemented with appropriate exercises and audio-visual equipment.

2. Design training programs to accomplish learning objectives.

3. Select and/or design appropriate training materials and coordinate their purchase or reproduction.

4. Arrange for, or advise host locations on, facilities required to accommodate class size and program design.

5. Coordinate program attendance, or advise host locations, to verify appropriate match between target audiences and participants.

6. Evaluate programs presented to ensure attainment of learning objectives. Modify program design as required.

7. Counsel participants' supervisor on appropriate ways to reinforce learning in the workplace.

8. Stay abreast of developments in the profession and needs within the organization and propose new programs as appropriate.

9. Prepare and submit annual budget proposals for assigned program areas.

10. Monitor expenses, by program, to stay within approved budget.

11. Advise field level training personnel on program design, instructional techniques, and evaluation techniques as requested.

Exhibit 3.1   (continued)

---

12. Carry out special projects and all other appropriate and reasonable duties that may be assigned from time to time.

III. Delegation of Authorities

1. *Personnel Authority.* This position has no delegated personnel authority.
2. *Financial Authority.* This position has approval authority for the purchase of goods and services up to $5,000 per purchase against approved budget.

IV. Working Relationships

1. *Departmental Staff*
   Must negotiate with other staff members to share the services of administrative support and secretarial staff over whom the employee has no supervisory authority.
2. *Service Departments*
   Must work effectively with purchasing, graphics, printing, and correspondence services in arranging for the procurement or production of training materials.
3. *Client Departments*
   Must provide for the balance of participation in program areas from various client departments served.
4. *Suppliers*
   Must manage the procurement and delivery of meeting facilities and support services from outside suppliers.

V. Working Conditions

This job is performed in both an office and classroom environment. Substantial travel is required with about 75 percent of the work being carried out away from headquarters.

VI. Qualifications

1. Must be able to work effectively with others over whom he or she has no organizational authority.

Exhibit 3.1   (continued)

2. Must be familiar with, and supportive of, current approaches to optimizing the utilization of human resources.
3. Must be familiar with the company's management philosophy and organizational structure.
4. Must be familiar with training program design and the utilization of audio-visual techniques.
5. Must be an effective public speaker.
6. Must be able to perform successfully under minimum supervision.
7. Must be sufficiently flexible and resourceful to cope with the inherent uncertainties of the profession.
8. Must have experienced sufficient organizational success to establish credibility with participants.

Results Areas with Performance Indicators

While job descriptions provide a detailed summary of the jobs described, they don't focus on *results*. Results areas with performance indicators pick up where job descriptions leave off.

"Results areas" reflect where individuals invest their time, talent, energy, and other resources. They are general categories in which work is performed.

"Performance indicators" are items that can be monitored to let you know how well a results area is being handled. They answer either of two questions: (1) "How do I know when I am doing a good job in this area?" or (2) "What happens when I don't do a good job in this area?"

Figure 3.5 shows examples of results areas with performance indicators.

Financial Results	Employee Relations
☐ Actual costs versus budget	☐ Staff turnover
☐ Cost per unit of output	☐ Absenteeism
☐ Net profit per sale	☐ Number of grievances

Figure 3.5 Example of results areas with performance indicators

How to Write Results Areas and Performance Indicators

In order to write a good list of results areas and performance indicators, you need to be familiar with the job being described. The most common approach is to have the person currently doing the job handle this project. Usually, two to three hours of staff time will be required. The following steps are typically involved.

1. *Drafting.* After generally explaining what's to be done, have the employee prepare a listing of results areas and performance indicators related to his or her job. *All* of the performance indicators that can be identified should be written down. Later, the list can be culled.

2. *Reviewing and approving.* Next, you review the employee's draft. During your review, be sure to note any differences between your understanding of the job and ideas contained in the draft. After these differences have been resolved, the draft is agreed to and approved.

3. *Finalizing.* With an approved draft, finalizing is a simple step of typing the information into an approved format. Appropriate identification information is added at this point.

4. *Updating.* Results areas and performance indicators should be reviewed annually. Changes can then be made as necessary to keep the information current.

When writing results areas, follow the guidelines below.

- Limit descriptions to one-, two-, or three-word statements.
- Generalize to accommodate changes of activities within certain categories that do not change. For example, use "project management" as a general description rather than list specific projects currently underway.

The Content of Performance Indicators

Performance indicators can be classified as pre-indicators, concurrent indicators, or terminal indicators, depending on when the information is available in relation to the results being achieved. In employee relations, for example, one pre-indicator is results from an employee opinion survey; an example of a concurrent indicator would be the number of grievances received; and a terminal indicator would be the rate of staff turnover. The earlier you can be alerted to impending performance problems, the better you can take action to prevent poor results.

When writing performance indicators, follow these guidelines:

- Identify *what* is to be measured, not how much or in what direction. Leave out words like "increase," "improve," and "decrease."
- Limit indicators to things that can be measured or counted; don't include statements of ideal conditions such as "good morale."
- Recognize that some indicators are "soft" numbers—that is, they aren't absolute, objective measures—they're only indicators. For example, the number of customer complaints is an indicator of customer satisfaction but not an absolute measure—some dissatisfied customers do not complain: they take their business somewhere else.

Limitations of Results Areas with Performance Indicators

Results areas with performance indicators are a significant step beyond job descriptions in gaining clarity of expectations.

EXHIBIT 3.2   Example of Results Areas with Performance Indicators

Instructor: Management and Supervisory Skills

Results Areas with Performance Indicators (in priority order)	*Time Allocation*
1. Program Presentation • Employee days of class time • Participant evaluations • Program reputation • Requests for participation	60%
2. Program Design • Attainment of learning objectives • New program offerings • Participant evaluations • Program costs	10%
3. Program Planning and Coordination • Participant to class size ratio • Materials availability • Facilities availability	10%
4. Administrative Responsibilities • Budget approvals • Actual expenses versus budget • Audit results	5%
5. Advise and Counsel • Project profitability • Project completion: actual versus planned • Requests for assistance	5%
6. Organizational Relationships • Acceptance of proposals • Ratio of participation • Access to colleagues	5%
7. Professional Development • Program participation-application • Articles published • Teaching contracts	5%

They focus on results to be achieved and on indicators that let you know the extent results are being achieved. This is much more helpful than focusing on duties or activities. However, still unanswered are the questions of *how much,* or *at what level,* these results are to be achieved. Performance indicators do not specify the desired level or the norm that should be reached or maintained. This is their basic limitation. Without some standard for comparison, the exercise of monitoring progress is empty. That's where *performance standards* come into the picture.

Performance Standards

Performance standards have long been a part of management planning. Basically they describe what constitutes satisfactory performance of a job. Figure 3.6 is an example of performance standards. Performance standards typically deal with input/output ratios, expense or income/budget ratios, errors or rejects/output ratios, timeliness measures, quantity of output measures, and so on. In their early development performance standards were applied to industrial production jobs and were commonly called production quotas. As recognition of their value grew, they moved into the office, where they were initially applied to clerical jobs. Today performance standards are finding applications in management jobs as well.

Performance will be considered satisfactory when

- frequency of lost time injuries is less than 4.0 per million employee hours worked
- hours paid for but not worked (excluding vacation) are less than 15 per 1000 employee hours worked
- pump and engine maintenance cost is less than $450 per unit per year
- warehouse turnover exceeds 200 percent per year

Figure 3.6 Example of performance standards

How to Write Performance Standards

Depending on the types of jobs involved, performance standards are developed and written either by the supervisor, the person filling the job, or a specialist, usually from an industrial engineering department. A higher level of acceptance and commitment can be expected when the employee has a hand in developing the standards. The following steps are typically involved.

1. *Planning.* The first step focuses on the results areas (described earlier on pages 70–74) to be covered by performance standards and on the performance indicators to be monitored. Typically, some 70 to 80 percent of an employee's time may be covered by performance standards.

2. *Prioritizing.* Having selected the results areas to be covered by performance standards, these areas should now be prioritized. Priorities may change during a performance period, but there must be agreement at the start between employee and supervisor.

3. *Establishing standards.* For jobs that have been in existence for some time, historical data (that is, what has been acceptable in the past) becomes the starting point for establishing standards. Appropriate adjustments are then worked out for the future. Past performance may be a satisfactory standard for the future, but higher or lower levels may be warranted. Initial standards for newly created jobs are derived either from expert opinion or from comparison to similar jobs in other departments or companies. These initial standards are adjusted as direct experience is gained and appropriate historical data becomes available.

4. *Reviewing and approving.* The last step is to review the standards that have been developed with your manager to obtain approval. This step is necessary to ensure organizational support for your plans and to moderate the levels of expectation among supervisors of common functions. It's important that you don't expect more or less of your staff than other supervisors do of similar groups.

Content of Performance Standards

Statements of performance standards tend to be less formal than job descriptions. Therefore, there is a range of style and format you can use, depending on how high into upper management the statements will be passed along. Statements that only you retain in working with your staff might be handwritten. Others, that are passed on to your manager, might be typed and conform to a standard company format. Some standards are negotiated with unions and become contracts. Exhibit 3.3 is an example of a set of performance standards. You might use it and the outline discussed below as a model.

- *Heading*. A heading simply identifies the employee covered by the standards. It can be by name or job title or both.

- *Results areas*. After a heading, the areas in which results are to be accomplished are identified. List them in order of priority.

- *Performance indicators*. In each results area, identify the performance indicators for which standards are established.

- *Performance standards*. Finally, identify the performance standard established for each indicator. Occasionally, a two-tier system is used—one tier identifying satisfactory performance and another tier identifying outstanding performance.

Limitations of Performance Standards

Performance standards bring substantial clarity to performance expectations. But they can have two limitations. One is that employees may concentrate on achieving standards simply because they are written down and ignore or exclude more important opportunities that aren't reflected in standards, such as implementing new equipment or methods and exploring new ideas. Also, some supervisors become overzealous in their use of standards and create "scorekeeping" competitions among staff members. Unless you are both able and willing to measure something, don't set a standard.

EXHIBIT 3.3   Example of Performance Standards

Instructor: Management and Supervisory Skills

1. Program Presentation
   Performance in this results area will be considered satisfactory when
   - 150 classroom days of instruction are presented annually
   - participant evaluations average 8.5 out of 10 for each program presented

2. Program Design
   Performance in this results area will be considered satisfactory when
   - participant to professional staff ratio is 20 to 1
   - supervisory evaluations indicate 80 percent of participants are able to apply subject matter taught

3. Program Planning and Coordination
   Performance in this results area will be considered satisfactory when
   - no program is cancelled due to lack of materials or facilities
   - participant to class size ratio is 0.94

4. Administrative Responsibilities
   Performance in this results area will be considered satisfactory when
   - expenses are within ±5 percent of budget
   - residential programs average participant-day cost, excluding salaries, is $100.00
   - nonresidential programs average participant-day cost, excluding salaries, is $35.00

5. Advise and Counsel
   Performance in this results area will be considered satisfactory when
   - project schedule objectives are met
   - project budget objectives are met

<u>**Exhibit 3.3**   **(continued)**</u>

6. Organizational Relationships
   Performance in this results area will be considered satisfactory when
   • participation from each segment of the company is in
     proportion to its share of the company's total manage-
     ment and supervisory staff
7. Professional Development
   Performance in this results area will be considered satisfactory when
   • five days of approved professional development work-
     shops/seminars are attended annually
   • three professional journals are regularly read each
     month

Managing by Objectives

   Managing by objectives is the process of sitting down with
your employees at the beginning of a project or work period and
agreeing on the results to be achieved. Objectives flow naturally
from performance standards. When actual performance falls
short of standard, an objective is set to bring performance back
in line. Also, new opportunities in an employee's results areas
become project-oriented objectives.
   Managing by objectives has two unique characteristics:
(1) it is results-oriented, thus clarifying who is to do what by

• Reduce absences in the department to two employee
  days per month, excluding vacation, by the end of third
  quarter 1982
• Publish a revised manual on purchasing procedures
  by July 1, 1983
• Eliminate filing backlog by March 1, 1982

Figure 3.7 Examples of objectives statements

when and (2) it works best when it involves employees in the managing process. Figure 3.7 shows some examples of objectives statements.

Below are some examples of the ways managing by objectives can contribute to an organization.

- *Improved performance.* Performance improves when employees know what they are expected to accomplish and have an increased sense of commitment when they participate in setting objectives.
- *Improved planning.* Mutual agreement on how results will be achieved brings improved planning to bear on work to be performed.
- *Improved coordination.* With a common purpose and sense of direction, the activities of an organization can be integrated to achieve expected results.
- *Improved control.* With plans developed and responsibilities detailed, key control points can easily be monitored for progress. You become aware of problems in time to deal with them.
- *Improved flexibility.* With plans and priorities established you can anticipate potential problem areas and have contingency plans to deal with problems that do arise.
- *Improved relationships.* Employees become more independent, and typically have greater freedom in decision making. They tend to see their supervisor as more supportive of their efforts.
- *Personal development.* Responsibilities are moved down to the worker's level in the organization, and employees develop more rapidly in their assignments. Also, each employee is expected to plan, organize, and control his or her own work area, thus developing three of the four functions of management.

Responsibilities Covered by Objectives

Each job assignment can be considered to have three components: (1) routine, (2) problem solving, and (3) innovation. These are shown in Figure 3.8. Innovation and problem solving

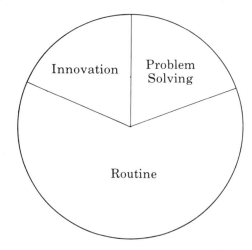

Figure 3.8 General components of a job assignment

are covered by objectives statements. (Routine is typically covered by performance standards.)

Routine.   This is the ordinary day-to-day activity of a job assignment. It is not necessarily easy to do. For example, it includes selling for salesmen, producing accounting reports for accountants, conducting training sessions for trainers. This part of a job is typically covered by performance standards and therefore needn't be covered by objectives.

Problem Solving.   This area includes the work done to return routine work to an acceptable level when performance standards are not being met. These problem areas should be written up as objectives in order to direct time and attention to them.

Innovation.   There is opportunity in nearly every job to do things differently and thereby do them better. Also, there usually are opportunities to stop doing work that no longer contributes to the department's purposes and to start doing other work that does. These are the areas to explore to find innovative objectives. These opportunities frequently get put off because of other demands.

How to Write Objectives Statements

Objectives are usually written by the person filling the job. Typically, an initial list of objectives is prepared at the beginning of a performance planning period and then added to, or changed, as the performance period unfolds. The following steps are involved in a managing by objectives system.

1. *Supervisory conference.* During this initial meeting between you and members of your staff, you pass along information you have about the direction your organization is setting for the coming work period. Also, you solicit ideas from staff members on areas of potential opportunity for problem solving or change.

2. *Drafting objectives.* Following the initial conference, staff members draw up a proposed list of objectives for their jobs during the next performance period.

3. *Review and approval.* You review and approve the objectives reflecting any changes appropriate and negotiated with the staff members. This sets the course for the employee during the coming period.

4. *Action planning.* The next step is to develop plans to achieve the agreed upon objectives. Typically, you should start with an objective statement that is optimistic. During the planning step develop a strategy to attain the objective. If a strategy can't be devised to achieve the optimistic objective this objective might need to be modified to make it more realistic.

5. *Periodic review.* With objectives set and plans underway, it's necessary and appropriate to monitor progress using periodic reviews. These sessions are best scheduled around key milestones in the plans, but should be held at least once every quarter.

Content of Objectives Statements

Statements of objectives should specify *what* is to be done by *when*. As appropriate, cost limitations or budgets should be included. The statements should definitely not include any reference to the means of accomplishing the objective. This would only limit the range of opportunity available when the action planning step (step 4) is dealt with. Follow the guidelines below when writing objectives.

Be Specific.   The statement should say exactly what is to be achieved and to what extent—for example: increase sales by 15 percent, reduce absenteeism by three employee days per month, remodel warehouse according to approved plans and budgets.

Use Measurable Objectives.   By being specific, objectives will be measurable, and you'll know for certain whether or not you've been successful at the end of the performance period.

Be Action Oriented   Objectives statements should say what is going to be done. By being action oriented, objectives are more easily measured. You'll know whether or not you did as you intended by the end of the period.

Be Realistic.   Good objective statements are realistic. While they might be optimistic at the outset, they should move into the realm of realism as the means to achieve them are developed. Avoid extremes, such as "100 percent" or "zero," that stand *no* chance of being accomplished.

Set Time Limits.   Good objective statements have a time limit for achievement built into them. People respond to deadlines. Without them things can easily be pushed farther into the future.

Examples of Objectives Statements

The most common mistakes in writing objectives statements are vagueness in defining the objectives and *how* they are to be achieved. Some of the following statements are good examples of objectives, some are not.

Increase market share from $8\frac{1}{2}$ to 10 percent by the end of 1984. This statement is satisfactory. It is specific, but doesn't say how the increase is to be achieved.

Improve customer satisfaction with after-sale service during 1983. This statement is vague in that it doesn't specify *what* will constitute improvement, such as reduction in the number of customer complaints or increase in the level of repeat business.

Complete the consolidation of the Mobile and Atlanta Districts by July 1, 1984, within approved budget. This statement is satisfactory.

Increase sales to retail outlets by 15 percent during 1984 through increased television and radio advertising resulting in an increase of 20 percent in the advertising budget. This statement would be satisfactory if it did not include *how* the increase in sales should be achieved ("through increased television and radio advertising resulting in an increase of 20 percent in the advertising budget").

Recruit, hire, and train two new sales representatives during the third quarter of 1984 at a cost not to exceed $10,000 and 80 hours of my time. This statement is satisfactory.

The Limitations of Objectives Statements

Objectives-setting has the same potential for limitations as setting performance standards. Staff members may become locked into achieving only the defined objectives and miss other opportunities that may come up during the performance period and that would contribute more to the business than the predetermined objectives. You can minimize this potential by being flexible and willing to consider reordering of priorities and by supporting these qualities in your employees.

Another potential danger is that some staff groups may develop competition over the *number* of objectives achieved, without regard to the actual contribution made by attaining each objective. In other words, they may sacrifice *quality* in order to achieve a greater *quantity* of objectives for the record.

A Simplified Approach: Performance Requirements

In jobs where employees do essentially the same things year after year, a simplified approach may be taken. Such jobs might include file clerks, laboratory technicians, and secretaries. For these situations, rather than the four elements in the systematic approach just described, the job description and performance standards can be merged into a form of *performance requirements*. In this simplified approach, the expectations can be worked out at the time of initial job startup. Then, they need only be updated as changes occur. When special projects are assigned, or problems develop, these can be handled in the form of objectives. Exhibit 3.4 is an example of performance requirements for a departmental secretary.

EXHIBIT 3.4   Example of Performance Requirements

Departmental Secretary

1. Taking Dictation
   Notes, letters, and memoranda will be taken by dictation. Reports will be drafted by the author in handwritten form. Shorthand should be taken at a minimum of 120 words per minute.

2. Typing and Editing
   All typed material shall conform to standard formatting with straight margins, no strikeovers, and no more than three corrections on any page. All work shall be proofread. All spelling and punctuation errors shall be corrected and suggestions on sentence construction are encouraged. Typing should be handled at a minimum of 50 words per minute.

3. Maintaining Files
   Two sets of files shall be maintained—a subject indexed file and a chronological file by author. All filing shall be completed weekly. Files shall be reviewed annually and most material three years or older shall be destroyed. (Exceptions will be discussed at time of reviews.)

4. Handling Incoming Mail
   Within 30 minutes of receipt, all incoming mail shall be opened (except that which is marked either personal

Exhibit 3.4   (*continued*)

or strictly personal), stamped in, and distributed within the office. Regardless of addressee, mail should be directed to the appropriate person for handling. Mail should be sorted into three categories—publications, correspondence not requiring a response, and correspondence requiring a response. All correspondence requiring file information for a response should be accompanied by the appropriate file.

5. Handling Outgoing Mail
   Mail shall be sent out on the day it is dated. All mail shall be sorted, addressed, and packaged according to established procedures to distinguish between intracompany handling and U.S. Mail Service handling. Personal mail shall be placed in the lobby mail drop.

6. Processing Invoices and Expense Accounts
   Invoices and expense statements shall be coded (including work orders), arithmetic verified, and proper approvals obtained. A summary of expenses, by work order, shall be maintained. A quarterly summary of expenses compared to budget shall be provided to the person responsible for each work order. Form of payment shall be determined by the person responsible for the expense—cash, field draft, check requisition, or routine check processing. Arrangements for temporary advances shall be handled as requested and records shall be maintained to see that they are cleared as indicated.

7. Maintaining Inventory of Office Supplies
   A one month's supply of commonly used office supplies shall be maintained. Current stock is to be checked weekly and orders placed as required. Where volume discounts are available, up to three months' supply may be ordered to take advantage of cost savings.

8. Making Travel Arrangements
   Make travel arrangements as requested utilizing the Airline Travel Guide and company procedures for ar-

---

Exhibit 3.4   (*continued*)

---

ranging for airline tickets, hotel, and rental car reservations. A current file of appropriate travel card numbers shall be kept for each staff member and used to obtain the best available service.

9. Answering Telephone Calls
   Answer telephones promptly with a friendly greeting and the name of the department or the name of the person to whom the telephone number is assigned. When answering the phone for someone out of the office, determine the nature of the caller's business and direct the caller to an appropriate other person or contact the absent staff member to return the call, as appropriate. When a caller is placed on hold, check back each minute to report the status of the situation.

10. Receiving Visitors
    Greet visitors, make them feel welcome, and inquire into the nature of their business. Direct them as appropriate. Announce visitors to staff members before ushering them into anyone's office.

11. Scheduling Appointments
    Maintain a forward monthly calendar for each staff member. (Know how to contact each staff member by phone at all times.) For those willing to delegate the task to you, make appointments as requested according to the forward schedule.

12. Personal Work Habits
    Arrive daily early enough to be ready for work at the beginning of the workday. Observe the normal lunch period and quitting time. Keep the work area neat and orderly. Limit personal phone calls and conversation.

How to Write Performance Requirements

Because of the organizational level covered by the simplified approach, performance requirements are usually written by the supervisor after a discussion with the employee doing the job. The following steps are involved.

1. *Initial conference.* In this initial meeting between you and your employee, each of you should voice your ideas about the job content and how it should be handled.
2. *Draft copy.* Following the initial conference, the ideas developed should be written up in draft form.
3. *Review and approval.* Both you and the employee should review and approve the draft copy, after negotiating any changes that are appropriate.
4. *Final copy.* Finally, the agreed upon draft copy is converted to a final copy. The employee receives a copy and you keep one for your files.

Content of Performance Requirements

Performance requirements cover the full range of duties and responsibilities assigned to an employee. They should concentrate on end-results to be achieved as much as possible and describe conditions that constitute satisfactory performance. Duties and responsibilities should be listed in priority order, so that when faced with conflicting time demands, an employee can decide what work to do first. Finally, the key elements of quantity, quality, cost limitations, and timeliness should be addressed, as appropriate.

Negotiating Performance Expectations

Staff members must be involved in developing the performance expectations that apply to their jobs for two basic reasons: (1) they have valuable information that will contribute to establishing appropriate expectations and (2) they'll be more willing to accept expectations that they've helped create.

The degree to which employees are involved will vary depending on the maturity level of the individual employee and on the particular element in the systematic approach to establishing performance expectations being worked on. With staff members who are low in either job or personal maturity you'll probably be very directive in deciding what is to be done and in deciding the performance standards that apply. On the other hand, employees who are high in both job and personal maturity may be able to develop their own standards for your review and approval. Figure 3.9 illustrates how employee contribution increases with the employee's maturity level.

Each of the elements in the systematic approach to developing performance expectations provides opportunity for employee involvement. However, some kinds of employee involvement are more important than others. In writing *job descriptions* the employee should be involved primarily as a source of information. Typically, a personnel specialist provides the expertise in formatting and brings consistency to the process. When detailing *results areas* and *performance indicators,* the employee, if qualified, should develop the first draft for your review and approval. On the other hand, you should negotiate *performance standards* and *objectives* through face-to-face discussions with the staff members involved. In these discussions, the participation of the employees should increase according to their maturity as shown in Figure 3.10. This participation allows development of a clear

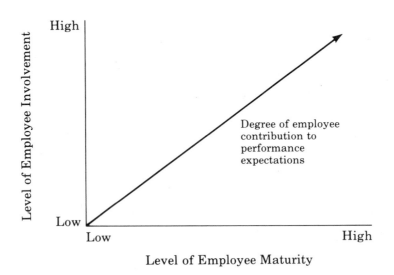

Figure 3.9 Relationship of employee maturity to employee
involvement in developing performance expectations

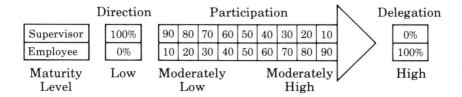

Figure 3.10   Percent of employee involvement
as a function of maturity

understanding of what is expected and development of a commitment to achieve the results agreed upon.

Supervisor's Role in Negotiating Performance Expectations

As a supervisor you have an active, responsible role of gaining an understanding with the employee on what is to be done and of obtaining the employee's commitment to accomplishing the job. While discussing and negotiating expectations you'll find yourself in the position of being any or all of the following.

Information Provider.   You have valuable, relevant information concerning past practices, practices in other parts of the organization, plans for the future, and an overall perspective. Any or all of this information may have a bearing on the final performance expectations developed by you and your staff.

Listener.   As the employee discusses his or her views and reactions to the expectations being developed, listen not only to content but also to feelings. Help the employee clarify both understanding and feelings by playing back what you hear.

Challenger.   As you elicit the employee's ideas, examine them to see that they represent an opportunity to achieve a worthwhile contribution. Challenge the person with low expectations to aim higher.

Reality Tester.   On the other hand, some employees, through lack of experience, may propose expectations that are too high. Check these out against reality. If appropriate, encourage the employee to modify his or her expectations.

Coach. Through your discussions provide guidance and encouragement. You may have high performance expectations of your workgroup, and as long as you reflect a positive, supportive attitude, workgroup members will be committed to reaching them. Most people prefer to be busy; they experience a sense of personal satisfaction from accomplishing something worthwhile. Your job is to insist on establishing challenging expectations and then see that they are accomplished.

Employee's Role in Negotiating Performance Expectations

You and your staff share in the negotiations of performance expectations. This increases the degree of commitment for the employee to achieve the agreed to results. The employee has the following responsibilities.

Information Seeker. A key benefit for the worker in discussing performance expectations is the understanding of the supervisor's view of what is to be done and at what levels of quality and quantity. The employee should take advantage of this discussion to obtain as much information as necessary to achieve understanding. He or she must avoid assumptions and ask questions to clarify and verify understanding.

Information Provider. Employees frequently have valuable information that contributes toward establishing realistic expectations. Such information should be provided during the discussion. This may be information from prior job experiences as well as information from the employee's area of knowledge and expertise.

Reality Tester. An employee should have a reasonable level of understanding of the demands being placed on him or her by the performance expectations being negotiated. Encourage the employee to speak up if the demands appear unreasonable. As a result of discussion, demands may be moderated, or the employee's view of reality may be modified. In either case, there is an increase in the probability of the employee being committed to the plan when these issues are resolved.

Innovator. Many employees have ideas on how to do things more efficiently or safely. Encourage employees to challenge traditional ways of doing things. Support them in questioning the need for work that appears unnecessary. Most work procedures can be simplified. Opportunities often exist to do something new and worthwhile but are never pursued because no one mentions the possibilities they represent.

Your Action Guide

Most employees want to do a good job. However, when they don't know what is expected of them, they can't perform at a satisfactory level. Therefore, agreement between you and each of your staff on what is to be done, what results are to be achieved, and the priorities on the use of time is mandatory to successful performance management.

There is an increased potential for different understandings of a job as the level of the job increases. The higher a person goes in an organization, the greater the potential discrepancy. Also, the longer the time span for completion of a work cycle, the greater the potential for discrepancy in ideas of the best use of time.

The nature of performance expectations can vary depending on the level of the job involved. Lower-level jobs can be covered adequately by a listing of duties and performance requirements, as shown in Exhibit 3.4. However, higher level positions need more elaborate delineation. This could involve four elements: (1) job descriptions, (2) results areas with performance indicators, (3) performance standards, and (4) objectives.

Regardless of the level of job involved, there is opportunity for employees to contribute to the development of expectations that apply to their work. The degree of contribution should depend on the maturity level of the employee. With employees near the low end of the maturity scale, you will need to be more involved and directive; with employees near the high end of the scale you should delegate or share the major portion of the decision.

- ✔ Have job descriptions written and kept up to date for all the jobs under your supervision.

- ✔ Have employees prepare results areas, performance indicators, and standards of performance for their jobs.

- ✔ Meet annually with employees to develop objectives for the coming year.

- ✔ Involve employees in each step of this process to the extent of their willingness and ability.

References

John O. Alexander, "Making Managers Accountable: Develop Objective Performance Standards," *Management Review,* December 1980.

Carrie L. Bennet, "A Managerial Job Description Program," *Defining the Manager's Job,* AMA Research Study no. 33 (New York: American Management Association, 1958).

Raymond G. Hunt and Cary Lichtman, "Role Clarity, Communication, and Conflict," *Management of Personnel Quarterly,* Fall 1970.

Robert A. Martin and James C. Quick, "The Effect of Job Consensus on MBO Goal Attainment," *MSU Business Topics,* Winter 1981.

George L. Morrisey, *Managing by Objectives and Results for Business and Industry* (Reading, MA: Addison-Wesley, 1977).

William E. Reif and Gerald Bassford, "What MBO Really Is," *Business Horizons,* June 1973.

Harold C. White and Michael N. Wolfe, "The Role Desired for Personnel Administration," *Personnel Administrator,* June 1980.

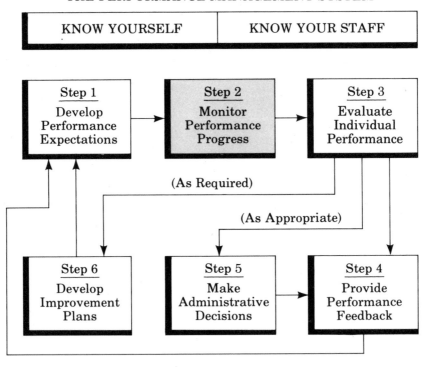

THE PERFORMANCE MANAGEMENT SYSTEM

KNOW YOURSELF	KNOW YOUR STAFF

Step 1
Develop
Performance
Expectations

Step 2
Monitor
Performance
Progress

Step 3
Evaluate
Individual
Performance

(As Required)

(As Appropriate)

Step 6
Develop
Improvement
Plans

Step 5
Make
Administrative
Decisions

Step 4
Provide
Performance
Feedback

DELEGATE RESPONSIBILITY AND AUTHORITY	MANAGE PERFORMANCE PROBLEMS	MANAGE GROUP PERFORMANCE

CHAPTER 4

Monitoring Performance Progress

As a result of reading this chapter you will

- Understand the need for monitoring the performance of your staff
- Be able to develop a performance monitoring system
- Know how to conduct interim reviews of employee performance
- Know what corrective action to take when performance is not on schedule

In chapter 3 the cornerstone of the Performance Management System, developing performance expectations, was laid. In this chapter, step 2, the process of monitoring the progress toward those expectations, is discussed.

Why Take the Time?

Monitoring performance progress is often neglected by supervisors because they're busy with what they see as more important issues. However, without some systematic method of checking on progress, there's little likelihood that expected results will be achieved.

You are responsible to your manager for delivering the product or service of your department to your customers on time, at acceptable levels of quality, within budget, and within appropriate company policies and procedures. To do this, you need to know how your department, as a whole, is doing relative to management expectations. Also, you need to know how each member of your staff is doing relative to your agreed upon expectations (discussed in chapter 3). With this information, you either confirm that everything is going along on schedule or you identify areas needing attention.

Performance monitoring also makes a contribution in the evaluation of work methods and employee performance. It provides the information you need to decide whether or not something can be done better. Were plans well laid out? Were things properly organized? Were coordination and communications adequate? Were the necessary resources available? Your answers to questions such as these will identify areas for potential improvement in the next performance period.

Finally, every supervisor is expected to evaluate employee performance. Such evaluations can't be an accurate reflection of an employee's performance without a good information base. By staying in touch with what is going on during a performance period, you'll know what was accomplished, how it was done, the problems encountered along the way, and how they were dealt with. Then, at the end of the period, you will be in an excellent position to reflect on the total period and arrive at an accurate assessment of the employee's contribution. This process will be developed further in chapter 5.

What You Should Monitor

Performance monitoring should be handled on two levels: the performance of individual members of your staff should be monitored, and the performance of your department as a whole should be monitored. You can monitor four basic areas:

- Results
- Effectiveness
- Progress
- Methods and procedures
- Work habits

Some of these areas apply to both individual performance and departmental performance; the rest apply to just one of the two performance types. The performance standards and objectives developed in step 1 of the Performance Management System become the primary focus of attention for monitoring individual performance. Additional items are presented here to supplement your monitoring procedures and to broaden your scope to include your departmental performance as a whole.

Monitoring Results

All companies and the departments in them exist to achieve results of one kind or another. As discussed in chapter 1, there are two basic results you are after: (1) increased *productivity,* which is the measure of how well a product or service is delivered to customers, and (2) increased *morale,* which reflects the level of satisfaction employees experience in their work.

Employee Satisfaction   Research has established a direct cause and effect between morale and productivity. A three-step relationship can be described. Basically, management decisions, policies, and procedures (known as causal variables) have a direct effect on the morale, motivation, and cooperation (called intervening variables) of workers. The intervening variables— that is, how employees feel about their work—have, in turn, a direct effect on productivity and profitability (known as end-result variables). Figure 4.1 shows this relationship and lists examples of causal, intervening, and end-result variables. In short, management decisions and policies can affect workers' attitudes . . . and a worker with a positive attitude is most productive. Many organizations periodically conduct employee

Causal Variables → Intervening Variables → End-results Variables

☐ Decisions	☐ Morale	☐ Productivity
☐ Procedures	☐ Attitudes	☐ Profitability
☐ Policies	☐ Loyalty	☐ Return on
☐ Objectives	☐ Motivation	investment
☐ Organization	☐ Cooperation	☐ Staff turnover
☐ Resources		☐ Absenteeism

Figure 4.1 Organizational variables
Adapted from Likert, *New Patterns of Management*

opinion surveys in order to monitor intervening variables, such as morale and worker satisfaction, in order to gauge productivity and other end-result variables.

Certain end-result variables such as turnover, absenteeism, and industrial accident rates can also be monitored within your department. These end-results are indications of the level of employee satisfaction and are generally less expensive to monitor than morale itself.

Quantity of Output.   Most departments and employees can measure the amount of work accomplished over a specified time period. You just need to clearly define the product or service to be monitored and the units in which it can be measured.

In many lines of work this is simple and straightforward. In a production operation of yarn, for example, it simply would be the number of pounds or yards of yarn produced. In a training department it would be the number of employee-days of classroom training delivered. In a legal, medical, or other service organization, it would be the number of cases or client conferences held. In a sales organization, it could be the number of sales, the amount of product sold, or an appropriate combination of the two.

Some lines of work are difficult to measure in terms of quantity. This is particularly true for departments that exist in a company primarily to provide a service that consists mainly of advice and counsel—for example, a public relations department, an engineering department, an accounting department, or a personnel department. Each of these can develop a way to measure the quantity of their output, but in all likelihood it will not be an accurate reflection of total contribution. These measures may need to be supplemented by measures of timeliness and various effectiveness measures, which are described on pages 100–102. Monitoring the quantity of output for individual employees and for your department as a whole will let you know how well you are meeting your output objectives.

Quality of Output.   All work accomplished can be examined in terms of its quality. Any quality assessment is made by comparing the product or service to some standard. The work being monitored for quality then either exceeds, equals, or falls short of what it is being compared to. In establishing procedures for monitoring quality, you must specify exactly what the product or service will be compared to. The most common bases of comparison are the standards specified in chapter 3, the expectations of your customers, and past experience.

Timeliness.   Monitoring timeliness is important when meeting deadlines is one of your department's requirements. Timeliness could be a very relevant measure for an accounting department or a construction operation, for example. Typically, you measure timeliness by comparing completion dates to established deadlines or schedules.

Another way to use time as a performance monitor is to observe the length of time it takes to complete a particular activity. In an order-filling operation, you might monitor the length of time from receipt of an order to shipment. The time required to clean and service an airplane is another example. In these applications, actual time is compared either to established standards or to previous experience. Both of these applications can be used for monitoring individual as well as departmental performance.

Income.   Some businesses and departments measure their results in terms of dollars of income rather than units of production. Sales departments generally follow this practice. While a sales organization could monitor the *number* of sales made, it is more relevant to consider the *dollar value* of those sales. While generally monitored on the departmental level, income at an individual level may also be used.

Costs. In addition to monitoring other areas, you'll probably want to stay abreast of the costs of producing results, typically for your department as a whole. Costs can be broken down into various subcategories depending on what is relevant to your operation. (Figure 4.2 shows an example of a cost breakdown for a manufacturing company.) Costs are typically monitored in comparison to budget or ratios.

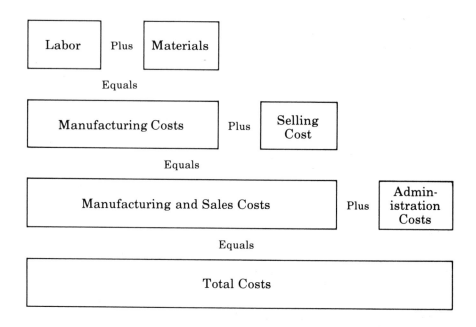

Figure 4.2 Breakdown of costs for a manufacturing operation
Adapted from Terry and Hermanson, *Principles of Management*

Monitoring Effectiveness

Monitoring effectiveness measures how well your department functions. This usually is an evaluation of both input (costs) and output (results) and is frequently expressed in a ratio. A number of such measures are available. A few of the more common ones are listed below.

- *Profit.* This is a calculation of income minus expenses, usually figured before taxes and often expressed as a percentage of sales.
- *Sales per employee.* Total sales divided by either the average number of total employees during the period or the average number of sales personnel gives a figure for sales per employee.
- *Return on investment.* Total profit divided by equity capital is the return on investment.
- *Training costs per employee.* Total training costs divided by the average number of employees trained during the period is the training costs per employee.
- *Employee turnover.* Total number of employees leaving during a period divided by the average number of employees on staff during the period gives a figure representing employee turnover.
- *Absenteeism.* Total number of days absent during a period (usually excluding vacations) divided by the number of scheduled workdays times the average number of employees during the period gives a figure for absenteeism.
- *Inventory turnover.* Total cost of goods added to inventory during a period divided by the total value of the goods in inventory at the end of the period is inventory turnover.
- *Professional staff utilization.* Calculating this depends on the nature of your operation. For example, it could be determined by dividing total client caseload handled during a period by average number of professionals on staff during the period; by dividing the average student enrollment by the average number of faculty; by dividing the total employee days of training delivered during the period by the average number of instructors; or by dividing the total number of employees hired during a period by the average number of employment interviewers on staff during the period.
- *Support staff utilization.* Average number of professional staff employed during a period divided by the average number of support staff employed during the period will give a figure for the extent of the use of support staff.

Support staff usually includes secretaries, technicians, clerks, and analysts.

- *Facilities utilization.* Depending on the nature of your operation, a variety of ratios can be calculated that will reflect the degree your facilities are used. Included might be such measures as total output divided by rated capacity of a machine; the number of hotel rooms occupied divided by the number of rooms available; the number of hospital beds occupied divided by total beds available; the average class size divided by classroom capacity.

- *Reject rate.* The reject rate is the total number of items not passing quality control standards divided by the total number of units produced.

- *Productivity.* This is calculated by dividing the total output for a period by the total costs incurred in generating that output.

Monitoring Progress

Monitoring results and effectiveness focuses only on end-of-period, or final, results. Monitoring progress toward results can give you an idea of what those results will be and indicate whether you should make interim adjustments in order to assure the achievement of your goals. Monitoring progress is applicable to both the individual and the department. Progress can be monitored by three different approaches, depending on the nature of your operation:

- Interim measures of results
- Interdependent events
- Substeps of projects

Interim Measures of Results.   A very common way to monitor progress is to divide a time period into segments, measure the results at the end of each segment, and then compare these results with desired final results. Interim measures can be made daily, weekly, monthly, or quarterly. If end-of-period results measures have been developed, monitoring them on a shortened time interval would be fairly simple, and quite appropriate. With this information you would know how well your operation was doing and you could make necessary adjustments to end the period within target.

Interdependent Events. In some types of operations direct cause and effect relationships can be established between particular events and output. Some of these you'll be able to control, others you won't. For example, in a manufacturing operation there is a direct relationship between sales and production. By monitoring sales, you can accurately forecast production output requirements even though your manufactured goods may temporarily go into inventory rather than go directly to the customer. On the other hand, a similar cause and effect relationship can be established between the number of calls made by sales personnel and total sales. As a supervisor in sales, you might be able to get your staff to make more calls in order to meet your sales goals.

Substeps of Projects. Project-oriented work is usually broken down into substeps during the planning phase. Budgets and deadlines can be established for these substeps that will form the basis for monitoring progress toward project completion. For example, in remodeling a plant or office there are specific steps that must be taken in proper sequence in order to complete the project. After being detailed, these steps can be monitored to gauge the progress of the project.

Monitoring Methods and Procedures

Work methods and procedures are additional areas of individual performance you can monitor. This provides information enabling you to decide whether or not work is being accomplished through the agreed upon procedures and systems. Are safe practices being followed? Are necessary reports and records being properly maintained? Are the methods employed by your staff in dealing with your customers and competitors up to the ethical standards you try to maintain?

An organization can go too far in establishing standardized methods and procedures. Employees need as much freedom as possible to express individuality and creativity in how they go about their work. However, in the areas of safety and other legal requirements, it is generally recognized that standardized procedures are best. Beyond that, monitoring work methods and procedures should be approached as an opportunity to offer suggestions for improvement when appropriate, rather than as enforcement of arbitrary procedures.

Monitoring Work Habits

Work habits are the personal approaches individuals take toward their work that either facilitate or interfere with its achievement. Included here are such things as housekeeping, attendance, punctuality, social conversation with co-workers or customers, personal telephone conversations, writing personal letters, and reading while on the job.

Monitoring work habits is appropriate in order to maintain discipline in a workgroup and to see that employees are actively engaged in their duties. However, as with work methods and procedures, there needs to be a modest range of tolerance. You need to know what's going on in your group and then assess its reasonableness within the context of current work demands, individual needs, and the potential of establishing undesirable precedence.

✔ Checklist of Factors to Monitor

- **Results**
    Quality of output
    Quantity of output
    Timeliness
    Income
    Costs

- **Effectiveness**
    Profit
    Sales per employee
    Return on investment
    Training costs per employee
    Employee turnover
    Absenteeism
    Inventory turnover
    Professional staff utilization

Support staff utilization
Facilities utilization
Reject rate
Productivity
- **Progress**
    Interdependent events
    Interim results
    Substeps
- **Methods and procedures**
- **Work habits**

Ways of Monitoring Performance

After considering the nature of your department's operation and selecting the appropriate items to monitor, you now need to decide how to monitor these and then develop the appropriate procedures. Several methods are available. Five of the most common are

- personal inspection
- customer contact
- records keeping
- interim progress reviews
- audits

An effective performance monitoring system will utilize several of these procedures and have built-in checks and balances.

Personal Inspection

Probably the most frequently used way of monitoring performance is looking at what's going on and deciding whether or not it is proper. By going to the work area and observing operations, you can monitor work methods and procedures as well as work habits. You will see firsthand whether or not safe practices are being followed, and whether housekeeping standards are being maintained. By inspecting the output of your operation you'll know if the appropriate level of quality is being maintained.

To get or obtain a true impression of day-to-day operations, personal inspections should not be announced ahead of time. Also, you should make them frequently enough to experience a valid, randomly scheduled sample. For instance, if you visit the work area every morning between 8:30 and 9:00, your visits will be anticipated, and what you see may not be typical of the rest of the work day. It's better to make a point of visiting at random times during the day and on random days of the week. At the same time, however, personal inspections should be open and direct. Supervisors have a legitimate right to know what's going on in their workgroup and to inspect the output of the group. Employees have the right to explain what they are doing and why. Be open about why you are there, ask questions, and listen to explanations. Don't conduct your inspection when no one else is around. You may draw some incorrect conclusions from what you see.

✔ Checklist for Making Personal Inspections

- Observe the quality of housekeeping in the work area.
- Observe work practices and assess the compliance to safety measures.
- Observe work methods being used and assess whether they conform with those that have been established as most efficient.
- Observe the quality of work being done to determine whether or not it meets acceptable standards.
- Assess the general level of morale by observing the degree of friendliness and cooperation among group members.
- Greet members of the workgroup, ask questions about both personal and business matters (as is relevant and appropriate) and answer any questions they might have.

Customer Contact

Some departments exist primarily to provide a service to other parts of the organization. Examples are employment offices, maintenance departments, data processing departments, and engineering departments. If you supervise this type of operation, one effective way to monitor the quality of your group's effort is to ask your customers for their evaluation. This information would augment data obtained through other means.

When your customers are outside your own organization, as in the cases of restaurants, hotels, and many sales operations, you can use periodic customer surveys to supplement unsolicited customer comments. These surveys are generally substantial undertakings and are usually handled by survey research firms to ensure a scientifically valid sampling.

As with personal inspections, customer contacts should be open and direct. Do not attempt to gather information on your staff in secret. To do so will only lead to a breakdown in the trust between you and your group.

Keeping Records

Some performance lends itself very nicely to being monitored through various records keeping procedures. This is particularly true when your concern focuses on quantity of output, costs, income, and timeliness. Quality measures can also be monitored in this fashion when they deal with objective data such as reject rates. Records can be generally classified into two groups—hand generated and computer generated.

Hand Generated Records.   A great deal of individuality is reflected through the various records kept by hand to monitor performance progress. However, they tend to fall into three types: planning formats, lists of expected performance, and graphs.

Planning formats that become monitoring devices when a project gets underway include simple listings of substeps of a project (Exhibit 4.1, page 108), PERT/CPM Diagrams (Exhibit 4.2, page 109), and Gantt Charts (Exhibit 4.3, page 110).

Simple listings of expected performance, actual performance, and any differences can be shown by a relevant time interval, such as weekly or monthly (Exhibit 4.4, page 112). Finally there are graphs, the most common being line graphs. Graphs typically show expected performance for the total year, with actual performance added to the graph on a weekly or monthly basis. (See Exhibits 4.5, page 113, and 4.6, page 114.)

EXHIBIT 4.1   Example of a Progress Status Chart

This exhibit shows a simple listing of a project's substeps for use as a progress status chart. The project is described, and the steps required to achieve it are listed along with the forecasted budget and scheduled completion dates. As each step is completed, the cost and completion date are recorded. When maintained, the chart presents a quick report of current status compared to original plans. By adding another column for accumulated costs, you might increase the chart's usefulness.

Project: Remodel Building #7 to provide 4 additional offices by October 31, 1983 at a cost not to exceed $17,500.

	Budget		Schedule	
Steps	Fore-cast	Actual	Fore-cast	Actual
1. Draw working plans	500	450	Aug. 15	Aug. 20
2. Obtain building permits	50	50	Aug. 31	Sept. 1
3. Form and pour foundation	2,500	2,750	Sept. 5	Sept. 5
4. Frame walls and roof	2,200	2,100	Sept. 10	Sept. 8
5. Install roofing	1,250	1,500	Sept. 15	Sept. 12
6. Install windows	750		Sept. 15	
7. Install exterior siding	3,800		Sept. 25	
8. Paint exterior	300		Sept. 30	
9. Install electrical wiring	650		Sept. 30	
10. Install heating/air conditioning	1,800		Oct. 5	
11. Insulate	750		Oct. 10	
12. Install sheetwork	900		Oct. 15	
13. Paint interior	350		Oct. 18	
14. Install interior doors and trim	700		Oct. 20	
15. Install electrical fixtures	150		Oct. 20	
16. Clean-up	150		Oct. 23	
17. Install floorcovering	250		Oct. 25	
18. Completion of Project (Total)	$17,250		Oct. 31	

EXHIBIT 4.2   Example of a PERT/CPM Chart

This exhibit shows a PERT/CPM chart (simplified for illustration) for the same project as in Exhibit 4.1. (PERT/CPM stands for Program Evaluation and Review Technique/Critical Path Method.) Numbers in the circles in the diagram correspond to the numbers of the steps. Numbers on the lines show the days required to move from one step to another. The "critical path" is the longest time path through the network, shown by the dotted line. When a step is completed, the circle representing that step on the chart is filled in with colored pencil. The advantages of a PERT/CPM chart are that it clearly presents all of the activities that are going on at the same time in a project and identifies where your attention must be focused (the critical path) in order to complete the project on schedule. Its shortcoming is that it deals only with schedules and not costs.

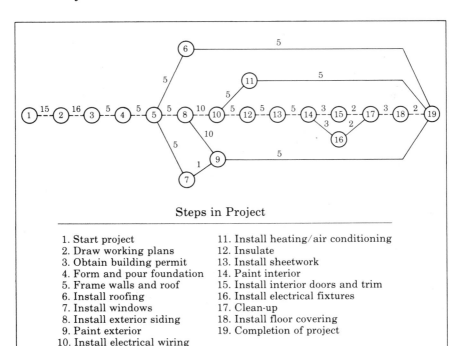

Steps in Project

1. Start project
2. Draw working plans
3. Obtain building permit
4. Form and pour foundation
5. Frame walls and roof
6. Install roofing
7. Install windows
8. Install exterior siding
9. Paint exterior
10. Install electrical wiring

11. Install heating/air conditioning
12. Insulate
13. Install sheetwork
14. Paint interior
15. Install interior doors and trim
16. Install electrical fixtures
17. Clean-up
18. Install floor covering
19. Completion of project

EXHIBIT 4.3   Example of a Gantt Chart

This exhibit shows a Gantt Chart (simplified for illustration) for the same project shown in Exhibit 4.2. The project steps are numbered and listed down the left side of the chart, and the project schedule is shown at the bottom. The schedule for each step is indicated by the line beginning at the starting point of the step and extending to its scheduled completion. When a step is completed, color in the circle at the end of the line representing the step. Much like the PERT/CPM chart, the Gantt chart deals only with time and reflects the steps that occur within the same time span. However, it does not identify the "critical" time path for completing the project on schedule. The Gantt Chart is appropriate for projects that have only a few concurrent steps and whose control is straightforward.

Exhibit 4.3   (*continued*)

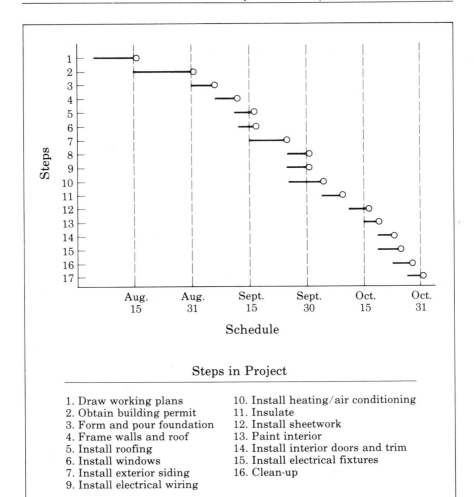

Schedule

Steps in Project

1. Draw working plans
2. Obtain building permit
3. Form and pour foundation
4. Frame walls and roof
5. Install roofing
6. Install windows
7. Install exterior siding
9. Install electrical wiring

10. Install heating/air conditioning
11. Insulate
12. Install sheetwork
13. Paint interior
14. Install interior doors and trim
15. Install electrical fixtures
16. Clean-up

EXHIBIT 4.4   Example of a Record for Monitoring Progress

This exhibit shows a listing of expected performance (sales volume in dollars) against which actual performance is compared. In the exhibit the total sales goal for the year is broken down by month into subgoals, reflecting seasonal trends. Actual sales for each month are recorded. The difference between forecast and actual is calculated, and a running total of the accumulated difference is maintained. At the end of each month, you can quickly see how the business is doing compared to the forecast and take steps to correct poor performance if necessary to reach the year-end goal.

Sales by Month—Actual Compared to Forecast

Month	Forecast	Actual	Difference	Accumulated Difference
January	$30,000	$29,000	−400	−400
February	40,000	41,700	+1,700	+1,300
March	30,000	29,600	−400	+900
April	25,000	23,000	−2,000	−1,100
May	40,000	39,000	−100	−1,200
June	35,000	33,700	+2,700	+1,500
July	30,000	29,400	−600	+900
August	25,000	26,100	+1,100	+2,000
September	30,000	32,300	+2,300	+2,300
October	35,000			
November	40,000			
December	30,000			
Total	$390,000			

EXHIBIT 4.5   Example of a Line Graph for Monitoring Progress

This exhibit shows a line graph display used to monitor monthly costs against forecast. It is an alternative method to Exhibit 4.4 for displaying similar data. A worksheet of data (similar to Exhibit 4.4) is required for constructing graphs.

Actual Costs Compared to Forecast Costs

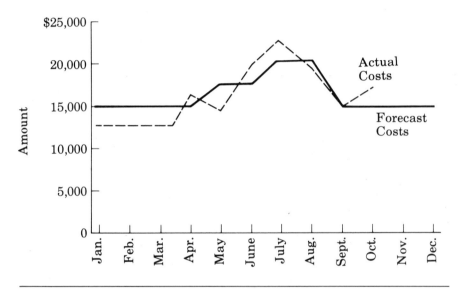

EXHIBIT 4.6　Example of a Line Graph for Monitoring Progress (Alternate)

This exhibit is similar to Exhibit 4.5, but it shows actual and forecast output of a machine as a percent of the machine's total rated capacity. Such information is helpful in monitoring over-all output as well as in detecting machine operating problems that might suggest maintenance, overhaul, or replacement. Many operators take pride in operating their equipment beyond rated capacity. However, this practice can cause machine failure if it is sustained over a long period.

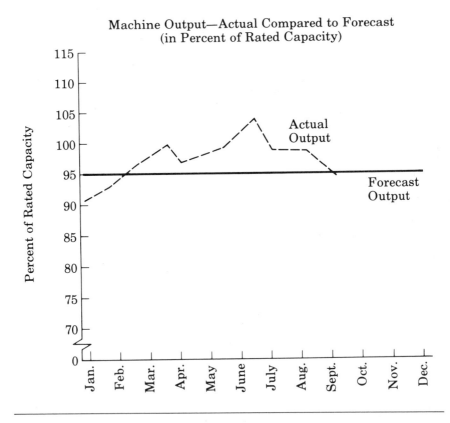

Machine Output—Actual Compared to Forecast
(in Percent of Rated Capacity)

Computer Generated Records. Computer generated records are of two different types. First are records that simply count and report items processed—for example, the number of checks issued, the number of data items entered, the number of invoices paid, and the number of programs run. The second type is records that involve some mathematical processing—for example, the value of goods in inventory, the total sales for a period, total expenses for a period, and many of the efficiency measures detailed in the previous section. Exhibit 4.7 (page 116) is an example of a computer generated record of error listings for an accounting section.

There is a tendency to go overboard in the use of computer-based monitoring because of computer capabilities. You should guard against this. Limit the data you receive to what is needed to help you stay up-to-date on individual workgroup progress.

Interim Progress Reviews

The most common, and the easiest, way to monitor progress is through interim progress reviews. These are communications between you and your staff about the progress of individual performance toward agreed upon results. They are typically built around data gathered through other monitoring procedures. Usually they occur at fixed time intervals—such as weekly, monthly, or quarterly—at the scheduled completion of key steps of a project, or they may be made at the request of either you or your staff member. Interim progress reviews can be any one, or a combination, of three different types—individual discussions, group discussions, or written reports.

Individual Discussions. Individual discussions occur privately between you and one member of your staff and may be either face-to-face or by telephone. In these discussions, you might review actual progress in relation to expectations, review any problems that have been encountered, help solve any current problems, and reorder priorities if necessary. Individual discussions not only keep you informed but also provide opportunity for you to reinforce good performance and help correct poor performance. Suggestions on how to conduct these discussions are presented later in this chapter on pages 119–123.

EXHIBIT 4.7   Example of a Computer Generated Report

This exhibit shows an example of a computer generated report for monitoring data entry errors from an accounting section. The report is on a billing section of a chemical company. For illustration purposes, it is important only to note that when an error is made, the report indicates both the section in which the error occurred and the employee's number who made it. From the report you can see that one employee (number 042) made 4 errors, employee number 25 made 7 errors, employee number 336 made 5 errors, employee number 728 made 9 errors, for a total of 25 errors in the section for the billing period reported. Additionally, the report provides the necessary adjustments in quantity and amount for making correcting entries.

SEP 12, 1981								ERROR SUSPENSE BY ACCOUNT						PAGE 12

CHEM ACCENT - E03

ACCOUNT 1030   TIME 03.10.07

JPL REF	REV	CO	OF	CT	QT	QP	SUB ACCT	EMPLOY ORIG	WORK ORDR	PROD	ASMS	BC	QUANTITY	AMOUNT	RPT LINE	ERROR REF
H8-51-04-M983		02	61	41			042	042			1080		3068	298.82		09-09-004
		02	61	41			042	042			1170		1496	11.35		
		02	61	42			042	042			1170		4491	893.69		
		02	61	91			042	042			1080		341	6.23		
		02	61	91			251	251			1010		27991	2,082.51		
		02	61	91			251	251			1030		45724	3,401.85		
		02	61	91			251	251			1040		13979	1,036.96		
		02	61	91			251	251			1040		164972	12,273.90		
		02	61	91			251	251			1030		6986	519.74		
		02	61	91			251	251			9207		7225	537.54		
		02	61	91			251	251			1170		33582	2,498.49		
		02	61	91			336	336			1040		7455	601.61		
		02	61	91			336	336			1010		45630	3,682.31		
		02	61	91			336	336			1110		25755	2,078.40		
		02	61	91			336	336			1080		43941	1,566.02		
		02	61	91			336	336			1060		14322	1,155.76		
		02	61	91			728	728			1010		315981	17,694.56		
		02	61	91			728	728			9210			.00		
		02	61	91			728	728			9209		-1636	-91.72		
		02	61	91			728	728			1170		6948	389.06		
		02	61	91			728	728			1110		76290	4,272.14		
		02	61	91			728	728			1090		76279	4,271.55		
		02	61	91			728	728			1080		135095	7,565.25		
		02	61	91			728	728			1060		3391	189.87		
		02	61	91			728	728			1040		54854	3,071.74		

ACCOUNT TOTAL   71,987.65

Section making error

Employee making error

Group Discussions. Obviously, a group discussion includes more than one other person meeting with you to review progress. The meeting may be of a project team or of several staff members working together on a common project. Group reviews of progress against expectations are appropriate when everyone attending the meeting needs to be informed of how individuals in the group are progressing. Occasionally, group discussions are appropriate when the individuals can help each other solve performance problems. Group discussions should be avoided under most other circumstances. It's usually not a good use of staff time to have members of your group in a meeting waiting their turns to report individually to you.

Written Status Reports. Written status reports vary substantially in their information and their frequency. They can report on the status of projects or ongoing activities. One of their major benefits is that they provide a written record of progress that you can refer back to at future times.

An example of a very simple written status report is a sheet or form on which employees make a check or tally mark each time a piece of work is completed, summarize these results and compare them to expectations. More elaborate reports summarize progress on a major project, compare progress to expectations, and detail problems encountered and anticipated. Weekly or monthly written progress reports are very common in sales departments. In addition to reporting progress in comparison to expectations, they often detail activities such as the number of sales calls made and the number of potential new customer contacts. Exhibit 4.8 is an example of a fairly complex monthly sales progress report.

Audits

Audits tend to focus on work methods and procedures rather than results. Common areas for audits include financial records keeping, use of proper authorities and procedures for disbursements, personnel policies and practices, plant safety practices, office and plant security practices, plant maintenance procedures, and purchasing practices.

EXHIBIT 4.8   Example of a Monthly Progress Report

This exhibit shows an example of a territory sales representative's monthly progress report. Each performance indicator is shown with actual performance compared to forecasts for both the current month and the year to date. This provides both the sales representative and the sales manager an easy way of monitoring progress. Items 2, 5, and 6 are clearly not doing as well as forecasted. This is noted in the sales representative's comments.

Territory: Austin #5

Month: May, 1980

Number of Dealer Units: 27

Number of Salaried Units: 9

| Performance Indicators | Current Month | | | Year to Date | | |
	Fore-cast	Actual	Per-cent	Fore-cast	Actual	Per-cent
1. Gasoline Sales (1,000 gal.)	1,160	1,160	100	7,500	7,400	98.7
2. Motor Oil Sales (gal.)	1,200	860	71.7	6,400	4,700	78.3
3. Coolant Sales (gal.)	200	190	95.0	900	960	106.7
4. Tire Sales (units)	700	1,050	150.0	3,000	3,200	106.7
5. Battery Sales (units)	120	73	60.8	500	387	77.4
6. Filter Sales ($1,000)	40	38.6	96.5	200	136.2	68.1
7. Rental Income ($1,000)	70.6	71.3	101.0	355	357	100.6
8. Dealer Conferences	15	15	100	75	72	96.0
9. Public Presentations	3	3	100	10	9	90.0
10. Audit Verification	3	4	133.3	15	15	100

Exhibit 4.8   (continued)

Comments: Continue to sell all the available supply of gasoline. Battery, oil, and filter sales are in trouble due to trend to self-service and discount store price competition. Need to develop some promotion angle. Vacation tire special turned tire sales slump around.

Signature: _Tim Austin_   Date: _6/3/80_

Audits are commonly conducted by company staff who are not members of the department or operation being audited. The auditors are typically experts in their field and may be either full-time or part-time members of an audit staff. Following a personal inspection by the auditor, a report is usually written detailing what was found and pointing out practices that deviate from established policy, authorized procedures, or sound business practices.

How to Conduct an Interim Progress Review

The interim progress review discussed on page 115 is the way most supervisors usually stay in touch with what's going on in their operations. It provides an opportunity for supervisors to influence the course of future events and offers each employee a chance to talk directly with his or her supervisor about progress.

Interim reviews usually occur at a fixed time schedule, such as weekly, monthly, or quarterly, but should also be made when a problem in performance progress is observed or when a significant project stage is completed.

Interim reviews vary both in timing and content according to the maturity level of the employee. Those employees who are at the low end of the maturity range should have more frequent reviews that focus primarily on problems and direct guidance.

Highly mature employees, on the other hand, need less frequent monitoring and less guidance. Their reviews are a summary of actual progress in relation to expectations, a recount of problems encountered and how they were handled, and a discussion of anticipated problems and proposed plans for dealing with them.

Objectives of Interim Reviews

Different interim reviews will have different points of emphasis. Overall, however, the following objectives should be accomplished:

- Agreement between you and your staff member on what was accomplished during the period under review
- Reinforcement, by you, of good performance
- Identification and solution of problems that may be interfering with performance
- Reordering of staff members' priorities for the next period to reflect your interpretation of demands placed on him or her by your management

The Supervisor's Role in an Interim Review

Your role in an interim review is directed toward achieving your objectives of knowing what's going on in your operation and influencing the course of future events as necessary. During the discussion you may do any or all of the following.

Listen.   Above all, you must listen as your employee updates you on progress, deviations from plans, problems encountered, and proposed solutions. Listen not only to content but also to feelings and reactions. Is the employee excited, discouraged, frustrated? Help clarify and verify what is being presented to you by summarizing your understanding of both facts and feelings and checking it out with the one talking to you.

Contribute.   In many interim reviews, progress will be in line with expectations. However, occasionally you'll need to deal with problems. When problems occur, you can contribute to their solution by directing the employee toward possible courses of action. The following list of alternatives suggests some of the options available.

- *Push for desired performance.*   Occasionally, you'll only need to re-emphasize the importance of goals in order to motivate others to achieve them.

- *Deploy more resources.*   Quantity and time objectives can often be met by putting more people and/or machines to work on a project. This also may involve authorizing overtime payments.

- *Seek out alternative sources.*   If one supplier can't deliver according to your schedule seek out others who are capable of meeting your needs.

- *Accept substitution.*   If the completion of a project or the attainment of a goal is being delayed by difficulties in meeting a quality standard, consider alternatives that can substitute for the originally specified item causing the delay.

- *Accept partial delivery.*   Occasionally, a large quantity of a product is requested to be placed in inventory for future use, when the *immediate* demand is for a considerably smaller amount. Accepting a partial delivery to meet immediate demands can work to the best interests of everyone.

- *Renegotiate original objective.*   After working at a project, it may become evident that the original objective simply can't be met. However, it may also be apparent that meeting the original objective in full is not a critical factor. In these cases, agree upon a modified objective at an interim review.

Provide Information.   As a supervisor you are a communications link between your staff and higher management. You should provide information regarding where the organization is headed, particularly since this information might affect both workgroup and individual priorities. Also, your experience may enable you to provide information that will contribute to the solution of performance problems.

Integrate.   An important role of supervision is the integration of the individual parts of an operation into a compatible whole. Is something being neglected? Is there duplication of effort? How can all the work to be done best be accomplished with the people available to do it?

Lead.   Perhaps the most important role you play in the interim review is that of leader. A leader keeps the efforts of a group directed toward a common goal. You must confirm and recognize good performance, correct poor performance, and keep interest and enthusiasm high. There are five techniques for getting people to do what must be done. Each is useful in different situations, and you should apply them as you feel is appropriate.

- Provide opportunities for employees to satisfy their interests, needs, wants, desires.
- Make a personal appeal—simply ask.
- Appeal to the individual's values by demonstrating a tie between those values and what you are asking.
- Offer a reward for the desired performance.
- Threaten punishment for nonperformance.

✔ Checklist for Conducting Interim Progress Reviews

- Have the individual involved summarize the status of progress against expectations.
- Review records which reflect the status of progress.
- Discuss extenuating circumstances which make it either easy or difficult to achieve expectations.
- Discuss any problems which may be interfering with progress.
- Reinforce progress that is at, or exceeding, expectations.
- Reorder priorities as may be required for the coming period.
- Moderate your degree of directiveness according to the maturity level of the individual.

The Employee's Role in an Interim Review

The interests of the workgroup are best served by openness on everyone's part coupled with an openminded view toward resolving any problems encountered. In keeping with this, the employee has the following responsibilities.

Provide Information.   The primary reason for an interim review is to update the supervisor on progress toward agreed upon objectives. The employee should be direct, open, and honest about progress made, problems encountered, and problems anticipated. This is no time to shade the facts or minimize the importance of problems. Get them out on the table so that they can be resolved during the interim review; otherwise they'll interfere with achievement during the remainder of the performance period.

Seek Information.   The employee should use the interim review to find out what changes need to be made in the priorities of your objectives, what new projects or opportunities exist, how these new areas of endeavor affect existing responsibilities, and how problems interfering with your performance can be resolved.

Your Action Guide

Monitoring performance progress of the workgroup and its individual members is important for two reasons: to alert you to performance problems so you can initiate corrective action and to provide an information base so you can prepare valid performance appraisals at the end of the performance period.

Effective monitoring procedures require you to identify what will be monitored and then develop an actual method of monitoring that supplies you with relevant data. As much as possible, individual employees should monitor and report their own performance so they, as well as you, will be aware of their levels of achievement. Accounting records provide verification of total group achievement, which should closely approximate a total of all group members' results claims.

The extent that you monitor individual performance will vary with each employee's maturity level. You'll monitor workers who are low in maturity frequently and you'll review their work habits as well as their methods and procedures. On the other hand, you'll monitor workers with high maturity less frequently and probably review only results accomplished. It's important to not neglect your highly mature employees. Because they may seem to always have things under control, there can be a tendency to isolate them and have minimal contact. At least give them quarterly progress reviews, scheduled in advance.

The interim progress review is the basic way you and your staff can keep up-to-date on progress. Use it as a motivational opportunity and a problem-solving opportunity. Employees generally like to talk about their successes, so don't neglect this aspect of the review as a means of reinforcing good performance, thereby maintaining employee motivation. Also, over time, develop an atmosphere of trust with your staff that supports their bringing problems to your attention before they develop into major trouble.

- ✔ Determine what needs to be monitored in your department, based on the primary objective of your group.

- ✔ Establish procedures for obtaining data on the variables to be monitored.

- ✔ Determine appropriate methods for providing data to everyone who is directly involved in the production of your group's output.

- ✔ Develop procedures for supplementing routine monitoring with personal inspections, progress reviews, and audits.

- ✔ Hold interim progress review discussions with all group members at least quarterly.

Finally, a word of caution. All of the time and effort devoted to monitoring performance progress must be kept in perspective. In and of itself, this activity does not produce anything except charts and graphs. The information is important but should not become an end in itself. Don't go overboard.

References

Louis A. Allen, *The Management Profession* (New York: McGraw-Hill Book Co., 1964).

Charles W. Barkdull, "Periodic Operations Audit: A Management Tool," *Michigan Business Review,* July 1966.

Barry A. Stevens, "Audit and Control of Performance in D.P.," *Journal of Systems Management,* August 1978.

Thomas A. DeCotiis and Lee Dyer, "Defining and Measuring Project Performance," *Research Management,* January 1979.

Harry F. Evarts, *Introduction to PERT* (Boston: Allyn & Bacon, 1964).

Henri Fayol, *Industrial and General Administration* (New York: Pitman Publishing Co., 1949).

Rensis Likert, *New Patterns of Management* (New York: McGraw-Hill Book Co., 1961).

Paul A. Mali, *Improving Total Productivity* (New York: Wiley-Interscience, 1978).

George R. Terry and Roger K. Hermanson, *Principles of Management* (Homewood, IL: Richard D. Irwin, Inc., 1974).

Spencer A. Tucker, *Successful Managerial Control by Ratio Analysis* (New York: McGraw-Hill Book Co., 1961).

THE PERFORMANCE MANAGEMENT SYSTEM

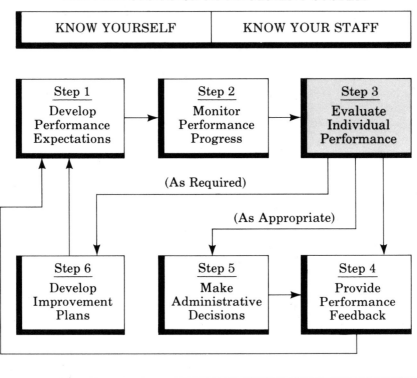

KNOW YOURSELF	KNOW YOUR STAFF

Step 1
Develop Performance Expectations

Step 2
Monitor Performance Progress

Step 3
Evaluate Individual Performance

(As Required)

(As Appropriate)

Step 6
Develop Improvement Plans

Step 5
Make Administrative Decisions

Step 4
Provide Performance Feedback

DELEGATE RESPONSIBILITY AND AUTHORITY	MANAGE PERFORMANCE PROBLEMS	MANAGE GROUP PERFORMANCE

CHAPTER 5

Evaluating Individual Performance

As a result of reading this chapter you will

- Understand the role of individual performance evaluation
- Know *what* to evaluate in order to achieve valid evaluations
- Know *how* to evaluate the appropriate elements of performance
- Understand the need for formal evaluation procedures
- Be able to avoid the common pitfalls that often lead to inaccurate evaluations
- Be able to complete fair and accurate evaluations for your staff

The third step in the Performance Management System is to evaluate the performance of individual members of your staff. As you monitor performance progress in step 2, you'll become aware of whether standards, goals, and objectives are being met. In this chapter we focus on evaluating the performance of individual employees.

Individual performance evaluations are never ends in themselves. They're "homework" that provides the information you need in order to make appropriate administrative recommendations, hold meaningful feedback discussions with staff members, and determine where performance improvement is required. They also provide a written record to substantiate actions you may take that differentiates among employees. These functions are discussed in chapters 6, 7, and 8 (steps 4, 5, and 6 of the Performance Management System).

Why Evaluate Performance?

The variety of ways performance evaluation results can be used is illustrated in the responses to a survey conducted among 130 companies. The results are summarized in Figure 5.1.

A systematic management information system on employee performance benefits the organization in two specific areas—decision making and proving the appropriateness of those decisions. It benefits individual employees in two general ways—by giving a basis for objective feedback and by preventing oversight of individuals.

To Aid Administrative Decisions

Who should be promoted? Who should be transferred or reassigned? Who should be laid off? What salary should an individual receive? What job title is appropriate in a hierarchy of titles? These kinds of decisions are made every day in large organizations; for best results they should be based on a systematic evaluation of performance results. (Administrative decisions are discussed in more detail in chapter 8.)

To Provide Documentation

Performance evaluation records can serve as excellent documentation of the reasons behind administrative decisions and

Purposes	Number of Companies Reporting
To determine merit increases	28
To tell employees where they stand	27
To determine training needs	23
To determine promotability	21
To evaluate employees	18
To determine advisability of transfer	13
To determine layoff or recall priority	7
To determine who should be demoted	7
To improve departmental efficiency	7
To determine disciplinary action	6
To determine who to retain at end of probationary period	6
To determine special talents	4
To validate psychological tests	3
To assure proper placement	2
Miscellaneous	4

Figure 5.1 Results of a survey among 130 companies on the
purpose of performance evaluation
From Richard S. Barrett, *Performance Rating*

actions. Also, they will provide you with backup in presenting recommendations to your management.

More and more frequently, administrative decisions by management are subjected to review by outside third parties. Depending on the circumstances of each case, the outside reviewer might be an Equal Employment Opportunity Commission (EEOC) investigator, a labor arbitrator, or a civil court judge. To justify decisions, management must provide evidence that the decisions were based on job-related issues that were fairly evaluated.

To Provide Feedback to Employees

Employees generally need to know how well they've performed in relation to what was expected of them. In the absence of specific feedback, they often form their own conclusions by comparing their experiences to their co-workers'—the kinds of assignments they receive, their salary, and whether or not they get promoted. These observations are often augmented by casual, day-to-day comments from supervisors. Because they may be random, incomplete, and often subjectively interpreted, these observations and inputs can sometimes lead an individual to wrong conclusions. A systematic method of performance evaluation, however, provides both the objective information and a standardized way of letting employees know how well they're doing relative to expectations. Providing feedback is discussed in greater depth in chapter 6.

To Assure an Employee Isn't Overlooked

A systematic performance evaluation program assures that an employee won't be lost in the bureaucracy of a large organization. Each individual gets recognized as a member of the workgroup and is acknowledged for his or her contributions.

To Aid in the Use of Human Resources and Career Development

A significant goal in evaluating performance is to enable you to identify areas where group members' talents aren't being fully utilized. By identifying areas of potential growth and development you contribute to both the organization and the employee. You can work to improve weak areas and offer staff members opportunities to more fully realize their abilities.

✔ Checklist of Uses of Performance Evaluations

- Making sound, equitable administrative decisions
- Documenting appropriateness of administrative decisions
- Providing feedback to employees
- Providing a basis for best use of human resources
- Counseling and coaching employees
- Developing performance improvement plans
- Predicting employee potential

How to Approach Evaluations

There are two approaches to evaluating employee performance; each is used to measure different factors. One approach looks at the qualities, traits, or behaviors necessary for effective performance and rates an employee against a profile of these characteristics. This is generally referred to as the *rating method*. Forms used in the rating method present a list of items to be evaluated with appropriate definitions. This might include such things as quality of work, quantity of work, communications skills, interpersonal skills, and decision making. A low-to-high scale is presented for each item, on which you are to mark your assessment of the employee's performance. The scale may have numbers, descriptive words or phrases, or simply low, moderate, high checkpoints.

The second approach is the *goals* or *objectives method,* which concentrates on performance planning where supervisor and employee develop goals or objectives to be accomplished and then later compare these goals with what actually did get achieved—i.e., with results. Forms used in the goals or objectives method are usually quite simple. They typically have a column for listing the objectives developed at the beginning of the period, may have a column for recording priority of the objectives, and will have a column for recording results achieved in relation to each objective listed. Typically, there is a summary assessment scale such as "Exceeds Expectations," "Meets All Expectations," "Meets Most Expectations," or "Fails to Meet Expectations."

Used alone, the rating method does not adequately focus on results. The objectives method, when used alone, lacks sufficient performance analysis. Therefore, most supervisors find a combination of the two most useful. The combination approach begins with performance planning and then evaluates accomplishments against plans. This is supplemented with the rating of a few relevant behavioral traits, thus providing a basis for coaching employees on performance improvement.

Regardless of the type of forms used by your organization, you must include in your evaluation a comparison of what was achieved with the standards and objectives developed at the beginning of your planning period. You should also consider any

extenuating circumstances which may have made it either difficult or easy to achieve those results.

Specific Factors to Evaluate

Ideally, the factors you evaluate should be both relevant
and ratable. The most accurate evaluations result when you
concentrate on observable, on-the-job *behaviors* of employees
and on the *results* they achieve. Personality factors can be important elements in how well an employee performs, especially
in interaction with others. But they should be evaluated with
caution and reservation because of the difficulty in objectively
assessing them.

Figure 5.2 shows the relationships of personality, behavior,
and results. Factors to be evaluated can be grouped into these
three general categories—*results* (box 5), *behavior* (box 4), and
personality (boxes 1, 2, and 3). Behavior and results are observable, while personality factors are not. Any evaluation of personality factors is *inferred* from observed behavior and results
produced.

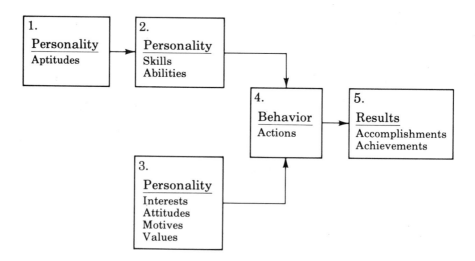

Figure 5.2 Relationships of personality, behavior, and results

Evaluating Results

You are undoubtedly interested in what your staff accomplishes. Because results are so often the "bottom line" of performance, they are frequently the prime subject for evaluation. In most cases, results are easily measured. In some jobs, results will be concise figures such as units of production, total sales, or total income generated. For other jobs, particularly those that perform a service rather than produce a product, some judgment may be required in evaluating results. Organizing your evaluation into the following four basic components, which also are discussed in chapter 4, will facilitate your evaluation.

Quantity.   How much was accomplished? How does that compare to what was expected? Did any circumstances beyond the employee's control affect the quantity achieved—either positively or negatively?

Quality.   How good were the results? How does quality of the work done compare to the quality expected? What relationship exists between quality and quantity? For example, some staff members may spend so much time trying for perfection that volume of output suffers; other staff members, in trying to meet volume standards, may let quality slip.

Costs.   What were the costs of achieving results? Consider such things as materials, tools, and services. How do costs compare to budget?

Timeliness.   Was work completed on time? If not, why? Were delays due to circumstances beyond the employee's control? Or were they due to poor planning and management?

Evaluating Behavior

Although they can't be measured as objectively as results, behavior factors are both ratable and important. In addition to placing results in proper context, an evaluation of behavior factors helps in planning career development of individual workers. This includes both planning for performance improvement in an employee's present job and planning for his or her future advancement. In evaluating behavior you'll look at work methods and procedures as well as work habits. Here are examples of behavior factors that you might evaluate.

- *Leadership.*   Consider both the employee's willingness to provide direction to others as well as others' willingness to accept and support his or her leadership efforts.

- *Planning.*   This is the ability to look ahead and develop a successful course of action. It includes being able and willing to get started in time to complete projects on schedule, to determine resources required, and to be prepared for contingencies that may arise.

- *Organizing.*   Consider how efficiently the employee goes about his or her work day. Does he or she match the work to be done with the resources available in an efficient manner? Are tasks logically grouped to minimize wasted effort?

- *Prioritizing.* Consider the employee's demonstrated skill in dealing with issues in the order of their urgency. Are important matters handled before unimportant ones?

- *Delegating.* Consider the employee's willingness and ability to assign work to others who are qualified and grant them the authority needed to carry it out successfully.

- *Controlling.*   Consider the employee's ability and willingness to keep assigned responsibilities on track by monitoring progress and taking action as required. This includes following up on work in progress and taking corrective action when necessary in order to achieve agreed upon objectives.

- *Problem solving.*   Look at the employee's ability to determine the source of problems, seek out relevant information, and consider alternatives, risks, and consequences of proposed action.

- *Decision making.*   Consider the employee's willingness to render judgment, take action, and accept responsibility for those judgments and actions.

- *Oral communications.* Consider the employee's skill in expressing ideas clearly and effectively in one-to-one conversations. Does the employee ensure clarification and verification of information transmitted in two-way conversations?
- *Written communications.* This is the willingness and ability to express ideas clearly and effectively in writing. Consider such things as legibility of handwriting, grammar usage, spelling, sentence structure, and precision.
- *Administrative skills.* Consider the employee's performance in maintaining accurate and complete records and reports. Also consider the appropriate adherence to administrative policies and procedures.
- *Interpersonal effectiveness.* Consider the employee's effectiveness in dealing with others. Is the employee sensitive and responsive to the feelings of others? Is he or she a disruptive influence in the workgroup?
- *Safety practices.* Does the employee follow safe work practices? Are appropriate safety devices and equipment used? Does the employee demonstrate concern for the safety of fellow employees?
- *Housekeeping.* Is the employee's work area generally neat and orderly? Are tools and other equipment properly stored when not in use? Are drawers and cabinets kept closed?
- *Punctuality.* Does employee report for work on time at the beginning of the workday and at the end of meal and rest breaks?
- *Attendance.* How many days of work has the employee missed, excluding vacation? How does this compare to the workgroup norm and standard?

Evaluating Personality

Personality is important to success, but it is difficult to evaluate the factors of personality for three reasons.

1. The ambiguity of the terms describing personality factors leads to evaluations that are biased by the evalua-

tor's understanding and makes the evaluations unreliable and invalid. For example, in one research project on the ambiguity of personality traits, definitions of dependability were obtained from 150 managers and supervisors who presented 147 different concepts, one person suggesting 6 different definitions.

2. There's no general agreement on which personality factors contribute to individual performance.

3. Most personality evaluations lack behavioral specifics, and employees are generally unable to change specific factors or the effect they have on performance. Therefore, including personality factors in an evaluation system leads to antagonism and defensiveness rather than performance improvement.

How Many Factors Should You Evaluate?

The number of factors you include in an evaluation depends on the purpose of the evaluation. Evaluations to be used for coaching and counseling an employee regarding his or her performance usually include many factors in order to give a more detailed performance analysis.

In a survey of the performance evaluation systems of 114 companies, 32 systems had 5 factors; 32 had 6 factors; 15 had 8 factors; and 12 had 9 factors. Thus it would appear that between 5 and 9 factors would provide adequate information for most purposes. However, in the same survey, one system included only 2 factors and another had a total of 132 factors.

Practicality plays a role in the number of factors you'll include. With more than nine factors there is a very high risk of overlap in evaluations from one factor to another.

Choose the Right Base of Comparison

In evaluating employee performance you compare the pertinent information you've collected on the employee to the appropriate established goals, expectations, or requirements and observe whether the employee exceeds, equals, or falls short of the standard. The base of comparison that you choose is extremely important. Choosing an inappropriate base for comparison, or not understanding the one you do use, can lead to false or misleading conclusions and evaluations. Here are the common bases of comparison used by supervisors:

- Supervisor's expectations
- Goals or objectives
- Performance standards
- Others doing similar work
- Past performance
- Your own performance
- Job demands

Supervisor's Expectations

Your own expectations of an employee are one of the most common bases of comparison, and certainly a valid consideration. You have certain expectations of your staff and they either fulfill these expectations or fall short of them. However, to be a fair and valid base of comparison, your expectations must be known to your staff and they must be comparable to expectations held by other supervisors. Talk with your staff about what you specifically expect. Chapter 3 discusses how to establish performance expectations.

Present Goals or Objectives

An excellent base against which to compare an employee's actual performance during a given period is the goal or objective he was to achieve. Typically the goal or objective will reflect your expectations. However, goals or objectives probably do not cover all the responsibilities of an employee's job. Therefore, they may not be adequate to provide a complete evaluation. In addition, circumstances beyond an employee's control frequently affect the achievement of goals or objectives and may make them easier or more difficult for the employee to achieve. This also must be considered in the evaluation process.

Performance Standards

When properly developed, performance standards represent the best available base of comparison. They typically cover the full range of duties and responsibilities and also reflect the supervisor's expectations of an employee. When properly supplemented with objectives, performance standards can become a complete base for performance evaluation. In your evaluation, however, be sure to consider and make allowance for any circumstances that made it either easier or more difficult than originally thought for the employee to achieve the results.

Others Doing Similar Work

In the performance evaluation process many supervisors make comparisons between employees doing similar work. This comparison can be helpful in two areas. First, when you evaluate employee behavior there are often no absolutes that you can use as a yardstick, and your own experience and expectations may not be applicable. Therefore, consideration of how others, particularly those who are successful, go about their work can be invaluable. Second, when you're considering which members of your group to recommend for promotion, transfer, reassignment, or lay off, you must compare your staff directly to each other to arrive at an appropriate recommendation.

Two potential problems can arise when you compare employees to one another. First is the makeup of an appropriate comparison group. Are they really doing similar work? Are members of the group comparable in knowledge and experience? The second problem is with the general quality level of the total group. Is it an average group, a substandard group or an elite group?

Past Performance

Performance in the current work period can be compared to performance in a prior work period. This type of comparison can be quite appropriate in performance counseling. You should have a feel for the general trend of progress being shown by members of your group. Is performance improving, declining, or holding steady? Use these trends to reinforce improvement and to spot problems when there's a decline. Generally speaking, however, administrative decisions should not be based on a comparison of current performance with prior performance. For example, a merit salary increase should be based on an employee's total contribution, not on performance improvement alone.

Your Own Performance

A very common practice is for a supervisor to compare an employee's performance to his or her own performance prior to becoming a supervisor. This tendency is particularly strong when the supervisor was promoted in the same department. It is one of the most unfair comparisons for several reasons.

- Depending on how long ago the supervisor did the work, it may have changed to the point that it's now an entirely different job.
- By virtue of being selected for promotion, the supervisor was probably an above-average employee, thereby representing too high a standard for comparing others to.
- People tend to have selective memories, remembering how well they did a job and losing touch with the problems they may have had.
- It's difficult for many people to admit that someone else can do something better than they can—a fact that can shade a supervisor's willingness to give high evaluations.

Job Demands

Some supervisors compare the results an employee achieves to the demands or requirements of the job. The employee either does or does not get everything done. Job demands may be reflected through job descriptions, or they may not be made a matter of record. It's hard to argue with this type of comparison base except to point out its lack of clarity and precision. Job demands, like objectives and expectations, must be made explicit, or they will be subject to individual interpretation. Also, demands need to be calibrated with capability. For example, consistent failure by an employee can indicate that the job is unreasonable rather than that the employee is incompetent.

Consideration of job demands appropriately leads to a comparison among similar jobs. This can result in a weighting among jobs, which would recognize that, although similar, some jobs are more demanding than others.

A Recommended System of Comparison

Now that we've looked at the various bases of comparison for performance, a perspective on evaluation emerges that incorporates three distinct analyses. First is a comparison of the results achieved by the employee and the performance expectations for the period. Second is a comparison of the demands of the employee's job to similar jobs. Third is a comparison of the results achieved by the employee to results achieved by other employees holding similar jobs.

Comparing Results to Expectations.   This first comparison is the main one in the process. It addresses the primary reason the employee is on the payroll—to achieve results. You can use it to measure expected standards, goals, and objectives as well as expected behavior. The starting point is the negotiation of expectations as discussed in chapter 3. Then by monitoring performance, as described in chapter 4, objective data is obtained that can be compared to the agreed upon expectations. Performance results can then be evaluated as either exceeding, equaling, or falling short of expectations. Performance expectations clearly incorporate what you as supervisor expect in terms of both results and behavior.

Comparing Job to Job.   Some jobs are obviously more demanding than others, even though they may have the same title and salary range. This can be due to extenuating circumstances beyond the employee's control. Or, it can be the result of organizational needs during the period—there either was, or wasn't, demanding work to be done. Economic fluctuations, for example, may vary the demands on some jobs. Or, it could be the result of career restrictions imposed by the employee. Occasionally, employees will turn down a reassignment or transfer that would increase the demands of their job. One way to fairly rate performance under varying job demands is to create a scale that takes into account the level of job demand. Figure 5.3 illustrates such a scale. Note how meeting expectations is evaluated differently under three different demand levels.

Comparing Employee to Employee. Comparing the performance results achieved by employees assigned to similar jobs will help ensure that employees who earn similar evaluations are contributing at comparable levels. It brings equity to your evaluation and ensures that employees are compensated in proportion to their level of contribution. This comparison also identifies employees at the high and low ends of the performance spectrum. Employees at the high end form a group from which to select candidates for advancement. Those at the low end form an appropriate group to consider for either performance improvement planning or termination. However, it's important to recognize that an employee is not automatically promoted or terminated by virtue of his or her placement in the performance

Performance Level	Level of Job Demands		
	Light for Job Level	Appropriate for Job Level	Heavy for Job Level
Exceeds expectations	Satisfactory	Outstanding	Outstanding
Meets all expectations	Satisfactory	Satisfactory	Outstanding
Meets most expectations	Marginal	Marginal	Satisfactory
Does not meet expectations	Unsatisfactory	Unsatisfactory	Marginal

Figure 5.3 Performance evaluation as a function of job demands

spectrum. Other issues, discussed in chapter 7, must also be taken into account.

Potential Pitfalls in the Evaluation Process

Performance evaluation is subject to many potential pitfalls. If not avoided, these lead to inaccurate, unfair evaluations from which improper administrative action may flow.

Ratability.   Some supervisors attempt to evaluate factors that are essentially unratable. To avoid this pitfall stick with what you can see, hear, or touch. Stay away from factors that are inferred. Factors such as interest in the job, loyalty, and attitude are not ratable with any degree of accuracy. When such factors *are* evaluated, your considerations will be based on inferences drawn from other observed behavior. Employees frequently react defensively when you discuss these factors with them. When you find yourself drawing conclusions about unratable factors, ask yourself the question "What have I seen or heard that has caused me to conclude that this employee lacks interest or has a poor attitude?"

Relevancy.   When you omit essential elements of the job, give undue weight to isolated events, or include factors that

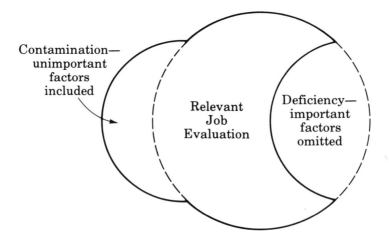

Figure 5.4 Job evaluation affected by contamination and deficiency

don't contribute to performance, you introduce irrelevancy into the evaluation process. This results in deficiency, distortion, and contamination, respectively. Figure 5.4 shows how a well-rounded job evaluation can become unbalanced by deficiency (relevant factors left out) and contamination (irrelevant factors included).

- *Deficiency*. Deficient evaluations overlook important elements of the job. For example, if credit collections are part of a sales representative's duties but the performance evaluation is based only on sales volume, the evaluation would be deficient.
- *Distortion*. Evaluations are distorted when they're unduly influenced by a single event. For example, a football player who drops the potentially winning pass in the end zone during the closing seconds of the game may be considered a poor performer without regard for how well he played during the rest of the game.
- *Contamination*. Contamination occurs when elements that don't contribute to performance influence the final evaluation. Two very common issues that can contaminate evaluations are personal appearance and congeniality. Employees who are neat and well-groomed or friendly and easy to get along with tend to receive better performance evaluations.

Variability. Evaluations of the employees in a group sometimes do not show appropriate differences in individual performance. When an adequate group size exists, a range of performance can be expected. If a range doesn't occur, it may indicate strictness, central tendency, leniency, or a halo effect.

- *Strictness*. Being overly harsh in the evaluation process results in lower than normal overall evaluations.
- *Central tendency*. Rating all employees as "average" is a way some supervisors avoid facing up to the consequences of valid evaluations in the high and low ranges.
- *Leniency*. Being overly easy in the evaluation process causes higher than normal overall evaluations.

- *Halo effect*. When the evaluation of one factor unduly influences the evaluation of other factors, either higher or lower, it is called a halo effect. When an employee does one thing particularly well, or poorly, you must avoid rating all factors correspondingly high or low.

Personal Bias.   Occasionally, performance evaluations may be influenced by a supervisor's personal bias. This results in an evaluation that doesn't reflect the employee's true level of performance. You can best minimize individual bias by involving others in the evaluation process who have knowledge of the employee's performance level. The following options are available.

- *Second-level reviews*. Have your completed evaluations reviewed and verified by an immediate manager. Take a second look at any points that are questioned. This reduces the chances of superficial or biased evaluations.
- *Group evaluations*. In a meeting, your observations can be supplemented by others, such as a functional manager or client manager within the company, who have an appropriate working relationship with the employee whose performance is being evaluated.
- *Multiple evaluations*. These are similar to group evaluations except that rather than meeting and arriving at a single evaluation through discussion each appropriate supervisor or manager completes an individual evaluation.
- *Staff review specialists*. Staff specialists can help reduce individual bias in a number of ways. Their range of involvement varies from examining completed forms for correctness and completeness to interviewing supervisors about employee performance and then actually completing the evaluation report. With proper training, specialists can contribute greatly to the process by maintaining quality and consistency.

Recency, Primacy, Reputation.   Don't let your evaluations be disproportionately affected by *recent performance*. They should reflect typical performance during the entire performance period. You shouldn't be unduly influenced by the *first impression* made by the employee; first impressions don't always reflect typical performance during the entire period. *Past performance* shouldn't influence the current period's evaluation. Limit the present evaluation to contribution in the current period; an employee's reputation as a good or poor performer mustn't be allowed to spill over into the present evaluation.

Timing of Performance Evaluations

How frequently should evaluations be completed? And how long should evaluation records be kept on file?

Frequency

The most common frequency for formal performance evaluation is annually. The frequency should, of course, tie into the performance planning schedule yet still be flexible enough to accommodate unique situations. For example, new employees and those recently reassigned should have their performance evaluated on a shorter interval, say at the end of 6 and 12 months, then annually. When a supervisor is reassigned, the outgoing supervisor should consider updating the record for those employees who have gone 8 to 12 months since their last evaluation. This procedure will provide current information for administrative decisions while the new supervisor is becoming acquainted. Occasionally, it makes sense to extend the time period. This would be appropriate, for example, when a major project is nearing completion. A more complete evaluation could be made by deferring the process to the end of the project.

Retention

People change. Therefore, decisions based on old information may not reflect the employee's present level of contribution. Also, when old records are available, supervisors may be unduly influenced by past performance rather than focus their attention on present performance and results. As a general guideline, records should be kept for two years. For an employee on an annual evaluation cycle, this means there would always be two reports on file—the one reflecting performance during the period just ended and another for the year before.

Who Gets to See Evaluations?

Who *has* access to performance evaluation records? Who *should* have access to them? Because of the acknowledged confidentiality of the information contained in evaluation records, these questions have plagued employee relations managers for some time. Three groups usually have access.

Department Management

The most logical people to have access to the results of the performance evaluations are the members of line management within the employee's chain of command—the immediate supervisor, second-level supervisor, etc. These are the people involved in making and/or approving decisions affecting the individual. Obviously, they need access to the performance evaluation records in order to make appropriate decisions. An employee's immediate supervisor also needs to have access to the records from time to time in order to be able to work effectively with the employee on performance improvement needs. Finally, the records may reflect valuable information on the employee's capability to fill future reassignment or promotion opportunities.

"Outside" Management Personnel

Typically, performance evaluation records are made available to other members of management outside the department on a "need to know" basis. This usually is when the employee is being considered for reassignment to the "outside" manager's jurisdiction.

The Employee

As part of a trend to provide people with access to records that affect them, such as credit and police records, a few states have passed laws giving employees a legal right to access to their own personnel files. In response to these laws, many companies have changed their policies to allow employees this right, even in states not legally requiring it. Therefore, your workgroup members may be entitled to review their performance evaluation records either as a matter of law or company policy.

Who's Involved in Evaluations?

Typically, supervisors are responsible for completing the evaluations of members of their workgroup. However, there frequently are reasons to involve others, who might include the employee's peers, other supervisors, and customers to whom the employee provides a service.

Peers

Peer participation has proven helpful under two circumstances. The first is with new employees who have been assigned to work with an experienced staff member. In this situation it is appropriate and helpful to ask the experienced staff member's assessment of the new employee's progress. This type of peer participation is very common. However, the second circumstance isn't. It involves asking for peer assessment of an employee's personal qualifications for advancement to supervisor. This type of peer participation has been studied and found helpful particularly in insurance sales.

Other Supervisors

A number of circumstances may develop that would justify other supervisors contributing to one of your employee's performance evaluation. The most common is when an employee has worked for more than one supervisor during the period under review. The current supervisor should seek input from the others. Occasionally, workgroups are organized so that some employees work for more than one supervisor. In these cases, all supervisors should be involved in the performance evaluation.

Customers

In many organizations employees are under the administrative supervision of one person but spend all or most of their time providing a service to someone else. Obviously, the one to whom the service is provided should participate in the performance evaluation. This situation exists in such diverse cases as secretaries working for many different staff members but also reporting to an administrative manager, and engineers providing technical support to assigned operating departments but also reporting to an engineering manager.

Your Action Guide

By the very nature of their job, supervisors evaluate the performance of their staff every day, regardless of whether their organization has a formal performance evaluation program. The daily evaluations are a necessary ingredient in the decision-making process supervisors constantly face as they make job assignments, coach and counsel employees on performance improvements, and make recommendations on salary changes, reassignments, and retention in service.

The most challenging stumbling block to fair and equitable performance evaluations is people's tendencies to react emotionally, or subjectively, to things, people, and events that they experience. These emotional reactions, which may be either positive or negative, get in the way of fair and equitable performance evaluation as supervisors react to the person rather than the results produced and/or they react to one or two episodes of performance rather than effort expended over the entire performance period.

A fair and equitable evaluation process focuses on *results* produced and *observable* behavior factors. Personality factors are carefully avoided because they are judged only by drawing inferences from observed behavior. Therefore, it's more appropriate to deal with the actual behavior you observe rather than generalize an inference about an employee's personality.

Any evaluation is made by comparing what is being evaluated to a pre-established standard, goal, or expectation and then observing whether actual performance or behavior equals, exceeds, or falls short. When evaluating performance, the base of comparison must be clearly defined and then be consistently used from employee to employee and from evaluation time to evaluation time.

Start by establishing a base for comparison for performance evaluation. The logical base for comparison is the agreed upon performance expectations negotiated at the beginning of the performance period. These performance expectations may be appropriately augmented with specific behavioral expectations that have either been discussed or are implied by the generally accepted norms of behavior in the workplace. The initial evaluation may be refined by additionally comparing the employee's job to other similar jobs in order to determine the degree of difficulty the employee may have been working under, and then by comparing the employee to other employees in similar jobs to be sure that employees who have similar performance evaluations indeed make similar levels of contribution.

- ✔ Evaluate the performance of your staff at the end of each annual performance period or at the end of a significant project.

- ✔ Discuss with staff members, at the beginning of the performance period, the major factors on which their performance will be evaluated.

- ✔ Gather data throughout the performance period to use in the evaluation process.

- ✔ Involve others who are appropriate in completing the performance evaluation, such as client managers, other supervisors and/or peers.

- ✔ Have the completed evaluations reviewed by your manager to ensure equity and objectivity.

- ✔ Destroy performance evaluation records after two years.

Following this sequence of events and not falling victim to the many pitfalls described will lead to sound performance evaluations. The information generated will be an appropriate foundation for feedback to employees, administrative decisions, and performance improvement planning.

References

Richard S. Barrett, *Performance Rating* (Chicago: Science Research Associates, 1966).

Elaine F. Gruenfeld, *Performance Appraisal: Promise and Peril,* Key Issues Series no. 25 (Ithaca, New York: Cornell University, 1981).

Marion E. Haynes, "Developing an Appraisal Program," *Personnel Journal,* January and February 1978.

Richard Henderson, *Performance Appraisal Theory and Practice* (Reston, Virginia: Reston Publishing Co., 1980).

Eugene C. Mayfield, "Management Selection: Buddy Nominations Revisited," *Personnel Psychology,* Autumn 1970.

Kenneth McFarland, "Why Men and Women Get Fired," *Personnel Journal,* August 1957.

THE PERFORMANCE MANAGEMENT SYSTEM

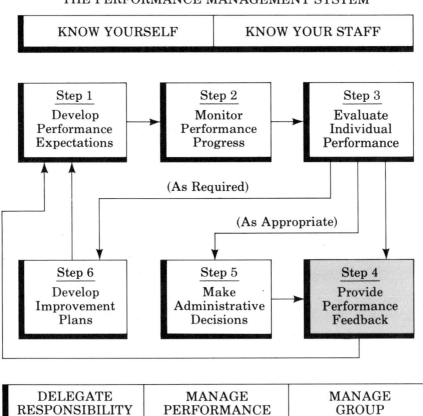

CHAPTER 6

Providing Feedback on Performance

As a result of reading this chapter you will

- Understand the different types of feedback and the importance of each
- Know when to provide feedback
- Know how to handle feedback effectively
- Be able to provide positive feedback in a way that enhances motivation
- Be able to provide negative feedback in a manner that increases the odds of success
- Be able to plan and conduct an effective formal performance review

All employees generally want and need feedback on their performance. They're interested in knowing how well they're doing in relation to what is expected of them by their management. Are they doing better than, as well as, or less than expected?

When there aren't any clear feedback channels, workers find other ways to satisfy their need to know, such as the grapevine or individual interpretations of what they see going on around them. For example, they may compare the assignments or promotions they receive with those of their co-workers and draw their own conclusions. Unfortunately, these conclusions may not be accurate because important information may be missing.

What Is Feedback?

Feedback is information provided to a person for the purpose of maintaining or improving performance. It is not advice, that is, telling someone what he or she ought to do. It is simply letting other people know how their performance affects you and/or your area of responsibility.

With some intended purpose in mind, a person selects a certain behavior or set of behaviors for achieving that purpose. The chosen behavior leads to the achievement of certain results. Feedback lets the person know the nature of these results. (See Figure 6.1.)

To be successful, feedback must meet three criteria:

1. The other person must understand the information.
2. The other person must accept the information.
3. The other person must be able to do something with the information.

Types of Feedback

Feedback comes in three varieties—neutral, positive, and negative—depending on the message that accompanies it. Neutral feedback is information with no expressed or implied quality dimension. Positive and negative feedback *do* have quality dimensions and are provided to either reinforce or correct performance. You'll find all three types of feedback necessary for effectively supervising your workgroup. Negative and positive feedback are often provided as a supplement to neutral, informative feedback.

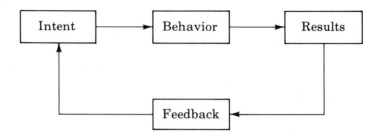

Figure 6.1 Simplified feedback model

Neutral Feedback.   As supervisor you typically have access to more information than members of your group. Consider ways of making available to your staff information that reflects how the group is doing as a whole and how individuals within the group are doing. Providing this kind of information to employees allows them to make informed decisions and keeps them from operating in the dark.

Neutral, informative feedback is straightforward information. It does not include any judgment by you of performance or behavior being either good or bad. Common examples of this type of feedback include total production figures for the workgroup, suggestions from customers for improvements in products or services, number and types of customer complaints, number of on-the-job injuries, number of copies made on the office copying machine, and other day to day facts.

With neutral, informative feedback, you assume that employees want to do a good job, and letting them know the results of their efforts is a way to help them achieve that goal. This assumption is undoubtedly true in many cases. However, at least three other assumptions are also implied with neutral feedback. One assumption is that if performance is below expectations, employees will know why. Another is that employees will know what to do to bring poor performance into line. A third is that the circumstances leading to the poor performance are within the control of the responsible staff members. In some situations these assumptions aren't appropriate.

Positive Feedback.   Feedback that has a positive quality factor built in is an excellent supplement to informative feedback. It is reinforcing and says to an employee "You did a good job. Keep up the good work." Positive, reinforcing feedback takes many forms. It includes praise, salary increases, promotions, and special privileges.

The most reliable form of positive feedback is praise and recognition from you, the supervisor. The other forms, such as pay raises and promotions, are significant but often beyond your direct control and occur too infrequently to be truly effective. Look for chances to praise good performance. By so doing, you'll encourage good performance and positive thinking, which will help assure a continued high level of performance. Don't get so caught up in other duties that you fall into the "no news is good news" trap.

Negative Feedback.   Feedback with a negative quality factor built into it is also an appropriate supplement to informative feedback. It is corrective and says to an employee "A change is required for the future." Negative, or corrective, feedback emphasizes that the current way of doing the job isn't acceptable—a new way must be found.

The key to successfully handling corrective feedback is to concentrate on planning for change. Explore alternative ways for the employee to handle the job. To accomplish this, ask the employee if she or he is experiencing the intended results. Then together search out alternative behavior that offers an increased probability of success for the future.

Sources of Feedback

Employees receive feedback on their performance from a number of sources. These can be generally classified into two categories: intrinsic and extrinsic.

1. *Intrinsic sources.* Intrinsic feedback is information on performance results gathered independently by employees in the normal course of doing their jobs. It may relate to quality, quantity, costs, and timeliness.

2. *Extrinsic sources.* Extrinsic feedback is evaluative information offered by others—supervisors, clients, peers.

Some very interesting research has been done on the different effects of intrinsic and extrinsic feedback on performance. It has been found that extrinsic feedback affects employees' attitudes toward the *source* of the feedback, while intrinsic feedback affects employees' attitudes toward their *job* and affects the quality of task performance. These findings are summarized in Figure 6.2.

From the results shown in Figure 6.2 you can see that extrinsic feedback sessions affect only the employee's attitudes toward the feedback experience and the person providing the feedback. Employees have positive reactions to positive feedback sessions and negative reactions to negative feedback sessions. Neither positive nor negative extrinsic feedback have any apparent effect on job satisfaction or performance level. To the extent that it can be measured, reactions to the feedback session are more toward the experience itself than toward the person providing the feedback.

Considering these findings, grave questions can be raised about the effectiveness of typical performance appraisal sessions as a means of providing feedback. The researchers found that the supervisor's evaluation, regardless of whether it was positive or negative, did not influence the employee's sense of being

Source and Type of Feedback	Employee's Reaction to Feedback	Impact on Employee's Relationship with Feedback Source	Impact on Employee's Job Satisfaction	Impact on Employee's Performance
Extrinsic				
Positive	Positive	Positive	No effect	No effect
Negative	Negative	Negative	No effect	No effect
Intrinsic				
Positive	No effect	No effect	Positive	Positive
Negative	No effect	No effect	Negative	Positive

Figure 6.2 Effects of feedback on employee attitudes
Adapted from Orelle and Herold, "Sources of Feedback: A Preliminary Investigation." Used with permission.

helped by the appraisal session, nor did it add to the employee's desire to do a better job. Both of these issues represent change within the person: a positive appraisal may make an employee feel recognized and pleased but it does not necessarily mean that the employee has received any new information that could be of help or increase the desire to do a better job.

In planning feedback, you must consider both its intrinsic and extrinsic dimensions. Extrinsic feedback should be utilized primarily to influence *attitudes*—to provide recognition and reinforce the desirable features of employee behavior. Intrinsic feedback processes should be developed so that employees will see firsthand how their efforts and performance measure up to agreed upon expectations, objectives and goals. This gives the employee direct feedback from the work itself rather than from you. Your supervisory role then becomes one of helping employees solve performance problems when the intrinsic feedback indicates that improvement is required.

Providing Extrinsic Feedback

Handling extrinsic feedback successfully requires a number of qualities and skills. Among them are honesty, courage, respect, confidence, and effective communications. These elements make handling feedback effectively a goal to strive for rather than a set of procedures you can immediately employ.

General Guidelines

The keys to handling feedback effectively are to minimize the chances of the employee becoming defensive, to deal with issues over which the employee has control, and to focus attention on problem solving and planning for the future. The guidelines below will help you minimize defensiveness. It's important to avoid a defensive reaction by the employee because it can cause him or her to reject the feedback, and it may have a detrimental effect on your relationship with the employee.

Be Selective.   Reserve feedback for key issues and situations. Don't get a reputation as a nitpicker or come across as insincere. When dealing with performance problems, arrange them in priority order and spend your time and energy in those areas that will nurture the important aspects of good performance.

Be Specific. Provide precise feedback so the employee will fully understand the nature of the feedback and the reason for it. It's much more helpful to tell someone "Your recommendation for changing the supply room layout has certainly reduced congestion and the amount of time required to fill requests," than it is to say "You've come up with some good ideas lately, keep up the good work." As a general rule, it helps you to be specific if you avoid using the expressions "always" and "never."

Be Prompt. Providing feedback is an ongoing, day-to-day responsibility. It can't be saved up and doled out in large portions quarterly, semiannually, or annually. When your goal is to reinforce or correct performance, make an effort to minimize the time lag between the behavior and the feedback. Unless the employee receives feedback promptly, he or she may repeat a mistake without knowing any better. Prompt feedback, capitalizes on the employee's heightened level of interest following the completion of a job.

Be Descriptive. Talk about what you see or hear and the impact that behavior has on your area of responsibility. Avoid drawing conclusions about the person from your observations. For example, it will be more effective to tell an employee "When you arrive late to work you hold up the rest of the crew and this puts everyone behind for the day," rather than, "Your coming in late simply demonstrates to me how totally irresponsible you are." Observations are generally accepted as fact while conclusions are often rejected as incorrect inferences.

Be Sensitive. Sometimes it will be appropriate to allow a brief cooling-off period so that both you and the employee can engage in a rational discussion of the problem performance. Be sensitive to the demands the other person is under. Is he or she particularly busy or under emotional strain? Also be sensitive to the setting. It's often appropriate to reinforce good performance in the presence of others, but corrective feedback should be reserved for private conversation. Remember, even excellent feedback given at the wrong time or place will frequently do more harm than good.

Explore Alternatives.   Usually people choose an action or course of action because it appears to be the only one available or appropriate. However, this frequently isn't the case. Alternatives usually do exist, but get overlooked under the stress of the moment. Effective feedback will encourage the employee to broaden his or her range of vision to include other possible alternatives.

Providing Positive Feedback

Positive, or reinforcing, feedback has positive effects on employees' attitudes. It should be used to bolster and maintain the morale of workgroup members. However, many supervisors are reluctant to give this type of feedback. They often see positive feedback as merely praise. And they feel either that it will come across as insincere or that employees are mature adults who don't need a pat on the back—they feel praise is for kids. But positive feedback is more than just praise. It is a way of letting people know that they are achieving the results you expect. If you're one of those supervisors who is afraid that your words of praise will come across as false or hollow, or if providing positive feedback on a job well done just doesn't come easily for you, the following guidelines will help, in addition to the general guidelines previously discussed.

Examine Your Attitudes.   The place to start in handling reinforcing feedback is with your own attitudes toward assessing employees' performance. All too often supervisors take good performance for granted and only single out for discussion the performance that doesn't measure up. For example, in talking with an employee who has done 12 assignments well and 3 assignments poorly, some supervisors might say, "These 3 assignments don't measure up; they need to be done over." This is a negative message that would be improved dramatically by at least an acknowledgment of the good performance. An alternative would be: "These 12 jobs were done well. However, these 3 need to be done over." Look for opportunities on a regular basis to compliment, praise, express your appreciation, or tell someone you like what was done, *and why.*

Be Honest.   Don't exaggerate the significance of the performance. Often supervisors will actually embarrass members of their staff by overstating the impact of the job. On the other hand, don't minimize the contribution. Compliment the employee for the actual work done, but don't get carried away.

Don't Demean.   Don't ruin the effect of your praise by adding a qualifier, such as, "That was an excellent piece of work, *considering that you're only a secretary.*" While such a statement may, in your mind, appear to build up the significance of the contribution, it comes across to others as downgrading, condescending, and demeaning. The whole effect of well-intended feedback is destroyed by the qualifier.

Don't Set a Person Up.   Many supervisors use a compliment to soften up an employee prior to giving negative feedback or criticism. Don't follow a compliment with negative feedback. It washes away the positive effect of the praise and causes your staff to tense up in anticipation everytime they receive a compliment. Hand out the praise and stop. Save the negative feedback for another time. Or don't preface it with a compliment.

Be Willing to Make It Public.   When you feel a member of your staff has done an outstanding job, let everyone in the group know about it. This not only gives the individual worker a pat on the back, it allows other group members to share in the good feelings of one of their own. Furthermore, it presents a role model for others to copy who hope to enjoy similar recognition.

Handling Negative Feedback

Negative feedback often has an adverse effect on the supervisor-employee relationship. It tends to generate defensiveness.

Even so, there are times when it's necessary and appropriate to work with employees at trying to improve their performance.

Problems that require corrective feedback usually can be seen as falling into two general categories of severity: minor and major. Minor problems tend to be with work execution and lead to less than optimum performance. Major problems tend to be violations of rules, policies, or norms of appropriate behavior. Successfully handling these various situations requires different strategies.

In minor problems, the employee's *intentions* are appropriate, but a less than optimum behavior is chosen as a means of achieving results. Either the employee didn't know *what* to do or didn't know *how* to do it. The net results are the same. The key to your success in these situations is for the employee to see you as helpful rather than critical. Try to be a coach rather than a boss. The following might be a typical sequence as you resolve a minor problem.

1. *Ask what was intended.* Ask the employee what she or he intended to accomplish. Then examine results to see the extent to which intentions and results are together or at variance.

2. *Explore alternatives.* Since results are at variance with intentions, the next question is "What else might you have done?" Look at as many options as the two of you can think of and consider the potential each has for success.

3. *Select an alternative.* After looking at all the alternatives, have the employee select an approach for handling similar situations in the future and agree upon a course of action. (Help the employee in this process as necessary.)

4. *Reinforce success.* Follow up with the employee, providing further help by answering questions, correcting errors, and reinforcing progress toward the desired level of performance.

In the category of *major problems,* the employee's intentions are at variance with acceptable workgroup behavior. It might be that an employee spends too much time socializing with fellow workers, so that everyone falls behind. Perhaps an employee misses too many workdays or works too slowly. The key to successfully handling these situations is to clearly define the boundaries of acceptable behavior and sell the employee on the value of operating within them. The following strategy has proven successful for many supervisors.

1. Get to the Point. Quickly and clearly describe the situation or behavior you are concerned about. This is no time for beating around the bush, watering down your feedback, or pulling your punches just to minimize the chances of an emotional reaction. Try a straightforward statement, such as "Your attendance record is unacceptable. You've missed an average of two days each week for the past month. I can't continue to tolerate this level of absenteeism."

2. Get a Reaction. After you've described your concern, stop talking and get a reaction from the employee. Get him or her talking about the problem under discussion. If no immediate reaction seems forthcoming ask for one. During this stage expect the employee to be defensive, to rationalize, and perhaps to even blame others. Demonstrate empathy and understanding for the situation. Be careful to not get caught up in debating or arguing points raised by the employee that might sidetrack the discussion.

3. Get Agreement. Get the employee to agree with you, at least partially, that the problem or situation can't be allowed to continue. This may require some real selling on your part to convince the employee that the behavior you are discussing is in fact inappropriate. If you can't obtain at least partial agreement, the following steps will be unrealistic, and you should simply demand compliance to the appropriate rules of behavior as a condition of continued employment.

4. Develop a Plan. With agreement that the action was inappropriate, work together to develop a plan for improvement. Don't expect too much too soon. It's better to have a modest plan that will be carried out than a demanding one that will be ignored.

5. Summarize.   Summarize your discussion in order to ensure understanding: Restate the problem, your expectations for the future, and the plan the two of you developed as a solution. Confirm the employee's understanding of these three key points.

6. Follow Up.   Set a specific follow-up date for getting back with the employee to review progress. Then be sure to get together as agreed. At this follow-up meeting provide appropriate feedback on progress being made toward the agreed upon goal.

Now that you're familiar with the guidelines for effective feedback, try putting them into practice. Here again are the five cases from chapter 1. Assume that they all do work typical of your department. You've asked each to meet privately in your office.

Providing feedback is an art that reflects the personality of the individual giving the feedback. Because of this, there's no single "right" answer for each case. However, your feedback should conform to the guidelines presented in this chapter and should emphasize the points mentioned after each case.

- *Merle*. Merle is an experienced employee who is interested in his work and seems motivated to do well. He has a good understanding of his responsibilities, plans well, and sets appropriate priorities.

    This is an opportunity to provide positive, reinforcing feedback to a valuable member of your staff.

- *Fran*. Fran is new in your workgroup, having recently completed a two-week orientation program for new employees. This is her first assignment to a regular position. She seems interested in her work and committed to doing a good job.

    This is an opportunity to begin building a positive supervisor– employee relationship by giving positive, reinforcing feedback to a new member of your workgroup.

- *Terry.* Terry has been a member of your group for three years. He knows his job and usually does it well. Occasionally he seems to need some recognition and acknowledgment of his contribution in order to maintain his level of productivity.

  > This is an opportunity to meet the ego needs of one of your staff. Provide positive, reinforcing feedback. In the process, be careful about minimizing it. Do not mention any shortcomings because of the potential negative impact of criticism on attitude.

- *Leslie.* Leslie has been a member of your group for two months. During this time she has shown interest in her work and has responded well to your training. You normally spend six months training new group members, and Leslie is on schedule in her development.

  > Like Fran's case, Leslie's is an opportunity to develop a positive supervisor–employee relationship with a new staff member.

- *Bill.* Bill has been a member of your group for seven years. He knows his job but seems to lack interest in getting it done. He was skipped over recently for promotion and since then has fallen off in his performance. He has been sulky and noncommunicative with you.

  > Bill is a remedial case. If you've previously talked to Bill about this problem, you may choose to concentrate on corrective feedback and on developing a plan to get things back on track. If you haven't discussed the problem before, emotional support might be more effective. Try something like "I understand how being passed over can make you feel. However, we can't let that destroy your future."

Receiving Feedback

So far, the emphasis has been on improving your skills in *giving* feedback. As a supervisor, you'll probably be involved mostly in that aspect of the process. However, *receiving* feedback can make a substantial contribution to your growth and development: there's no better way to find out how well your actions achieve your intended results. Look for opportunities to elicit feedback from others—superiors, peers, and subordinates. When you do so, keep the following points in mind.

- *Don't "hang" the messenger.* When you have organizational power over the person giving you feedback (such as an employee), you must avoid any reaction that could be interpreted as retaliation. Be open to receiving the information you requested.

- *Understand what you're being told.* Ask questions to clarify your understanding of the feedback. Ask for examples. Are there times when you do something and other times when you don't? What makes the difference? Play back your understanding of what you've been told for confirmation. All too often, emotional reactions to feedback can cloud your understanding: confirmation of the message becomes an important step in the process.

- *Check out the information.* It's important to know if the information you've received is just one person's point of view or if others generally agree with it. Ask others to comment on the information. In doing so, you'll probably gain further insight into your impact on others.

- *Decide what to do with the information.* In this step you acknowledge your right to choose your own behavior and your responsibility to accept the consequences of that behavior. You can't be all things to all people. You must select those areas for change that make sense to you. These should be areas in which you'd be more effective if you changed and areas in which the new behavior would fit with your self-image.

- *Develop a plan.* Having chosen the behavior you want to work on, develop a plan to bring about the desired change. Is some specific training required? Look for opportunities to practice the new behavior, both on and off the job. Look for evidence to confirm the value of the new behavior. Are you satisfied with the results or is further change desired?

Handling the Formal Performance Review

It was emphasized earlier that providing feedback is a daily, ongoing responsibility. If this is the case, why should you go through the ritual of a periodic formal performance review? The main reasons are:

- To look at a significant period of performance, such as a year, in order to focus on normal rather than extraordinary events
- To place the events within the time period into an appropriate perspective
- To look at what performance during the period means for the future
- To develop plans for the employee's growth and development

To be successful, there are several points to consider before, during, and after your discussion of a performance review with an employee.

Before the Discussion

Before the discussion is a period of planning and preparation for both you and the employee. This period may begin as much as a month prior to the actual discussion.

The first step of preparation is to update yourself on the employee's performance for the total period under review. People normally remember recent events and significant events, but they tend to forget the normal day-to-day experiences. Updating yourself will include reviewing available records and gathering any additional data you may need from other sources, such as other supervisors or clients. Concentrate on gathering objective information rather than opinions and hearsay.

Once you've gathered information, the second step is to decide on the major points of emphasis for your planned discussion. What approach will elicit the best response? What motivates this particular individual? Think through potential trouble spots. How would you react if you were on the receiving end of this discussion? Finally, make a brief outline of the key points you plan to cover.

The third step is to arrange for the meeting with the employee. Start by selecting a private place for the discussion. This can be your office, the employee's office, a conference room, or an off-site meeting place. The important criteria are that you do not want to be interrupted or overheard; therefore, a restaurant would be inappropriate. Then select a mutually convenient time and make an appointment with the employee. You want to pick a time when you both will be in as positive a frame of mind as possible. Delay the discussion if either of you isn't feeling well. Avoid stressful times caused by either work or personal demands. Be clear about the purpose of the meeting and encourage the employee to do some preparation.

During the Discussion

Your employee may react in ways that will be detrimental to your goals if the discussion is not properly handled. Threat to self-esteem and defensiveness are the two most common detrimental employee reactions. They tend to be evoked when there's substantial variation in the employee's view of his or her own performance and your view of that same performance, when there's substantial criticism, and when there's no opportunity for the employee to influence the outcome of the discussion. These reactions can be minimized by having clear, agreed upon performance expectations, by concentrating on objective measures of results that are readily available to employees, and by conducting a collaborative problem-solving discussion, characterized by a spirit of helpfulness and working together.

Opening the Discussion.   It's important to start off on a positive note, because this sets the stage for all that follows. Be available at the appointed time and place. Greet the employee in a friendly manner and take a few minutes for the employee to become comfortable. As much as possible you should behave like your usual self. If you typically transact business with employees from behind your desk, then that's where you should sit now. On the other hand, if you typically operate in a more informal style, that would also be appropriate for this discussion.

At the outset, engage the employee in general, but related, conversation. For example, you might talk about the practice in your department of holding this type discussion and the benefits an employee can expect as a result of it. Ask the employee to describe prior experiences with these discussions and reactions to them. While you're talking in this general way, observe the employee for signs of stress. These might include a tense and rigid posture, limited response to questions, or an elevated voice pitch. Continue the general discussion until these signs subside, usually three to five minutes, then move on to setting the specific agenda for the discussion, the amount of time you have available, and the part you expect the employee to play. After you've agreed on these items, you're ready to develop the discussion.

Developing the Discussion. The major portion of the discussion should focus on specific job duties and responsibilities—what was accomplished, how that measures up to expectations, and implications for the future. The best outline for this portion of the discussion is either a job description or a listing of results areas as described in chapter 3. A performance evaluation form of *general* performance factors is not a good outline for the discussion. If you permit the employee to inspect the evaluation form as part of the discussion, wait until you've completed your discussion of duties and responsibilities.

As you develop the discussion, involve the employee by asking questions to draw out ideas and by eliciting reactions to the ideas you express. During this phase, the amount of time each of you talks should be about equal. When the employee is talking, listen attentively and make notes of things to follow up on later and of ideas you want to remember.

There are several ways you can involve the employee and effectively maintain the balance of the discussion time between the two of you.

- *Display a supportive attitude.* Support the employee's right to see things differently from you, and support the employee's right to choose a particular course of action, as long as he or she is willing to accept the consequences of that choice. When you are supportive of others, they are more willing to express their ideas.

- *Encourage continued conversation.* Encourage elaboration on subjects through such simple techniques as using silence appropriately, restating the employee's opinions, feelings, and attitudes, and asking for more information by saying such things as "Tell me more about that," or "Could you give me an example of that?"

- *Be open to new information.* Demonstrate an interest in new information by adopting a tentativeness about your own point of view. If the other person feels you aren't open to considering new information, she or he probably won't voice any.

- *Try to relax.* When you are relaxed and open, the other person will find it easier to relax. When you appear under stress or pressure, the other person will be more tense, anxious, and eager to end the experience.

- *Ask appropriate questions.* Some questions encourage conversation while others limit it. Learn to ask questions that cause the other person to think and go into some detail with the answer. Generally, avoid questions that can be answered with a yes or no. Some questions that may prove useful are:

  - What parts of your job do you enjoy most? Why?
  - What parts of your job do you enjoy least? Why?
  - What parts of your job do you find difficult? What makes them difficult for you?
  - What could I do to make things better for you?
  - How do you feel about your prospects for the future?
  - How could you improve your value to the company?
  - What are your career goals for the next three to five years?
  - What do you see as your major strengths?
  - What is your understanding of your duties and responsibilities? Priorities? Schedules? Standards? Expected results?
  - What would you like to talk about?

Needless to say, a discussion can't be conducted simply as a series of questions. You should add your own thoughts and opinions on the various topics as they're discussed. These will be either a confirmation of the employee's view or a clarification when you see things differently.

Review your outline. When all issues have been covered, including those introduced by the employee, it's time to close the discussion.

Closing the Discussion. Every discussion should end on a positive note for the future. This will be easy with employees whose performance equals or exceeds expectations. All you need to do is encourage continued contribution. However, when performance has fallen short of expectations it may be difficult to be positive. Here you should show confidence in the employee's ability to improve his or her performance and encourage the pursuit of whatever improvement plans have been developed. Emphasize your willingness to help, and be supportive of the employee's efforts.

In closing, summarize the key points covered and the agreements you've reached, then check the employee's understanding of these issues. The best way to do this is to ask the employee to summarize. Then you can check to see that the two of you are together. Summarizing the discussion yourself doesn't really confirm the employee's understanding.

After the Discussion

Following the discussion, you'll have certain administrative responsibilities to complete. Also, there may be additional information to be obtained and/or confirmed before the discussion can be finalized. The following steps are usually involved.

Summarize for the Record. Write a brief summary of the discussion. This should include key points discussed, employee reactions, and plans or action items developed. You may want the employee to read and edit a draft of the summary to be sure you are in agreement. Some supervisors have the employee write the summary. Consider which is best for your department. Exhibit 6.1 is an example of a form for summarizing performance discussions.

EXHIBIT 6.1   Example of a Performance Review Summary Form

		CONFIDENTIAL
	DISCUSSION SUMMARY	(WHEN COMPLETED)

NAME TITLE	DEPARTMENT	DISCUSSION DATE
DISCUSSION TYPE ☐ Performance ☐ Career ☐ Salary **CALL UP DATE (NEXT DISCUSSION)**	**PARTICIPANTS**	

Summary:

Exhibit 6.1   *(continued)*

Items of particular interest:

PREPARED BY:		REVIEWED BY:	
SIGNATURE	DATE	SIGNATURE	DATE

Complete Administrative Details. Fill in whatever forms are required by your organization and route them, as appropriate, to your manager and/or the personnel office. Handle these details promptly. The longer you delay, the greater the chance you won't remember details required for the record.

Follow Through on Commitments.   If in the discussion you agreed to do something, follow through on it. Setting aside or forgetting even something as simple as an employee's request for information can have a serious impact on the employee's attitude. It indicates a lack of concern and interest on your part.

Obtain Feedback.   To help develop your skills in handling these discussions, you may want to obtain feedback from your staff. Exhibit 6.2 is a questionnaire designed for this purpose. For best results, someone else, such as a personnel specialist should coordinate use of the questionnaire.

✔ Checklist for Formal Performance Reviews

- Update yourself on the employee's performance during the entire period under review.
- Select a private meeting place and a mutually convenient time.
- Make an appointment with the employee approximately one week before the discussion.
- Give the employee your complete attention during the discussion.
- Engage the employee in the discussion by asking for opinions and points of view.
- Have the employee summarize the key points covered and agreements reached at the end of the discussion.
- End on a positive note—voice confidence for the future.
- Complete appropriate administrative procedures.
- Get back with the employee if you agreed to do so during the discussion.

EXHIBIT 6.2   Example of a Form for Evaluating Performance Reviews

REACTION TO JOB PERFORMANCE DISCUSSION
(Please check one response to each question)

1. When did you have your last formal job performance discussion?

   ____ Within the last 12   ____ More than 24
        months.   months.

   ____ More than 12 but   ____ I don't remember
        less than 24 months.   ever having one.

   Additional Comments: _____

   _____

   _____

2. How did you feel when your boss told you he or she wanted to have a performance discussion with you?

   ____ Excited—I was inter-   ____ Unsure about what
        ested in discussing   was going to happen.
        the subject.

   ____ O.K.—It's part of the   ____ Dreaded the idea.
        normal routine.

   Additional Comments: _____

   _____

   _____

3. How did you feel when the discussion was over?

   ____ Excited about my   ____ Glad it was over for
        performance and   another year.
        prospects.

   ____ So-So—it was pretty   ____ Really turned off.
        routine.

Exhibit 6.2   *(continued)*

Additional Comments: —————————————————

—————————————————————————————

—————————————————————————————

—————————————————————————————

4. How would you describe your part in the discussion?

___ Actively involved.   ___ Responded when
                                  asked a question.

___ Asked a few ques-   ___ Sat quietly and lis-
    tions.   tened.

Additional Comments: —————————————————

—————————————————————————————

—————————————————————————————

—————————————————————————————

5. Do you know where you stand with your boss; that is,
   how well your job performance meets his or her expectations?

___ Yes, this was clearly   ___ I'm not sure, my boss
    covered.   didn't seem to get to
                                   that point.

___ I think so, there   ___ No, we didn't talk
    were some pretty   about that.
    clear signals.

Additional Comments: —————————————————

—————————————————————————————

—————————————————————————————

—————————————————————————————

Exhibit 6.2   (continued)

6. How would you describe your boss's behavior during
the discussion?

____ Open, direct, and   ____ Guarded, indirect
interested.   and ambiguous—
                                hard to figure out.

____ A bit nervous and   ____ Really uptight—
unsure, but we got   would rather have
through it okay.   been doing some-
                                thing else.

Additional Comments: _____

_____

7. How satisfied were you with your boss's answers to
your questions?

____ Completely—I got a   ____ Not very—most an-
clear, open response   swers were ambigu-
to all questions.   ous generalities.

____ Fairly well—we   ____ Not at all—questions
were able to talk   were ignored or re-
about my concerns.   jected as unim-
                                portant.

Additional Comments: _____

_____

8. Do you have an identified performance improvement
goal to work on?

____ Yes, with a plan and   ____ I remember some-
follow-up schedule.   thing being men-
                                tioned.

____ Yes, but we didn't   ____ No, apparently ev-
develop any plans.   erything is okay.

Exhibit 6.2 (*continued*)

Additional Comments: _____

_____

9. To what extent did you have an opportunity to influence the performance improvement goal?

___ None—I wasn't asked. I was told.

___ Very little—I suggested some things but they weren't seriously considered.

___ Considerable—I suggested several things and we agreed on a mutual plan.

___ Not applicable—I don't have an improvement goal.

Additional Comments: _____

_____

10. What have you done about your performance improvement goals?

___ I've begun or completed work on the plan we developed.

___ I'm not too excited about it. I'll probably ignore it and hope it goes away.

___ I've given it some thought but haven't actually done anything yet.

___ Not applicable—I don't have an improvement goal.

Additional Comments: _____

_____

When Your Performance Is Reviewed

This section highlights some of the necessary contributions that *you* should make to ensure success when *you* are the one being reviewed.

Before the Discussion

When your manager informs you of an impending performance review, work to arrange a mutually convenient time. Make sure you allow yourself sufficient time to prepare. Then proceed to take the following preparatory steps.

1. *List key results areas.* The first step is to identify and list your key results areas. You may already have done this at the beginning of the performance period. (See chapter 3.) You want to be able to clearly describe your job, as you see it, in terms of duties, responsibilities, and results to be achieved.

2. *Identify accomplishments.* Go to the records and summarize what you accomplished in each of your results areas. In the process, note any variations from the prior review period. If some results areas show a downward trend, objectively consider why—avoid making excuses, look for facts.

3. *Consider rating yourself.* If your manager gave you a copy of the performance evaluation form to be used, fill it in. If you didn't get a form, consider each results area. Did you exceed, equal, or fall short of your agreed upon expectations?

4. *Analyze your performance.* What are your strengths? What do you enjoy doing? What do you do well? Where have you had difficulty? What were the reasons for it?

5. *Identify an improvement goal.* What do you believe would make a contribution to your performance? What knowledge and/or skills would you like to work on during the next few weeks?

During the Discussion

The discussion provides the means not only for reviewing performance during the review period but also for reconciling any differences between you and your manager on the content of your job, and for exploring opportunities for the future. In order to be able to experience these outcomes, you must participate actively in the discussion. The following suggestions should contribute to a meaningful experience.

Discuss Your Performance Objectively.   It's often quite difficult to separate performance from self. After all, a lot of you is reflected through your performance. That's why it's especially important to avoid becoming defensive, hostile, or antagonistic. Try to stay objective about what you've achieved during the period under review rather than make excuses for any shortcomings.

Try to Understand Your Manager's Point of View. Listen to your manager and ask questions to be sure you understand what he's said. Ask for examples and particular incidents. Summarize and play back what you've been told in order to confirm your understanding. To really understand another person you must have an open mind to what you are being told. Don't discount the value of the other person's perspective. Be open to suggestions; your manager probably has some good ideas on how you could do your job better. Don't assume you're the only one who is in a position to know what's going on.

Express Your Own Point of View.   Offer information you have as well as your ideas and opinions, not to make excuses, but to gain mutual understanding. Discuss problems you ran into in getting things done. Don't cover up problems to avoid appearing unable to handle things. It's usually better to be open and up front with these difficulties so they can be worked out. Finally, be willing to express feelings. Such statements as "I enjoyed that" or "I don't believe I'd like to do that" or "it has been a really tough year" add a valuable human dimension to the discussion.

Set Specific Goals.   Leave the meeting with specific goals to be achieved during the coming performance period. The nature of the goals will probably depend on your degree of success in the past period: it may be to expand beyond your present job or it may be to improve in some area in order to measure up to the requirements of your job.

After the Discussion

Now that the discussion is over, there are some additional points you should consider. Basically, these focus on understanding, putting things into perspective, and getting underway to achieving your goals.

Think Through What You've Been Told.   Spend some time reflecting on what you were told during your performance discussion. Does what you were told correspond with your perception and with what others tell you? What are the implications of the feedback you've received? You are responsible for your own future. You must decide what course of action to pursue and live with the consequences of your choice.

Request Another Meeting.   If, in your reflection, you are unclear on any of the issues discussed, ask for a follow-up meeting. Then review and confirm your understanding and/or ask for any additional information you feel you may need to make an informed decision about your future.

Take Action. Having given due consideration to all relevant information, make a decision and take action. All too often people delay getting started on improvement plans and become preoccupied with other activities until the plans are forgotten. To avoid this, develop a detailed action plan. What steps must you take, and in what sequence, to achieve your goal? Lay out a schedule for each step in your plan. Then mark on your calendar appropriate check points and completion dates to monitor your progress. Consider taking a commitment with yourself to provide some appropriate incentive to achieve your goal. For example, you might decide to buy yourself a new garment when you complete your plan, or take a weekend trip to a favorite place. These self-administered incentives can be an excellent way to keep your mind on your plan.

✓ Checklist for Preparing for Your Own Formal Performance Review

- Summarize the key elements of your job.
- Reflect on the period to be covered during the discussion and list your accomplishments.
- Try to be objective in assessing and discussing your performance.
- Express your own points of view, opinions, and preferences.
- Be open to new ideas and suggestions.
- End the discussion with specific goals to be achieved during the next performance period.

Your Action Guide

Everyone needs feedback: they need to understand how their performance compares to expectations. You can approach feedback in two ways.

First, assure that intrinsic feedback is provided to employees through their normal work process by building systems that reflect quantity and quality of output. Intrinsic feedback has been proven to be most effective in bringing about improvement in performance levels.

Second, recognize the direct relationship between the types of extrinsic feedback and their impact on supervisor-employee relations. Use positive feedback to build morale and reinforce good performance. This approach takes you out of the role of critic, or "bearer of bad news," and places you in a supportive, helpful role. When employees do well, *you* acknowledge their accomplishments. When they do poorly, the *system* advises them of their poor performance, and you help seek out ways of improving.

Feedback is best handled on an event by event basis. Try to minimize the time lag between the event and the feedback on it. In addition to timely, ongoing feedback, a regularly scheduled formal performance review discussion is an integral part of an effective performance management system. It provides an opportunity to review performance over a significant time period, place accomplishments into perspective, and determine the implications of past performance on the future. These reviews are most effective when they are supportive, collaborative problem-solving experiences. No new information is introduced—the employee should be able to gauge his or her own performance against expectations, and extraordinary events should have been dealt with when they occurred. As you review various aspects of the employee's job, provide reinforcement for those things done well and offer help, direction, and encouragement to improve in those areas where results did not measure up.

A good review will be a two-way conversation centering around key on-the-job issues. Its aims are mutual to employee and supervisor. The question is "How can you best work together in order to experience the rewards of the work place?"

The key to feedback is the simple notion of respect for the employee as a person. Feedback is not an excuse for demeaning or embarrassing someone in front of others. Most people want to be effective in their work and feedback is an important ingredient in that effectiveness.

- ✔ As much as possible, build into each job a way for the employee to see firsthand the effects of his or her effort and whether or not efforts are successful.

- ✔ Look for opportunities to provide positive feedback to group members.

- ✔ Reserve negative feedback for important and critical areas.

- ✔ When providing feedback tie it to specific performance rather than express general or overall opinions and judgments.

- ✔ Don't save up feedback—provide it soon after the event it relates to.

References

James C. Conant, "The Performance Appraisal: A Critique and an Alternative," *Business Horizons,* June 1973.

Edward J. Feeney, "Getting Back to Basics, Management's Key to Productivity," *Manage,* April 1980.

Martin M. Greller and David M. Herold, "Sources of Feedback: A Preliminary Investigation," *Organizational Behavior and Human Performance,* vol. 13, 1975.

Gary P. Latham and Edwin A. Locke, "Goal Setting: A Motivational Technique That Works," *Organizational Dynamics,* Autumn 1979.

Norman R. F. Maier, *The Appraisal Interview* (New York: John Wiley & Sons, 1958).

Nile Soik, "How to Conduct the Employee Performance Review: A Step-by-Step Procedure," *Journal of the American Society of Training Directors,* November 1958.

Alvin F. Zander, ed., *Performance Appraisals Effects on Employees and Their Performance* (Ann Arbor: The Foundation for Research on Human Behavior, 1963).

THE PERFORMANCE MANAGEMENT SYSTEM

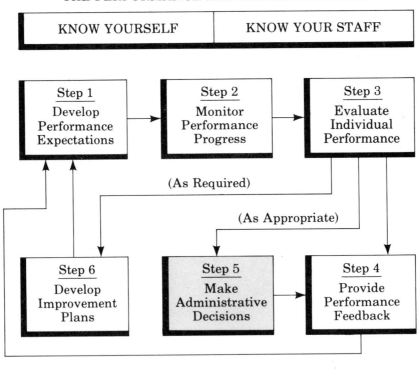

CHAPTER 7

Making Administrative Decisions

As a result of reading this chapter you will

- Understand the key elements of salary administration
- Be able to make equitable salary recommendations for members of your staff
- Be able to recommend appropriate members of your staff for promotion
- Know what to consider in determining whether to terminate an employee

Supervisors participate in several administrative decisions, usually by making recommendations. These decisions may include transfers, reassignments, promotions, salary changes, and whether or not to keep a staff member on the payroll. In this chapter, we'll look at three of these decisions: salary determination, promotions, and termination.

Making Salary Decisions

Probably no aspect of employment involves more emotion than pay. It's the final measure of what one's services are worth. In determining what an employee should be paid, you'll consider such factors as past and present performance, potential job level, position of current salary within the applicable salary range, competitive salaries in the community, rate of inflation, and economic success of the company.

Many companies have adopted salary policies designed to assure a direct relationship between performance and pay. For example, a survey taken among Fortune 500 companies showed that 93 percent claim to subscribe to a merit-reward philosophy of salary administration for nonsupervisory employees. However, on the basis of survey results it was concluded that for blue collar, clerical, and professional-technical employees only about 6, 14, and 19 percent of the companies respectively attempt to give emphasis to job performance factors when making wage and salary increase decisions.[1] These results are quite startling and lead to unending speculation as to the reasons behind them. Perhaps one reason is the lack of a rational salary administration model—one that takes all the key elements into account.

According to Adam's Equity Theory, feelings of satisfaction or dissatisfaction over pay, among other things, is related to an employee's observations of how much others are paid in relation to his or her own pay. Employees are satisfied when they see their pay as proportionate to their input. They generally can accept the fact that others get paid more because they put in more. Employees become dissatisfied when they see themselves putting in more but receiving the same or less than others, or when they put in the same and receive less. Therefore, it is imperative to workgroup satisfaction that a rational system for determining individual salaries exists and that the system recognize and respond to the potential areas of perceived inequity discussed in the following section.

The three main areas where equity in pay is usually looked for are: within the community, among jobs within the company, and between performance levels within the company. In equity between levels of performance, we're assuming that a salary range exists for each job, rather than a flat rate, and we're assuming that placement within that range is based on performance rather than longevity.

As a supervisor, you probably won't be determining the salary administration policy and procedures for your organization. In all likelihood, there will already be an established set of procedures in place. Look at the following system as a model that incorporates the key considerations that should be present in any decision-making system. As you compare your present decision-making system to the model, see if there are any missing pieces in your policies and procedures. If so, you might recommend that your personnel staff do some redesign on your present system.

Establishing Equity Within the Community

Equity in pay within the community, from the company's point of view, is controlled by two constraints: (1) a maximum salary level that does not exceed some appropriate cost limit nor upset the wage equilibrium in the community labor market and (2) a minimum salary level that will attract and hold a sufficient supply of qualified manpower. From the employees' point of view, equity in the community means salary opportunity equal to that offered by alternative organizations with which employees might associate.

What Is the Community?   In establishing community equity, the starting place is to define community. For professional and managerial employees, the community may be national in scope. On the other hand, for blue-collar and clerical employees, the community might be quite localized. The determining factor is the geographic dispersion of organizations the company competes with for employees in a given category. If you recruit nationally, you have a national community for salary purposes. If you recruit locally, you need only concern yourself with the local community.

The Salary Survey.   Equity in the community is established through salary surveys. Through a survey, participating companies exchange salary information on comparable positions. Usually included in the information exchange are starting salaries, salary ranges, and an actual frequency distribution of employee salaries. Other information might include education level, age, and experience.

In recent years there's been an increasing concern about salary surveys, due to the implication that companies get together and limit salary opportunities. In practice, this has not been the case. A salary survey reflects conditions at a specific point in time—that is, when the survey was taken. It has always been inappropriate during a salary survey to discuss a company's intentions, concerns, or plans for the future. However, to avoid allegations of wage fixing, three practices have emerged to replace the individual company-conducted survey. Each has the common objective of keeping company identities secret.

- Rely on existing surveys conducted by universities or government agencies such as the Bureau of Labor Statistics.
- Establish a survey within the framework of an existing professional or trade association.
- Companies interested in participating in a salary survey join together and hire a survey or accounting firm to gather, process, and distribute the data.

Selecting the right companies to include in a survey is a critical step in the process. The key is to include companies that actually represent alternative employment opportunities for your staff. This may result in more than one survey group depending on the category of employees involved. Since one objective of the survey is to assure employees of equal salary opportunity within the community, one valuable aid in your selection of participating companies would be to ask employees what companies they believe should be included.

Determining Salary Policy.   Determining salary policy begins with establishing a salary budget for a specified period—usually six months or a year. Setting the budget typically takes into account the economic success of the company, general economic conditions in the nation, and the amount the organization will have to spend in order to attract and hold the number and quality of employees needed to run the organization. This is where the community salary survey makes a contribution.

From information obtained through the survey, management can determine its salary policy relative to the position it wants to maintain in the community. Some companies, for example, are satisfied to set their salary schedule equal to the average of the top half, or even top quarter, of participating companies. Whatever policy your organization chooses to adopt, its salary schedule can be based on information obtained through the survey rather than on speculation. Remember, the survey reflects information as of the time it was taken. In establishing a salary schedule, you must also take into account any conditions that may impact future salary levels, such as inflation and changes in employment opportunities in the community. Increasing demand for a particular skill will drive up the salary range for that skill.

Establishing Equity Among Jobs

Equity among jobs within a company is determined by a consideration of the relative value of jobs themselves, without regard for the employees who are doing them. Some jobs are more valuable simply because of the contribution they make to the company's goals. The value of other jobs may be more subtle. An objective method for determining the relative values of jobs will help prevent feelings of inequity.

Information from the community wage survey will indicate the range of salaries appropriate for comparable jobs. However, it's highly unlikely that all of your company's job classifications will be comparable to other jobs in the community. To establish equity among jobs, a method is needed to relate the jobs not covered in the survey and to provide orderly salary advancement through a hierarchy of job classifications. This calls for a means of job analysis and the establishment of a salary grade structure—activities normally performed by salary administration specialists from the personnel department.

There are several methods of job evaluation you can use. One of the easiest is the weighted factor–ranking method. First, factors that affect job value are selected and defined. Next, definitions for each of the factors are developed and agreed upon by management. Finally, the factors are then subjectively weighted (assigned a number) to reflect their relative degree of importance in determining salary grade placement. For example:

- *Factor 1: Job complexity.* This factor measures the mental requirements of the job. It includes breadth of responsibility for equipment, products, and records as well as the mental skill and effort required to handle the job.
- *Factor 2: Supervision.* This factor measures the extent of supervision required over the job. It includes the extent of contact and availability required by the employee's supervisor and the extent to which work is reviewed. *High* ratings on this factor indicate a *low* amount of required supervision.
- *Factor 3: Physical effort.* Measured here are the physical requirements of the job—such things as lifting, standing, carrying.
- *Factor 4: Working conditions.* The exposure to unpleasant environmental and physical hazards such as moving machinery parts and heights are considered under this factor.

The next step is to rank all jobs under each factor. Under each factor, the job for which that factor is most significant is listed first. Now multiply each rank position value by the weight assigned to the factor, and finally, add up the factor values for each job. This yields a number for each job that reflects its value relative to the other jobs. From this list, salary grades can be determined. Figure 7.1 is an example of this process.

The dollar value of the salary grade ranges is derived from the community wage survey using the comparable jobs for which survey data was obtained. Jobs in your company that aren't comparable to jobs in the community survey gain their salary range from their rank in relation to jobs that *do* compare in the community survey. This produces a full salary grade schedule, with all jobs assigned to a grade based on relative job value. See Figure 7.2 and Exhibit 7.1 for examples of salary grades and schedules.

1.

Ranking by Factors*

1 (3)	2 (3)	3 (2)	4 (2)
Job a	Job c	Job b	Job b
Job b	Job b	Job c	Job e
Job c	Job d	Job a	Job a
Job d	Job a	Job d	Job b
Job e	Job e	Job e	Job c

*Factor weights are shown in parentheses.

Step 1. Each job is placed in a relative order under each factor, which is rated in degree of its importance.

3.

Rankings by Sum of Weighted Factor Values

Job b (38)—Grade 4
Job c (34)—Grade 3
Job a (33)—Grade 3
Job d (29)—Grade 2
Job e (16)—Grade 1

Step 3. Jobs are put in order of their factor weight totals and graded by their relative importance.

2.

Values for: Job a = 5 X (3) + 2 X (3) + 3 X (2) + 3 X (2) = 33
Job b = 4 X (3) + 4 X (3) + 5 X (2) + 2 X (2) = 38
Job c = 3 X (3) + 5 X (3) + 4 X (2) + 1 X (2) = 34
Job d = 2 X (3) + 3 X (3) + 2 X (2) + 5 X (2) = 29
Job e = 1 X (3) + 1 X (3) + 1 X (2) + 4 X (2) = 16

Step 2. The reverse rank order position of each job under each factor is multiplied by the weight of the factor. (Factor weights are in parentheses.) The results are added for each job to produce sums that can be ranked objectively to each other.

Figure 7.1 Calculation of relative job values by weighted factor–ranking method

Salary Grade	Monthly Minimum	Monthly Maximum
10	$4,695	$6,575
9	3,755	5,255
8	3,005	4,205
7	2,405	3,365
6	1,925	2,695
5	1,540	2,155
4	1,230	1,725
3	985	1,380
2	785	1,100
1	625	875

Figure 7.2 Example of salary grade structure

EXHIBIT 7.1   Example of Departmental Salary Schedule

Engineering Department Salary Grade Schedule

Job Code	Classification	Salary Grade	FLSA Status (E: exempt N: nonexempt)
905	Engineering Department Manager	10	E—Exec.
910	Engineering Supervisor	8	E—Admin.
915	Engineering Group Leader	7	E—Admin.
918	Consulting Engineer	9	E—Prof.
920	Senior Engineer	8	E—Prof.
925	Engineer	6	E—Prof.
928	Senior Engineering Technician	6	E—Prof.
930	Engineering Technician	5	N
935	Senior Engineering Draftsperson	5	N
940	Engineering Draftsperson	4	N
010	Executive Secretary	6	E—Admin.
030	Administrative Assistant	5	N
015	Senior Secretary	4	N
020	Secretary	3	N
025	Typist	2	N
060	Reproduction Machine Operator	1	N

Establishing Equity Between Performance Levels

Equity between levels of performance is somewhat more complex to establish. An employee's salary, at any point in time, should reflect the company's assessment of that person's past, present, and future contribution within an established salary structure. This relationship can be expressed by the formula:

$$\text{Salary} = \left(\frac{\text{Present}}{\text{Performance}} + \frac{\text{Past}}{\text{Performance}} + \frac{\text{Future}}{\text{Performance}} \right) \times \frac{\text{Salary}}{\text{Range}}$$

where: Present performance   = Scale rating (1 to 10) based on accomplishments versus objectives

Past performance = Sum of discounted present performance ratings for a specific number of prior years

Future performance = A ranking of employees into groups based on potential for advancement

Potential = A considered judgment based on past and present performance, individual interests and aspirations, present organizational level, and opportunities within the company

This formula is based on a two-stage evaluation process. The first stage is an evaluation of present performance on a 1 to 10 scale considering accomplishments versus objectives. The second stage is a ranking of employees into groups according to their potential for advancement. This is a subjective assessment predicated on the assumption that a company will cast its lot with the best employees it has available. Such a system is applicable only if there's a sufficient number of employees to give a statistically valid distribution.

Present Performance. An employee's present level of performance is the key to the formula. Present performance is evaluated by comparing an employee's accomplishments against the standards and objectives established for the job at the beginning of the performance cycle discussed in chapter 3. Here you must consider three questions: (1) To what extent were standards and objectives achieved? (2) How easy or difficult were the standards and objectives relative to the employee's job level? (3) How easy or difficult was it to achieve the standards and objectives under prevailing conditions? The supervisor's assessment of each of these three factors should be recorded, and an overall evaluation of present performance made on a 1 to 10 scale. Employees who achieve challenging standards and/or objectives under difficult conditions would have a present performance rating of 10. The rating will vary between 1 and 10 for each member of the group.

Past Performance.   An employee's past performance is relevant in determining salary level to the extent that she or he can be expected to continue a performance trend. Obviously, there needs to be a limit on how far back into the past you should look and the extent to which the past should be considered. Recommended limits are to go back a maximum of three years in the same salary grade and discount the past performance ratings (the sum of the discount factors always equals 1). In actual application of the formula, decisions would need to be made on these two points. The decisions are generally based on practicality, common sense, and individual preferences. The rating earned in each previous year is multiplied by the weighting factor, which reduces its overall value. The discount factor increases with the age of the performance rating. Thus the older the performance rating is, the less weight it has in present considerations.

For example, assume prior present performance ratings of 9 in year one, 10 in year two, and 9 in year three. Also, assume discount factors of 0.6, 0.3, and 0.1, respectively. This would yield a past performance rating of 9.3:

$$= 0.6 \times (9) + 0.3 \times (10) + 0.1 \times (9)$$
$$= 5.4 + 3.0 + 0.9$$
$$= 9.3$$

Future Performance.   The company's expectations of an employee's future performance is relevant in determining salary level in that it represents a realistic consideration of potential within the company. Future performance expectations are based on considerations of past and present performance, individual interests and aspirations, present organizational level, and opportunities available.

To derive a future performance rating, rank employees by considering their potential to advance. Then divide the total ranking into ten subgroups. The future performance rating is the subgroup the individual falls into. It will vary between one and ten for each member of the group.

Present Versus Future Performance.   Next, the relative weighting between present and future performance must be considered. It can be said that when an employee is hired, salary is based totally on future performance, and at retirement it is based entirely on present performance with due consideration to prior performance. This suggests that the importance of the present and future performance ratings should be weighted according to how long the employee has been on staff. One relationship between these two ratings is shown in Figure 7.3. Note how over time the weight of future performance diminishes and the weight of present performance increases. The selection of ten years of service as the intersect of the two curves may appear at first to be an over-generalization. That individuals vary significantly in their potential at any given point of service is accounted for in the ranking on potential. At issue in weighting the two values of present and future performance is the question, at what point does the company's willingness to pay for *potential* performance equal its willingness to pay for *present* performance? Perhaps it is at 5, 7, 10, or even 15 years. But at some point the two become equal, and from there on *present* performance dominates. See Figure 7.3.

Factors for weighting present and future performance can be derived from the curves at the point appropriate for the employee's length of service with the sum of the two factors always equaling one.

Salary Factor.   A salary factor that is equitable between performance levels can now be calculated. It is equal to the three prior years' performance ratings discounted, plus present performance weighted for length of service, plus relative future performance, or potential, weighted for length of service, all divided by 20. (Because of weighting constraints, past performance may equal 10, and present plus future performance may equal 10.) This factor is divided by 20 to convert it to a percentage. This value can now be applied to the employee's salary grade range to derive current salary level.

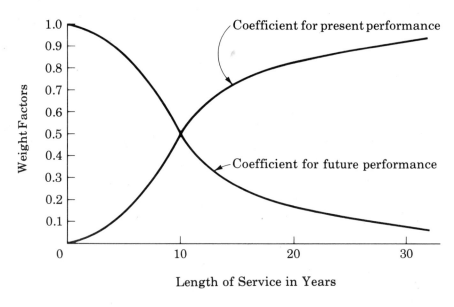

Figure 7.3 Relative weighting of present and future
performance in salary determination

Current Salary Level. An employee's current salary
level should reflect the value of past, present, and future performance within the company's salary grade structure. This can be
calculated by taking the salary grade range and multiplying it
by the salary factor and then adding this amount to the salary
grade minimum. Three examples will help illustrate how to apply this system in actually determining a salary. In each case
the employee is assigned to a classification that has a salary
grade minimum of $1,750 per month and a range of $525 per
month.

- *Example 1*. This employee has 12 years of service.
  Present performance rating is 8 and for the three prior
  years it was 7, 7, and 6. Future performance rating is 5.
  Processing this data through the system yields a current
  salary of $2,110 for this employee. (Note: this does not
  indicate what salary action is due since we do not know
  the employee's current salary level.)

Salary =

$$\left(\frac{\begin{array}{c}(8 \times 0.6) + (5 \times 0.4) + (7 \times 0.6) \\ + (7 \times 0.3) + (6 \times 0.1)\end{array}}{20}\right) \times 525 + 1{,}750$$

- *Example 2.* This employee has five years of service. Present performance rating is 9 and for the three prior years was 9, 8, and 8. Future performance rating is 10. The model yields a salary of $2,233.

Salary =

$$\left(\frac{\begin{array}{c}(9 \times 0.2) + (10 \times 0.8) + (9 \times 0.6) \\ + (8 \times 0.3) + (8 \times 0.1)\end{array}}{20}\right) \times 525 + 1{,}750$$

- *Example 3.* This employee has one year of service. Present performance rating is 3 and there are no prior performance ratings. (An employee promoted to a new salary grade likewise would not have a prior performance rating until after a year in the new grade.) Future performance rating is 1. The model yields a salary of $1,781.50 for this employee.

$$\text{Salary} = \left(\frac{(3 \times 0.1) + (1 \times 0.9)}{20}\right) \times 525 + 1{,}750$$

The formula can easily be computerized, and this should be seriously considered. Many of the individual salary increase decisions made at review time are in fact quite mechanical. A computer printout would give the "ideal" salary treatment for an individual based on an objective application of the formula. A manager would decide to either confirm or alter the computer-derived proposal. The decision would have the advantage of first being objectively determined and then being subjected to management judgment. Such an approach would help reduce arbitrary judgments by managers who consider extraneous factors when making salary decisions. Employees would be assured of being paid in fair proportion to their contribution of effort, skill, knowledge, and ability as reflected through past, present, and future performance.

Other approaches to salary administration can have the three elements of equity built into them (see Exhibit 7.2.) See Exhibit 7.2 for an example of a fixed-rate progression system that's based on length of service modified by merit.

Now that you have an understanding of the ingredients of effective salary administration, review some salary increase

---

EXHIBIT 7.2   Example of a Merit Pay Plan on a Fixed-rate Progression Schedule

I. Progression to Standard Rate

- Employees whose Overall Evaluation is *Satisfactory* will progress to the Standard Rate in accordance with the published progression schedule.
- Employees whose Overall Evaluation is *Outstanding* may be recommended for progression increases of either larger amounts or on shorter intervals to appropriately reward outstanding performance.
- Employees whose Overall Evaluation is *Inadequate* will not receive any salary adjustments until their performance is improved to at least a *Satisfactory* level. They will then progress to the next step on the progression schedule and begin accumulating time toward subsequent progression.

II. Merit Rate

- To receive the Merit Rate level of pay, an employee must demonstrate *Outstanding* overall performance on a continuing basis.
- In the event an employee receiving the Merit Rate drops to *Satisfactory* on overall performance, he or she will have sixty days to return to *Outstanding* or receive a reduction to the Standard Rate.

Exhibit 7.2   *(continued)*

III. Application of General Increases

Salary Position at Time of General Increase	Performance Level at Time of General Increase		
	Outstanding	Satisfactory	Inadequate
Merit Rate	Move immediately to new Merit Rate level.	Stay at current salary or move to new Standard Rate level whichever is greater.	Stay at current salary—special case subject to individual action.
Standard Rate	Move immediately to new Standard Rate level.	Move immediately to new Standard Rate level.	Stay at current salary.*
In Progression	Move immediately to corresponding step on new schedule.	Move immediately to corresponding step on new schedule.	Stay at current salary.*

* Employees in this situation will be eligible to receive the General Increase when their performance improves to the point where it is warranted.

recommendations for the following seven employees. In considering the cases, keep the following in mind:

- Salary increases may range from 0 to 15 percent of current salary.
- You'll be setting salary administration precedent.
- You want to hold salary costs to a minimum.
- You want to keep all seven employees and you want them to feel satisfied with their increases.
- All seven employees are comparable in education and experience. They all came to work last year at the same salary. Their employment opportunities with other companies are good.

- The salary determination formula presented in this chapter will not apply because adequate information on the employees isn't provided.

Fran. Fran's job is interesting, has comfortable working conditions, and offers security as well as opportunity. Fran's overall performance evaluation is *Meets All Job Requirements.*

> Fran's is an ordinary situation with nothing unusual to take into account. Fran is doing everything you expect; therefore, a salary increase of 10 percent would be appropriate to reinforce the current level of satisfactory performance.

Merle. Merle's job is also interesting, has comfortable working conditions, and offers security as well as opportunity. Merle's overall performance evaluation is *Exceeds Job Requirements.*

> While similar to Fran's, Merle's situation is different in one very important respect: his performance exceeds job requirements. Therefore a salary increase of 15 percent, the maximum available, is an appropriate reward for performance beyond expectations.

Pat. Pat is average in ambition and initiative and is evaluated as *Meets All Job Requirements* on overall performance. Pat's job is considered a "dead-end" without much opportunity for advancement.

> Pat should receive a 10 percent salary increase to reinforce satisfactory performance. While you may want to consider an appropriate reassignment in the future, the fact that Pat's job is considered a "dead-end" should not influence your present salary recommendation.

Leslie. Leslie's job is dirty, unpleasant, and uncomfortable but is seen as offering both security and opportunity. Leslie's overall performance evaluation is *Meets All Job Requirements.*

> A 10 percent salary increase would be appropriate to recognize and reinforce Leslie's present performance. The unpleasant working conditions should be factored into the job evaluation and be reflected in the job's salary grade.

Jerry. Jerry's job is interesting, has comfortable working conditions, and offers security as well as opportunity. Jerry has let you know of a job offer from another company. You expect Jerry will stay with you if you come close to matching the other company's salary. You evaluated Jerry's overall performance as *Meets All Job Requirements*.

> Jerry should also receive a 10 percent salary increase to recognize and reinforce a satisfactory level of performance. As a supervisor you must avoid the temptation to try to outbid competitors in order to keep employees. If you establish a practice of responding to these outside offers, you can expect to hear about a lot more of them in the future. Under ordinary conditions, nearly everyone can find an offer somewhere that exceeds a current salary.

Noel. Noel's job also has comfortable conditions and offers security as well as opportunity. Noel's overall performance evaluation is *Meets Most Job Requirements*. You don't want to lose Noel since replacements for his job are hard to find.

> Noel's performance doesn't measure up: he meets only most of his job requirements, not all of them. However, you want Noel to stay on the job. An increase of 5 percent could be warranted in this case, along with specific development plans to bring Noel's performance up to job requirements. Noel should be told that 5 percent is below average but appropriate for his level of demonstrated performance.

Rae. Rae is assigned to a boring, dull, and monotonous job that seldom requires any action but must be attended closely at all times. Replacement is expensive because at least six months of training is required. Rae's overall performance is evaluated as *Meets All Job Requirements*.

> As in Leslie's job, Rae's working conditions should be factored into the job analysis and salary grade. Rae's performance warrants a salary increase of 10 percent. In addition, job rotation should be considered to allow more variety in job duties for Rae.

✔ Checklist for Determining Salary Recommendations

- Become thoroughly familiar with your company's salary administration policy and procedures.
- Be sure that all jobs under your supervision are properly graded under your company's job evaluation program.
- Complete or update performance evaluations for all staff members.
- When clear distinctions in performance exist, establish corresponding distinctions in salary levels. However,

avoid salary differences that can't be supported by performance evaluation or that reflect a degree of precision greater than performance evaluation can justify.

- When individual performance warrants, use the full range of salary increase authorized by your company's salary administration program.

The Promotion Decision

A decision to promote someone has major consequences for both company operations and the individual employee involved. And once made, a promotion is difficult to reverse due to the stigma of failure that often accompanies demotion.

An effective procedure for selecting employees for promotion must incorporate three basic elements: (1) a method for determining the qualities necessary for success in the new position, (2) a method for assessing candidates' qualifications, and (3) an equitable way of selecting among qualified candidates.

Determining the Qualities Necessary for Success

The starting place for any selection procedure is a definition of what you are seeking. This requires some form of job analysis and the development of a list of job requirements.

What Is a Job Analysis? A job analysis begins with a description of what employees holding the job do. This is the same starting place as used for preparing a job description (see chapter 3). If you have a job description for the position, then this step will already be accomplished. Next, the job analysis tells what is required in order to successfully carry out the necessary duties. These are the actual job requirements. At this stage focus attention on qualities that spell the difference between success and failure and list them in terms of knowledge, skills, and behavior. (Exhibit 7.3 is an example of a list of job requirements.) Avoid generalities such as high school graduation. This part of the analysis will be an elaboration on the last section of the job description, if one exists. After the list is com-

EXHIBIT 7.3 Example of Job Requirements

Qualifications of Candidates
for First-level Supervisor in Plant Operations

A. Technical Knowledge/Skills

1. Thorough knowledge of the mechanical operation of assigned unit.
2. Thorough knowledge of chemical operation of assigned unit.
3. General knowledge of each of the crafts involved in the maintenance of assigned unit.
4. Thorough knowledge of product specifications.
5. Thorough knowledge of product end uses.
6. Thorough knowledge of how assigned unit interrelates with other units of the plant.
7. Ability to determine source of problems, seek out relevant information, consider alternatives, analyze risks, and recognize the consequences of proposed action.

B. Management Knowledge/Skills

1. Demonstrated understanding of the economics of a business with appropriate concern for costs and efficiency of operations.
2. Ability to effectively plan and organize own activities as well as those of assigned workgroup to effectively utilize manpower, tools, and equipment.
3. Ability to exercise control to assure task completion including follow-up and taking appropriate corrective actions.
4. Ability to take charge and be accountable for own actions, support company policies, and keep appropriate others properly informed.
5. Ability to set appropriate priorities.

C. Interpersonal Skills

1. Ability to communicate effectively both orally and in writing.

Exhibit 7.3   (*continued*)

---

    2. Ability to listen, understand, and respond to others as appropriate.

    3. Ability to influence the assigned workgroup to maintain appropriate levels of quality and quantity of output.

    4. Ability to resolve conflict between and with workgroup members.

    5. Ability to resolve performance problems through motivating to improve or disciplining as appropriate.

D. Personal Qualities

    1. Interest in the job of supervision and commitment to workgroup success.

    2. Willingness to be on the job beyond scheduled hours when required by plant conditions.

    3. Commitment to high ethical standards whether dealing with outsiders, management, or workgroup members.

    4. Ability to maintain stability of performance under stress and opposition.

    5. Ability to look at problems in a new way, to change past practices when required to improve operations, and to get the job done with available resources.

---

plete, assess the importance of each quality in terms of successfully fulfilling the job. The following categories would be appropriate:

- critical to successful performance
- important to successful performance
- moderately important to successful performance
- helpful but not necessary to successful performance

How to Complete a Job Analysis.   When you decide that a job analysis is appropriate, you have three choices for how to get it completed. In selecting one of these choices, consider such things as your objective and the degree of support you need for the results.

- *Do it yourself.* You probably are quite familiar with the requirements of jobs under your supervision. However, when working alone you may lack objectivity and may have some trouble selling your results to your management.

- *Use a staff specialist.* Most personnel departments have staff members qualified to write job descriptions and complete job analyses. This brings both objectivity and credibility to the project.

- *Use a task group.* Another effective way is to convene a task group that has supervisory responsibilities over the target position. When augmented by a staff specialist this is a very effective approach. The major benefit is acceptability of the outcome by those involved. It works best when the target position exists in several departments and/or locations.

Assessing Candidates' Qualifications

After drawing up the job specifications, your next step is to develop a means for evaluating candidates' ability to meet the specifications. Sometimes this is fairly simple, other times it's more complex. Consider Figure 7.4.

As you can see from the figure, ability is only one of three major factors contributing to performance. Performance is a

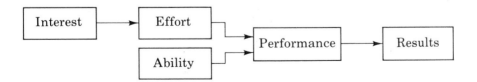

Figure 7.4 Basic elements of successful performance

result of the effort put forth and individual ability, both innate and acquired through training and experience. Often, a modest amount of ability is combined with extraordinary effort to achieve a high level of performance. Unfortunately, the converse is also true on occasion. Interest leads to effort. That is, when someone is interested in a particular job, effort comes easily. When there is a lack of interest, there tends also to be a lack of effort.

When assessing candidates' qualifications for promotion you must evaluate the extent of their interest and ability to perform in the future job assignment. Typically, the best assessment of interest is made through a discussion with the candidate. Some companies gauge interest by publicizing promotion opportunities and allowing employees to express their interest in being considered.

The best assessment of ability is made by observing abilities demonstrated while employees carry out their current job assignment. This is consistent with the adage that present performance is the best indicator of future performance. However, sometimes there isn't enough similarity in the two jobs to make a valid prediction.

The qualities that are common to both the present and future jobs can be illustrated by the two overlapping circles in Figure 7.5. In many situations there's sufficient overlap or simi-

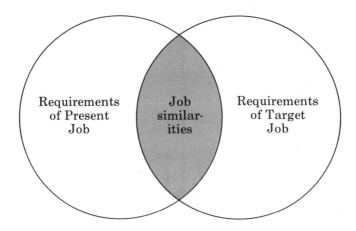

Figure 7.5 Comparison of present and future job requirements

larity between the present and new positions, and present performance is quite adequate for determining qualifications for promotions.

On the other hand, there also can be enough difference in the requirements of the present and future jobs that very little overlap exists between the two circles in Figure 7.5. These situations call for additional assessment techniques. Two of the most common are written tests and simulation exercises.

Written Tests. Written tests, recommended by their developers to aid in making promotion decisions, have been marketed for many years. Under research conditions, however, very few have been found to make significant contributions. Tests can be put into three general categories.

- *Tests of knowledge, skills, and ability.* Some companies develop their own tests that focus on the specific requirements of jobs. General tests in this category include verbal ability, mechanical ability, clerical ability, and supervisory practices.

- *Tests of interests, values, attitudes, and motives.* These are generally referred to as personality tests. They have not been very effective in predicting on-the-job performance for three reasons:

  1. The results can be easily distorted.
  2. They lack reliability.
  3. Few, if any, have been designed for occupational prediction.

- *Tests of intelligence.* Intelligence, or mental ability tests, have been used by the military for several years. They have potential application in evaluating candidates for promotion where there is a significant increase in the mental requirements in the future job.

Simulation Exercises. Simulation exercises attempt to place the candidate in a real-life opportunity to display qualities considered important in the job. These exercises have shown promise as a supplementary technique. Their contribution directly relates to the selection or development of an exercise specifically designed to bring out the appropriate qualities for observation and evaluation. Simulation exercises can be generally sorted into four categories.

- *In-basket exercises.* In an in-basket exercise the candidate receives a packet of materials containing instructions, background material (such as an organization chart and a calendar), and a series of items to handle. It's as though the candidate arrived at work and began handling the items in an in-basket. Items usually included are letters to be answered, telephone messages to handle, and reports. During a specific time period the candidate handles as many of the items as possible. Usually the candidate is interviewed following individual work on the exercise as a part of the assessment process.

- *Role play exercises.* Role play exercises vary substantially depending on the job. Typically, they're one-to-one discussions where the candidate assumes the new position and deals with a typical problem or situation. If the target position is at a supervisory level, the candidate might have to conduct a performance discussion, terminate a hypothetical employee, or handle a personal or disciplinary problem. If the target position is in sales, the candidate might have to handle an irate customer.

- *Leaderless group discussions.* When leadership and oral communications skills in a group context are important, leaderless group discussions allow these qualities to be assessed. Typically, five to eight candidates are put in a group and given a topic to discuss. They are also usually expected to develop a group response to the topic. An example of such a topic is: "What are the important qualities of an effective supervisor?" While the discussion is in progress the candidates are observed and evaluated on relevant qualities.

- *Business games.* Business games take many forms. Some are computer based. Some have the actual manufacture of a product as part of the design. Some are in workbook format requiring written responses to a sequence of situations. All place the candidates in the position of running a company or department. They may share elements of planning, organizing, making decisions, setting priorities, controlling operations, and taking corrective actions in response to changing conditions. As in the other exercises, candidates are observed and assessed while the exercise is in progress.

Assessment Centers.   You can substantially improve effectiveness of your selection techniques by using appropriate tests and/or exercises in combination. A popular way of doing this is through the use of assessment centers. An assessment center is a standardized program that brings a group of candidates together for assessment. While together they complete a series of tests and participate in a series of simulation exercises and interviews. A staff committee gathers data on the candidates and then discusses each one and arrives at an assessment decision.

A Word of Caution.   Guidelines issued by the Equal Employment Opportunity Commission require that anything used to aid in the selection of candidates for promotion must be validated. That is, there must be statistical evidence to demonstrate that there's a direct relationship between performance on the selection device and performance in the target position. You should never use a device that hasn't been validated. Statistical validations can be handled either by qualified staff specialists or by outside consultants.

Selecting Among Qualified Candidates

Employees are often selected for promotion to reward good performance and to recognize years of service. Both of these are important considerations in the promotion decision but they're *secondary* to the employee's qualifications to perform the assignment. Your selection process should integrate all three factors of *performance, service,* and *qualifications.* This can be done either mathematically or judgmentally by an individual or a group.

Mathematical Integration.   A mathematical integration of performance, service, and qualifications requires a formula that gives due consideration to each element. This usually means assigning weights or values to the three elements. For example, you might weight performance as (2), service as (1), and qualifications as (3). All the candidates can now be ranked separately on the three elements. Reverse order rank positions are multiplied by the weights of the elements and totaled to determine the appropriate candidate to promote. Figure 7.6 illustrates this procedure.

1. Rankings on Each Element (Weights in Parentheses)

Performance (2)	Service (1)	Qualifications (3)
1. Jones	1. Brown	1. Hardy
2. Smith	2. Jacobs	2. Arnold
3. Hardy	3. Jones	3. Brown
4. Brown	4. Hardy	4. Jones
5. Jacobs	5. Arnold	5. Smith
6. Arnold	6. Smith	6. Jacobs

2. Reverse Order Ranks Multiplied by Weights and Totaled

$$\text{Jones:}\quad (6 \times 2) + (4 \times 1) + (3 \times 3) = 25$$
$$\text{Smith:}\quad (5 \times 2) + (1 \times 1) + (2 \times 3) = 17$$
$$\text{Hardy:}\quad (4 \times 2) + (3 \times 1) + (6 \times 3) = 29$$
$$\text{Brown:}\quad (3 \times 2) + (6 \times 1) + (4 \times 3) = 24$$
$$\text{Jacobs:}\quad (2 \times 2) + (5 \times 1) + (1 \times 3) = 12$$
$$\text{Arnold:}\quad (1 \times 2) + (2 \times 1) + (5 \times 3) = 19$$

3. Order of Preference

1. Hardy: 29	4. Arnold: 19
2. Jones: 25	5. Smith: 17
3. Brown: 24	6. Jacobs: 12

Figure 7.6 Example of mathematical integration of promotion considerations

The ranking on qualifications usually involves a consideration of on-the-job performance, and any supplementary assessment procedures utilized. Seldom is the qualifications evaluation a straightforward, easily determined numerical value.

Judgmental Integration. A more popular approach is to judgmentally integrate the three elements. To simplify the process you can consider present performance to be a prerequisite for consideration. Once a candidate meets this prerequisite, it's given no further consideration. The pool of qualified candidates is then ranked on the basis of predicted ability to successfully perform the job. Candidates are selected from the top of the list with length of service judgmentally moderating the final decision. For example, if Jones and Hardy have nearly equal qualifications, but Hardy has substantially more seniority Hardy would be selected.

EXHIBIT 7.4   Example of Pair-comparison Analysis for Prioritizing Candidates for Promotion

	1 Jones	2 Smith	3 Hardy	4 Brown	5 Jacobs	6 Arnold	Number of X's
1 Jones			X	X		X	3
2 Smith			X	X		X	3
3 Hardy							0
4 Brown						X	1
5 Jacobs						X	1
6 Arnold							0
Total Blanks	0	1	0	1	4	1	
Total X's	3	3	0	1	1	0	
Sum of Blanks & X's	3	4	0	2	5	1	
Priority	4	5	1	3	6	2	

Exhibit 7.4   (*continued*)

Procedures

1. Draw a matrix large enough to handle the number of candidates being considered.
2. List candidates down the left column and across the top, being careful to maintain the same sequence.
3. Working across, one row at a time, compare the candidate in the left column to each candidate listed across the top. If a candidate listed across the top is better qualified than the one in the left column, place an "X" in the box.
4. When the individual comparisons are complete, count the number of blank boxes in each column and record this on the appropriate line at the bottom. Then, count the number of X's across each row and record this in the last column to the right. Transfer these data to the appropriate line at the bottom of the matrix.
5. Add the number of blanks and the number of X's in each column.
6. Assign priorities with the lowest total of blanks and X's receiving the highest priority. In the event of a tie, look back to where the 2 candidates were compared and prioritize according to that prior decision.

Individual supervisors can follow this procedure, as well as groups who must make a promotional decision. For groups, it's usually helpful to have some structure to focus the discussion. Exhibit 7.4 is an example of such a structure. This structure limits each decision to a choice between two candidates. Arrive at decisions either through consensus discussion or by voting, depending on the guidelines chosen by the group at the start of the meeting.

✔ **Checklist for Recommending Employees for Promotion**

- Identify the qualities required for successful performance in the future position.
- Complete, or update, performance evaluations on all staff members who are prospective candidates for promotion.
- Analyze performance in employee's present assignment that is similar to performance required in the future assignment.
- Where similarity between the present and future positions is insufficient to form a valid conclusion, consider supplementary evaluation techniques.
- Establish a rational, objective procedure for comparing all qualified candidates in order to arrive at a final recommendation.

The Termination Decision

Company-initiated terminations generally fall into one of three categories:

1. Layoff due to lack of work
2. Discharge due to violation of company policy or unacceptable behavior in the workplace
3. Requested resignation due to poor performance

Performance evaluation data can be a factor in each of these termination decisions, except in cases where your decisions are restricted by union agreements.

Layoffs due to lack of work usually take into account length of service, performance, availability of other work and willingness to accept reassignment. Discharges usually consider the severity of the rule violation, prior record of violations, and performance. Requested resignations usually consider performance, length of service, availability of suitable replacements, qualifications for other assignments, and attitudinal variables such as willingness to try and cooperativeness.

Layoffs Due to Lack of Work

While no supervisor wants to cut off an employee's source of income, layoff due to lack of work is probably the easiest termination decision to make. There's usually no personal stigma associated with layoffs. A layoff is the result of circumstances beyond the control of the individual employee. While this generally is true, if it's not restricted by labor contract provisions, an organization may choose to use layoffs as an opportunity to do some culling of the workgroup.

Rather than going strictly by the "last in, first out" rule, you should view length of service as a moderating force in your final decision, with performance and availability of alternative opportunities also being considered. For example, if you have two employees with nearly equal service, but one is clearly a better performer, lay off the one with the poorer performance record. However, a *substantial* difference in length of service probably should not be discounted. If the poorer performer has less service, the decision should be straightforward. Occasionally there may be a sufficient difference in performance to warrant displacing an employee with even slightly more service. Another option is to consider reassigning an employee with a good performance record.

✔ Checklist for Recommending Employees for Layoff

- Consider appropriate alternatives to layoffs, such as reassignments or transfers.
- Use layoffs as opportunities to upgrade the general quality of your staff.
- Be sure your final recommendation is supported by performance evaluation information.
- Have your recommendation reviewed by someone else to verify fairness, equity, and objectivity.

Discharges Due to Violations of Company Rules

This kind of termination is slightly more difficult to handle than a layoff. However, terminations usually are based on clear-cut episodes that either do or do not warrant discharge. Your decision should also be appropriately tempered with other considerations. What's the employee's performance history? Is there a history of rule violations? How severe is the present violation? A good record can override a violation of moderate severity. But a violation of modest severity can justify discharge for an individual with a poor performance record or a history of prior violations. Handling discharges will be explored in greater depth in chapter 10.

Requested Resignations Due to Poor Performance

You must consider several issues in deciding to terminate an employee because of poor performance. Is the performance marginal or is it unacceptable? What are the prospects for improvement? Has performance declined due to some episode in the employee's life? How long has the employee been on the payroll? Is a replacement readily available? How willing and cooperative is the employee? What alternative assignments exist?

Look at all of these factors together. You may choose to not terminate a marginal performer because he or she has been around for a long time or because a replacement isn't readily available. You might decide to find the employee a different assignment that's more suited to her or him. You may choose to endure a period of poor performance because you expect the employee to recover from some personal trauma and return to an acceptable level of performance. Any course of action you choose will probably be influenced to some degree by the employee's willingness to try to improve and the degree of cooperation he or she displays.

Termination for inadequate performance must be supported by performance evaluation records. You must be completely honest in discussing evaluation results and highlight the particular problem areas for the individual. If after a reasonable time period you don't find improvement, a decision to terminate the employee can be made with confidence that it is both proper and reasonable. Before you finalize your decision, however, review it with a third party to verify its fairness, equity, and objectivity.

Your Action Guide

Individual performance evaluation (step 3 in the Performance Management System) provides valuable input into several significant administrative decisions (step 5 in the system). These decisions in turn serve as a supplementary form of feedback to employees on their performance (step 4 in the system). An effective decision-making system will assure that what an employee is being told about her or his level of performance is consistent with what she or he is experiencing in terms of salary treatment, job assignments, promotions, and termination or retention in service.

Performance is only one of several important considerations in these decisions. For example, in a salary decision the range of salary opportunity available must play a role. If an employee's salary is the top amount available for the present job assignment, typically an increase can't be granted. Promotions can only be made when openings exist, and then the primary consideration should be candidates' qualifications. Occasionally, this results in a top performer in a present assignment not being promoted because someone else is better qualified for the new job. Likewise, retention in service can be affected by issues other than performance, including the length of service, availability of alternative assignments, and prospects for making a contribution in the future.

Interestingly, most any supervisor faced with decisions of salary, promotion, and termination will take performance into account to some degree. The objective of this chapter has been to provide a framework for structuring that process, in order to give consistency to the decisions and their considerations.

ᐅ Review your company's policies and practices that apply to the decisions being made.

⟋ Develop an appropriate structured way to give due consideration to all relevant elements in the decision.

⟋ Use only current, up-to-date performance evaluation data in the decision process.

⟋ Make sure that the administrative decisions affecting staff members are consistent with the verbal feedback they receive on their performance.

References

J. Stacy Adams, "Toward an Understanding of Inequity," *Journal of Abnormal and Social Psychology,* vol. 65, no. 5, 1963.

William C. Byham, "Assessment Centers for Spotting Future Managers," *Harvard Business Review,* July–August 1970.

William A. Evans, "Pay for Performance: Fact or Fable," *Personnel Journal,* September 1970.

Marion E. Haynes, "Selecting First-Level Supervisors," *Personnel Management Review,* December 1976.

F. H. Hunt, "R&D Management: A Personnel Ranking System," *Personnel,* May–June 1969.

A. L. Kress, "Job Evaluation for White-Collar Workers in Private Sector Employment in the United States," *International Labor Review,* October 1969.

Edward E. Lawler, "Merit Pay: Fact or Fiction," *Management Review,* April 1981.

THE PERFORMANCE MANAGEMENT SYSTEM

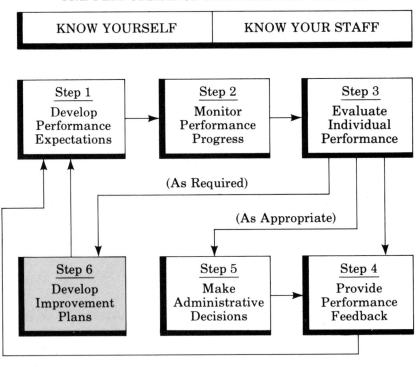

KNOW YOURSELF	KNOW YOUR STAFF

Step 1
Develop Performance Expectations

Step 2
Monitor Performance Progress

Step 3
Evaluate Individual Performance

(As Required)

(As Appropriate)

Step 6
Develop Improvement Plans

Step 5
Make Administrative Decisions

Step 4
Provide Performance Feedback

DELEGATE RESPONSIBILITY AND AUTHORITY	MANAGE PERFORMANCE PROBLEMS	MANAGE GROUP PERFORMANCE

CHAPTER 8

Developing Performance Improvement Plans

As a result of reading this chapter you will

- Understand the elements which contribute to performance
- Understand the importance of employee participation in performance improvement planning
- Understand the importance of goal setting in achieving performance improvement
- Be able to develop performance improvement plans with your staff

Occasionally, after evaluating individual performance (step 3 of the Performance Management System) you'll find a need for performance improvement. This obviously will be the case when results don't measure up to expectations. Presented in this chapter is a strategy to help you successfully develop performance improvement plans.

The Elements of Performance

When performance is defined as the results an employee achieves, many contributing factors become clear. Some of these are within the employee's control, others are not. Three in particular emerge:

1. *The employee.* The individual's knowledge, skills, interests, values, attitudes, and motives.
2. *The job.* The requirements and demands of the job and the opportunities it provides for interesting, challenging work with built-in feedback.
3. *The situation.* The organizational context in which the job is performed, including climate, supervision, available resources, administrative systems, and organizational structure.

You need to examine each of these groups for ways they can be improved. A change in any one of them may dramatically affect performance and results. All too often, a shortfall in performance is automatically assumed to be entirely the employee's fault. Consider the following case as an example.

Tom is an accounting clerk working for a small company. He was hired about three months ago to replace an employee who was retiring after 43 years of service with the same company. One of Tom's duties is to summarize the company's gross sales figures by sales districts each month. The general manager expects the summary report on his desk by the third working day of the following month. The first month that Tom was totally responsible for the report, he completed it on the fifth working day. In the eyes of the general manager, Tom's performance needed improving. It didn't meet the general manager's expectations.

When the accounting supervisor talked to Tom about the report being late she found that Tom was interested in completing it on schedule and knew procedurally how to pull the report together. She also found that Tom's predecessor had a very informal but effective network of contacts in the district sales offices that he relied upon for information. Tom was not privileged to the same sources and had to rely on formal systems that took longer to deliver the same information.

Tom's inability to deliver the summary report on schedule was primarily due to an incompatibility between the report's due date and the administrative procedures for generating the report. He might be able to deliver the report on time if he were to do one or more of the following:

- Negotiate a *revised* due date with the general manager consistent with current administrative procedures
- Revise formal administrative procedures for getting the required information more quickly
- Visit the sales offices to develop access to his predecessor's informal network

Improving the Employee

The employee is probably the most difficult of the three factors to change. When, after a full performance analysis, you determine that the employee needs to change, there are several approaches you can take.

Build on Strengths. The first thing you need to do is establish a positive orientation toward the employee and the performance problems being experienced. Acknowledge that no one is perfect. Realize that attempting to eliminate all of an employee's weaknesses is unrealistic. Everyone is a combination of strengths and weaknesses—in most people, strengths outweigh weaknesses. Improvement efforts are most successful when you examine ways to make greater use of *existing* talents rather than try to develop *new* or deficient ones.

Build on Likes. A significant correlation has been observed between what a person likes to do and what she or he does well. Establishing cause and effect between likes and performance is not nearly as important as attempting to match interests with the work to be done. To the extent you can allow people to do things they like to do, you also can increase the odds of good performance. This doesn't suggest that work be ignored, or left undone simply because no ones likes to do it. Rather, it is a challenge to you as supervisor to make the best possible match between those on your staff and the work of your section or department.

Relate to Personal Goals.   Performance improvement efforts should relate to and be compatible with the employee's personal goals and career interests. When an employee has strong career interests, capitalize on them by demonstrating how the improvement you seek in the employee's performance will contribute to the realization of those interests. This process establishes a mutually beneficial outcome. This recognizable relationship between personal goals and improvement plans will increase the employee's motivation to achieve the desired improvement.

A word of caution is necessary regarding personal goals. People's ambitions and interests are subject to change as the individual is exposed to new experiences. Therefore, don't assume that career interests and personal goals will remain the same. Consider them in short-range improvement planning and then from time to time talk with employees to keep abreast of their current interests.

Improving the Job

Changing the particular assortment of tasks assigned to an employee provides certain opportunities for improving performance. Job content contributes to poor performance when it's either boring and demotivating, beyond the skills level of the employee, or composed of inappropriate or unnecessary tasks. These problems can be addressed in several ways.

Necessary Tasks.   The starting point in examining a job for ways to improve performance is to question whether each task in the job is actually necessary. It's very common to continue doing something, even after it isn't useful or necessary.

Also common is duplicating the work of another section because of distrust in the other section's ability to do the work properly. This is particularly evident in records keeping. In examining a job carefully, you should reduce the job to its essential elements.

Appropriate Tasks.   When the essential tasks are identified, the next question is where these tasks should appropriately be performed. This analysis should consider appropriateness in terms of department or section and appropriateness in terms of the skills and authority of staff members. In regard to the former, you may find tasks that should be turned over to administrative or technical support sections such as accounting, employee relations, purchasing, engineering, and inspection. In regards to skills and authority, you may find employees doing work substantially beneath their skills that can be reassigned within your section. On the other hand, you may find employees attempting to do work for which they do not have the required knowledge, skills, and/or authority.

Job Design.   The outcome of an analysis of job tasks is a job design. It takes into account the necessary and appropriate tasks to be performed and groups them into jobs that offer interesting and challenging work to the members of your staff. Two concepts typically incorporated into job design are job enlargement and job enrichment. Job enlargement involves grouping together more tasks requiring a similar level of skill so employees can more closely identify with an end product. Job enrichment involves increasing the levels of responsibility and freedom.

Job Rotation.   Job rotation can be a simple but effective way to reduce or eliminate boredom, thereby enhancing motivation. It simply means having employees swap jobs for a while. In addition to renewing employee interest, it provides the added benefit of cross-training among your staff. When considering job rotation, follow these guidelines:

- Rotate jobs that are of nearly equal complexity. You need to minimize the risk of an employee either being unable to handle the new job or not being challenged by it.

- Have employees change jobs for a significant period of time. The duration of the assignments can vary, but should be long enough to expose an employee to a full range of duties and allow the individual to experience the results of decisions made on the job.

- Standards of performance should be realistic. When establishing performance expectations make them challenging for the employee's level of knowledge, skill, and experience. Don't be too lenient simply because the employee will only be in the job a short while, but also don't set up a failure by being too demanding.

Special Assignments.   From time to time opportunities become available for staff members to serve on committees, study teams, or task forces. Use these opportunities to provide variety and renew interest among your staff as well as to provide a means for staff members to contribute to the solution of company and community problems.

Improving the Situation

The situation or environment the job is performed in offers many opportunities for changes that potentially could improve performance. Consider in particular the following points.

Organization.   Consider the way the workgroup is organized. Are lines of communication and responsibility clear and appropriate? Is interaction with other departments and customers clear and as effective as possible? Is the number of hierarchical levels appropriate? For example, should area coordinators or group leaders be established to improve performance of the section?

Area Layout.   Examine the way the work area is laid out. Is it as efficient as it might be? Could wasted effort be eliminated or travel flow be improved by rearranging the work area? Is adequate storage space available and convenient to the work area?

Resources.   Each employee is allocated certain resources—tools, equipment, money, time, services—to use in accomplishing his or her results. All of these resources need to be reviewed to see that they're adequate and consistent with the priority of the work.

Schedules.   Schedules can be controlled or changed for the benefit of the work that must be accomplished. Are they appropriate? Do all deadlines fall at the same time of the month creating a slack period in between? Could deadlines be better spaced during a week or month? Do normal schedules provide adequate time to get the job completed?

Supervisor.   Do you over- or under-supervise the employee? In chapter 1, supervisory styles were discussed in relation to the maturity level of the employee. Have you made an appropriate match between your style and your employees' maturity levels? If you are too far out of line the employee will be frustrated due to either too little or too much guidance. Other things you should consider include the extent to which you communicate, how much you delegate, the standards you set, how much you follow up on work in progress, what you reward, the methods you endorse, and the extent that you allow or encourage your staff to take risks.

Dynamics That Affect the Planning Process

Egos tend to be very fragile. And, if it is to be successful, planning for performance improvement must be handled in a way that doesn't damage the employee's ego. Insight into how you can effect improvements without hurting individual ego can be gained by looking at the results of several studies in interpersonal situations. These studies look at the dynamics of (1) power, (2) interpersonal bargaining, and (3) criticism, as they relate to performance improvement discussions or similar situations.

The Dynamics of Power

One significant study of the dynamics of power looks at the distribution of power in performance improvement discussions. The study was based on the concept that it takes one unit of

Portion of 1 power unit held by supervisor	Compe-tition	Collaboration										Powerless-ness
	1	1	0.9	0.8	0.7	0.6	0.5	0.4	0.3	0.2	0.1	0	0
Portion of 1 power unit held by employee	1	0	0.1	0.2	0.3	0.4	0.5	0.6	0.7	0.8	0.9	1	0

Figure 8.1 The power spectrum

Adapted from Blake and Mouton, "Power, People, and
Performance Reviews." Used with permission.

power to make a decision. This unit can be fully retained by a supervisor or an employee, or it can be shared. This concept resulted in the power spectrum shown in Figure 8.1.

Looking at Figure 8.1 you can see that outside the range of collaboration are competition and powerlessness. In competition both supervisor and employee seek to retain the full unit of decision-making power. Each attempts to force compliance on the other. On the other extreme is powerlessness, where neither has decision-making power. This situation is typical of situations where the decision is either a function of policy or is made by higher management.

Within the range of collaboration the power distribution may vary from 1/0, where the supervisor wields all the power, to 0/1, where the employee makes the decisions. Actual relationships in the workplace usually fall between 0.9/0.1 and 0.6/0.4 or 0.5/0.5.

As a result of experiments conducted in the study, two relevant correlations were found. One correlation has to do with the amount of personal satisfaction an individual enjoys with a decision. As influence on the decision increases, satisfaction with the decision also tends to generally increase. The optimum point of satisfaction for both supervisor and employee in a given decision was found to exist between the 0.6/0.4 and 0.5/0.5 distribution of power. This relationship is shown in Figure 8.2. While this point doesn't provide the greatest satisfaction for either party, it does provide a moderately high level for *both*.

The other correlation relates power and responsibility. The feelings of responsibility for the outcome of the decision are at a peak for both supervisor and employee near the 0.5/0.5 power

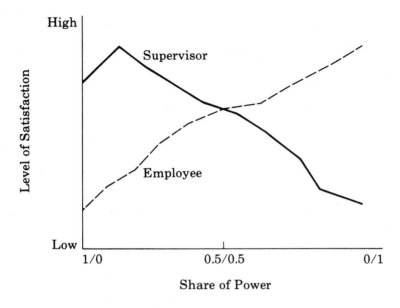

Figure 8.2 Relationship between power and satisfaction
Adapted from Blake and Mouton, "Power, People, and
Performance Reviews." Used with permission.

position. Feelings of responsibility decrease as an individual's influence on the decision decreases. However, at no point does the supervisor feel a lack of responsibility for the performance of workgroup members. These results are shown in Figure 8.3.

Two kinds of discussions were analyzed in the study:

1. A formal summary by the supervisor of the employee's past performance based on an appraisal rating procedure

2. A collaborative discussion between supervisor and employee based on a goal-setting process

Of necessity, the first type of discussion was close to a 1/0 power distribution. This is because the ratings were solely determined by the supervisor. The second type of discussion, however, approached a 0.5/0.5 power distribution with both the supervisor and employee involved in determining impediments to performance and planning to eliminate them.

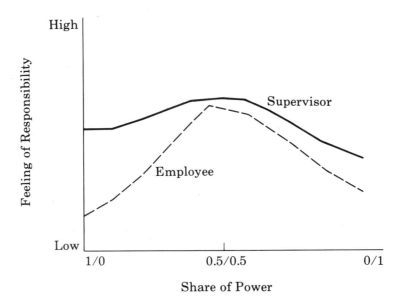

Figure 8.3 Relationship between power and responsibility
Adapted from Blake and Mouton, "Power, People, and Performance Reviews." Used with permission.

In the first discussion there was no feeling of satisfaction experienced by the employee, and while the supervisor had a high sense of responsibility to effect change, the employee had none. Additionally, this type of discussion resulted in feelings of isolation between the people involved rather than a pulling together to reach a common objective.

In another study, which also looked at power, the relationship between the influence of different degrees of power and the development of interpersonal trust was considered. One conclusion of this study was that the greater the power one person has over another, the more likely it is that the less powerful person will be suspicious of the more powerful person. This leads to reduced chances for the development of interpersonal trust.

A second conclusion was that, even with a substantial power differential, a cooperative strategy is more likely to develop trust and thereby maximize the mutual gain from the relationship.

Think about these ideas and try putting them to use. You'll reduce the impact of the traditional power difference between yourself and members of your workgroup. Through collaboration and cooperation you can establish and maintain trusting relationships.

The Dynamics of Interpersonal Bargaining

A successful performance improvement session ends in agreement between you and the staff member on a course of action, with commitment from the staff member to carry out the action. This interaction is quite similar to a bargaining session in which the participants have different interests but are dependent on each other in order to avoid a mutually detrimental outcome. These "bargaining" discussions can be affected by two important elements that you must consider and try to avoid: threat and face-saving.

The Element of Threat.   When one or both parties engaged in bargaining threaten the other party at the start of negotiations, the likelihood that agreement will be reached is reduced.

Used as a means of influence, threat implies that harm will be inflicted unless the threatened person modifies his or her behavior in the desired manner. In performance improvement planning, the harm to be inflicted by a supervisor could range from withholding promotion or salary advancement to demotion or termination. The harm to be inflicted by the employee could range from neglect of duties to absenteeism or tardiness to resignation.

The Need to Maintain Face.   When participants in a bargaining situation are made to look foolish or weak, they're likely to retaliate against whomever caused their humiliation. Furthermore, they'll retaliate even though they know that to do so may sacrifice their chances of a positive outcome.

The need to maintain face is expressed through two sets of actions—face-saving and face restoration. Face-saving is action to prevent someone else from doing something that would cause you to appear foolish, weak, or incapable in the eyes of others. In performance improvement planning this could be seen in an employee's attempt to prevent you from submitting a derogatory report to higher management or to prevent any action clearly visible to peers, such as suspension, reassignment of duties, demotion, or discharge. Face restoration involves attempts to seek redress from someone who has already caused an individual to look foolish or weak.

Employees generally seek to project a positive self-image to supervisors, higher management, and peers within the workgroup. Conflict in accomplishing this may be met with attempts to maintain or restore face, which will be detrimental to the working relationships within the group.

The Dynamics of Criticism

The effects of criticism in terms of negative extrinsic feedback have been discussed as part of step 4 of the Performance Management System in chapter 6. Let's look at how criticism can affect planning sessions.

A study involving 92 performance improvement discussions looked at the effects of criticism, among other things. Analyses of these discussions found that praise tended to be general while criticism tended to be specific. Also found was that employees reacted defensively about 54 percent of the time when criticized, and constructive responses to criticism were rarely observed. Defensive reactions usually took the form of denying the shortcomings cited by the supervisors, blaming others for the performance deficiency, and various other forms of excuses designed to minimize the individual employee's responsibility.

Importance of Self-Esteem. Employees in the study were asked to rate their own performance prior to engaging in the performance discussion with their supervisor. Only two placed themselves below average on the scale. All others saw themselves as average or above, with the mean being at 77 percentile. After the performance discussion, the employees were asked how they thought their supervisor had rated them. This time the mean dropped to 65 percentile. A total of 81.5 percent saw their supervisor's evaluation as being less favorable than their own evaluation of their performance. Obviously, the discussion had been an ego-deflating experience, and therefore it's not surprising that they reacted defensively.

Impact on Performance Improvements. The real issue, of course, is the extent to which the supervisor's objectives were achieved. Was he or she successful in bringing about performance improvement? The answer is an unqualified no. Those who received an above average amount of criticism actually improved less than those who had received less criticism.

This conclusion was reached in the following manner. After the original discussions between employee and supervisor, each employee was asked to identify the one aspect of his or her performance that had received the most criticism. Follow-up investigations were then carried out 10 to 12 weeks later. These investigations found that performance improvement in the most criticized areas was actually considerably less than the improvement in other performance areas. It appears clear that frequent criticism represents such a strong threat to self-esteem that it disrupts rather than improves subsequent performance.

A Recommended Approach

Using the concepts of *what* you can change in order to improve performance and using ideas regarding the dynamics of power, you can create an integrated approach to developing improvement plans. This approach is built on a foundation of mutual trust and respect between supervisor and employee and utilizes a basic collaborative, problem-solving strategy. But remember, when working with people there are no guarantees, only increased probabilities.

Working relationships are built on your day-to-day interaction with your staff. These relations are very much reflected in the way you arrive at and communicate goals and expectations. You can demand compliance to specified work goals and methods, but this approach, typically, will result in a minimum level of performance—usually just enough for an employee not to lose his or her job. Another approach is to sell employees on the merits of the work goals and methods that you yourself have developed. This practice gains slightly more commitment because employees are allowed to understand your thinking. Although they may not agree with you, they can at least see that you have supportable reasons for your directives. Still another approach is to allow employees to participate with you in developing work goals and methods. This usually results in substantial commitment to achieving results because of the employees' involvement and identification with the decisions. Finally, you can delegate areas of appropriate responsibility to qualified employees. With this approach you'll reap the rewards of the effort, ingenuity, and commitment of self-motivated individuals. In chapter 1 each of these styles was shown to have merit when matched appropriately with an employee's maturity level. That view still holds. However, most employees move quickly through the maturity levels that require the more directive management styles when they're in an environment supportive of such growth. Don't over-direct employees who are able and willing to operate with greater independence. Allow them the opportunity to get involved with you.

As you consider these various options, some significant issues emerge: A supervisor who operates in the more directive ways implies that the employee isn't capable, can't be trusted, lacks interest, and is, in effect, just an implement to carry out the ideas generated by the supervisor. At the other end of the spectrum, a supervisor who operates in a less directive way allows for the ideas of his or her staff to contribute to achieving the results of the unit. This leads employees to identify with the supervisor *and* with the workgroup.

The strongest, most important relationship you as a supervisor can foster is positive identification with the work unit and with you as the leader of the unit. People need, and constantly seek, identification with groups that enhance their self-esteem. They prefer to be members of winning teams as long as they are accepted and supported as worthwhile members of the team.

You can achieve this positive identification by caring about your employees, by respecting them, by showing feelings, by enlisting their respect. In turn, you gain respect by meriting it. For this, there is no substitute for integrity or for a value system that is fair, reasonable, and flexible. The following strategy helps you achieve these qualities of authenticity and underscores the positive elements of your relationship with your staff.

A Collaborative Problem-Solving Strategy

When you encounter inadequate performance, you have a problem. The employee also has a problem. The best way to deal with it is to work together to overcome it. Here are the key steps in this problem-solving process:

1. Analyze the problem
2. Set an objective
3. Develop a plan
4. Implement the plan
5. Follow up

Analyze the Problem

Begin by discussing the problem with the intent of analyzing it and determining its cause. This analysis should be broad in its perspective. Don't assume that the employee is at fault; include all the elements in the performance equation (employee, job, and situation) as possible causes of the shortfall in performance results.

The climate of the discussion will either contribute to or detract from its potential for success. To contribute to success enter the discussion with an open mind. While it's helpful to give some prior thought to the performance problem being addressed, you must avoid an approach that might suggest your mind is made up. To do otherwise will minimize the available opportunity for the employee to contribute to the discussion.

Next, you need to eliminate the status and power differences that traditionally exist between employee and supervisor. This will contribute to trust in the relationship and allow movement toward the 0.5/0.5 position on the power spectrum. Rather than telling the employee what's wrong and what should be done to correct it, encourage and involve the employee in the analysis. Essentially, be a coach rather than a boss.

Finally, during the analysis be careful to avoid criticism, threats, and other activities that might cause the employee to appear foolish, weak, or incapable. To do otherwise will invoke a variety of defensive behaviors that will be detrimental to future performance.

Using these ideas, one might start out a performance improvement discussion this way:

Supervisor: "Jim, I've been looking over your weekly summaries and see that our inventory is over target. I'm concerned about this, as I'm sure you are, and would like to discuss some possible ways to bring it down to your targeted level."

Jim: "I'm open to any suggestions you have. I'd sure like to finish the quarter on target."

Supervisor: "I'm sure you would. So, let's work together and examine all the ingredients that go into your achieving results. Maybe that way we can get our fingers on the problem. Why don't you start at the point you first get involved with the work flow and tell me how each step in the process is coming and what problems you've run into."

Jim: "Okay. To get started, I have to receive input from three different groups—field sales offices, manufacturing, and logistics. From these inputs I try to maintain a production schedule that meets our customers' needs, minimizes inventory, and keeps the plant operating smoothly. Lately, our investment in inventory has been on the increase."

Supervisor: Are you having any trouble getting timely, quality input figures from those sources?"

Jim: "No, the actual results figures from each location come in on schedule. However, a couple of sales districts have been a little optimistic in their next month's projections."

Supervisor: "What do you mean, 'optimistic'?"

Jim: "Well, most districts have made downward adjustments in their original sales forecasts. But two districts maintain that they expect to catch up in a month or two, so they are unwilling to make similar adjustments."

Supervisor: "Do you believe that is what is causing our inventory to build?"

Jim: "It probably is. I haven't felt justified in adjusting their figures. I'm sure they wouldn't buy my estimates."

Set an Objective

Following a complete analysis of the performance problem, the next step is to set a performance improvement objective.

EXERCISE 8.1

Which of the following statements are improvement objectives? Which are results objectives?

1. *Increase production by 7.5 percent by the end of the third quarter.*
2. *Develop effective working relationship with the quality control department by end of the current year.*
3. *Reduce costs of delivery by $3,000 by end of first quarter.*
4. *Learn to do statistical analysis required in inventory control by March 15.*
5. *Reallocate work among staff to better match assignments with individual skills and interests by June 30.*

Objective statements 2, 4, and 5 are performance improvement objectives. Statements 1 and 3 are performance results objectives. While objectives 1 and 3 represent an increase in performance output, they don't address impediments to performance as statements 2, 4, and 5 do.

This is not a performance results objective. Rather, it's an objective to improve or change something that appears to be blocking good performance.

Any statement of your objective should meet the basic criteria presented in chapter 3. It should focus on outcome—what is to be achieved. It should be specific, include a time commitment, and be realistic. However, it should not specify how the objective is to be accomplished. For performance improvement plans, it is better to have a sequence of short-term, realistic objectives than to have one long-term, optimistic objective. This approach allows the reinforcement and motivation realized from goal attainment to hold the employee's interest.

Now, let's tune back in on the discussion between Jim and his supervisor to see how an improvement objective might be set. (The analysis stage continued to explore all other possible causes of the inventory buildup.)

> *Supervisor:* "From what you're telling me, it seems that if we could get these two districts to make the downward adjustments in their sales forecasts that other districts have made, we could do a better job of production scheduling. Is that the way you see it?"
>
> *Jim:* "Yes, I believe so. However, we can't just tell them to adjust their figures, and I can't take it upon myself to adjust the figures for them."
>
> *Supervisor:* "I realize that, Jim. Don't overlook the fact that there are several ways to get something done. However, before we get into that, let's set an objective. What do we want to come out of this effort?"
>
> *Jim:* "Reduce inventory to the targeted ceiling by the end of the current quarter."
>
> *Supervisor:* "I agree with that as your objective. However, in addition to that, we need to set an objective to clear up the problem you're experiencing of continuing to receive overly optimistic figures from those two districts."
>
> *Jim:* "Okay, I see what you mean. How about: Get the sales forecast figures for those two districts reduced by 6 percent."
>
> *Supervisor:* "Is 6 percent an appropriate figure?"

Jim: "That's what the other districts did and they are on target with their new figures."

Supervisor: "Okay, what's a reasonable target date for getting this done?"

Jim: "Well, I need the new figures for next week's calculations; so, the sooner the better. How about Thursday? That gives us three days to work on it."

Supervisor: "That might be a little optimistic. Let's take that as a tentative target until we decide upon a course of action. If necessary, we can adjust it by a day or two."

Develop a Plan

With an objective set that will remove the impediment to good performance, the next step is to develop a plan to reach the objective. Planning involves several specific steps:

1. Select a Strategy.   The first step is to select a strategy to accomplish the objective. This is the time to become creative. If you start with a challenging objective you may need to be very innovative in devising a strategy to carry it out.

2. Identify Action Steps.   Once you have an appropriate strategy, you need to break it down into distinct steps. When doing this, list each action to be taken in carrying out your strategy.

3. Develop a Schedule.   Look at each of your action steps. How long will each take? Which ones can either overlap or be carried out at the same time? With these data you can now develop a schedule for your total effort.

4. Allocate Resources.   The final step is to allocate resources to carry out each of the action steps. Resources could include talent and time of individuals, time of machinery, and money.

Again return to the discussion between Jim and his supervisor. This time, the conversation picks up with the objective and moves through the development of a plan.

Supervisor: "Okay, our objective is to get the sales forecast figures reduced by 6 percent by Thursday. How can we do that?"

Jim: "I'm not sure. But however we do it, I don't want to alienate the district staff. They could cause me real problems if they wanted to."

Supervisor: "I agree we have to be careful. But what are some of the ways, good or bad, that we could get the job done?"

Jim: "Well, we could get the general sales manager to contact them, as long as he didn't say it was because of me."

Supervisor: "Yes, we could do that. What else?"

Jim: "I could talk to them again. You could talk to the district managers. Or, I guess we could even get some of the other district managers to talk to them."

Supervisor: "So, we've identified four options. Which one is most likely to get results? That is, get the figures adjusted without alienating the district staff."

Jim: "Having the general sales manager handle it would certainly be most effective, if it were done properly."

Supervisor: "Those districts that have adjusted their forecasts, have they formally advised the general manager of their revisions?"

Jim: "I don't think so. I think they've informally made the adjustments."

Supervisor: "Therefore, if the general manager requested revised figures from everyone, these two districts wouldn't be singled out for special treatment."

Jim: "That's right. And those figures really should be formally adjusted. I'm sure several other people are using the wrong numbers."

Supervisor: "Great! What do we need to do to make it happen?"

Jim: "We need to meet with the general manager and show him some data to back up our recommendation that he request adjusted sales figures from the districts. I can get the data together. Perhaps you could call and get us a date on his schedule. Then both of us can attend the meeting."

Supervisor: "You have all of the right steps, and I believe you can carry it forward alone. You set up the meeting and present your data and recommendation. I'll be here to back you up if I'm needed."

Jim: "Well, okay, if you think I can handle it."

Supervisor: "I know you can. Just let me know when you get the meeting scheduled so I'll know whether or not we can make our Thursday target."

Implement the Plan

With a plan developed, it's now time to implement it—get it under way. Ordinarily, in performance improvement, this will be the employee's responsibility. However, in any particular plan there may be action steps that you agree to carry out. When this is the case, don't delay. Your actions underscore your level of interest. If you don't take action that you agreed to, you demonstrate a lack of interest and commitment in working with the employee to help overcome his or her performance problem.

Follow Up

One of the most effective ways to cause an employee to take action on an improvement plan is to set a follow-up date at which time the employee will review progress. Most people don't like to tell their supervisor that they haven't gotten around to implementing the agreed upon plan. To avoid this potentially embarrassing situation, they'll initiate action in order to have something positive to report on the follow-up meeting.

This point was particularly well illustrated in a study in an industrial setting. Employees who had been given suggestions on areas of their performance needing improvement were asked whether or not they had done anything in response to the suggestions. Thirty-eight percent had; 62 percent had not. When the two groups were studied in order to find an explanation for this difference between them, it was found that everyone who had done something had a follow-up meeting scheduled with his or her supervisor. The vast majority of those who had done nothing did not have a follow-up meeting scheduled.

EXERCISE 8.2   Practice Case in Performance Improvement Planning

The objectives of this case are to demonstrate the importance of performance planning and review and to provide practice in analyzing performance problems and developing improvement plans.

Background

Leslie is an experienced sales representative assigned to a developed territory where significant potential exists for the company's product. A performance planning and review system has existed for about five years. However, Leslie was accustomed to operating independently—setting goals, scheduling, planning, and so forth—without counsel from the regional sales manager. End of period reviews were cursory—typically, no improvement plans were developed.

You were assigned as regional sales manager, Leslie's immediate supervisor, three years ago. On reviewing Leslie's performance record, you decided to get actively involved to develop specific plans to address the areas where performance wasn't up to standard. You've been pleased with the results you and Leslie have achieved over this period and are now contemplating how to approach the future and maintain the performance level.

Instructions

Study the performance summaries on Leslie over the past three years (see pages 242–244). Try to visualize what has happened during this period. Elements to consider include: a new supervisor who institutes a system for addressing performance problems, the loss of some existing customers to the competition, and the successful introduction of a new product line. What else comes through from an analysis of the summaries?

1. Analyze the expected results for the three years. What's happened during this time? What do you believe has

Exercise 8.2 (continued)

caused it? Which year represents the best statement of expected results?

2. What was Leslie's overall performance during this period? What were some of the problems being experienced?

3. What do you think the performance improvement plans did for Leslie? Could they be improved? If so, how?

4. How do you think Leslie felt about you and the job during this period.

5. From the last performance summary, which shows only the key result areas, what do you think Leslie's expected results should be for the coming year?

6. How would you propose to supervise Leslie during the next year? Consider maturity level as discussed in chapter 1. Also, what degree of involvement should you allow Leslie in performance planning and what extent of performance monitoring do you consider to be appropriate.

7. What will be the nature of your feedback to Leslie when you meet to review accomplishments and plan for the following year?

EXHIBIT A   Performance Summary

Name: Leslie M. Hawkins   Job: Industrial Sales Representative
Performance Period: 4/1/81 to 3/31/82   Review Date: 4/7/82

Results Expected	Results Achieved	Improvement Plans
I. Product Sales		
Sell 100 Model 701 Motors	Sold 105 Model 701 Motors	Increase sales calls to an
Sell 200 Model 710 Motors	Sold 192 Model 710 Motors	average of 6 customers daily.

Exhibit A   (*continued*)

II. Customer Service

Maintain all existing accounts	Lost 3 accounts to competition	Develop plan by 5/15 to monitor competition.
Receive no more than 10 customer complaints	Received 7 customer complaints	Analyze causes and develop plan by 6/1.

III. New Business Development

Increase market share 5%	Increased market share 2%
Sell 5 new accounts	Sold 5 new accounts

IV. Public Relations

Make 3 speeches a month	Averaged 3 speeches a month	Provide Public Relations Dept. list of newspapers in territory to receive news releases.
Publish 2 positive news items a month	Averaged 1 news item a month	

V. Administrative Responsibilities

Submit all reports on schedule	All reports submitted on schedule
Operate within ±5% of approved budget	Expenses were 4.6% over budget

EXHIBIT B   Performance Summary

Name: Leslie M. Hawkins   Job: Industrial Sales Representative
Performance Period: 4/1/82 to 3/31/83   Review Date: 4/10/83

Results Expected	Results Achieved	Improvement Plans
I. Product Sales		
Sell 100 Model 701 Motors	Sold 120 Model 701 Motors	Introduce new model into
Sell 200 Model 710 Motors	Sold 165 Model 710 Motors	territory on 9/1.
II. Customer Service		
Maintain all existing accounts	Lost 1 account (out of business)	
Receive no more than 5 customer complaints	Received 2 customer complaints	
III. New Business Development		
Increase market share 3%	Lost 1½% of market share	Develop promotion plan for
Sell 5 new accounts	Sold 4 new accounts	new model by 8/1.
IV. Public Relations		
Make 3 speeches a month	Averaged 3 speeches a month	
Average 2 positive news items a month	Averaged 2 news items a month	
V. Administrative Responsibilities		
Submit all reports on schedule	All reports submitted on schedule	
Operate within ±5% of approved budget	Expenses were 2.7% over budget	

245

EXHIBIT C   Performance Summary

Name: Leslie M. Hawkins   Job: Industrial Sales Representative
Performance Period: 4/1/83 to 3/31/84   Review Date: 4/10/84

Results Expected	*Results Achieved*	*Improvement Plans*

I. Product Sales
Sell 130 Model 701 Motors — Sold 132 Model 701 Motors

Sell 190 Model 710 Motors — Sold 189 Model 710 Motors

Sell 60 Model 801 Motors — Sold 82 Model 801 Motors

II. Customer Service
Maintain all existing accounts — Maintained all existing accounts

Receive no more than 5 customer complaints — Received 4 customer complaints

III. New Business Development
Increase market share 2½% — Increased market share 3%

Sell 5 new accounts — Sold 6 new accounts

IV. Public Relations
Average 3 speeches a month — Averaged 2.5 speeches a month

Average 2 positive news items a month — Averaged 2.5 news items a month

Exhibit C *(continued)*

V. Administrative Responsibilities

| Submit all reports on schedule | All reports submitted on schedule |
| Operate within ±3% of approved budget | Expenses were 1.8% over budget |

EXHIBIT D Performance Summary

Name: Leslie M. Hawkins   Job: Industrial Sales Representative
Performance Period: 4/1/84 to 3/31/85   Review Date:

Results Expected	Results Achieved	Improvement Plans

I. Product Sales

II. Customer Service

III. New Business Development

Exhibit D (*continued*)

IV. Public Relations

V. Administrative
   Responsibilities

Leslie's Case Analysis

The key point in Leslie's case is the positive change in results achieved over the three year period. The last year's performance calls for an increase in Leslie's involvement in future planning and a decrease in the frequency of performance monitoring. Feedback should be reinforcing, utilizing the specific results to support the feedback.

Leslie should be given primary responsibility (about 90 percent) for setting next year's goals and have a quarterly review conference scheduled for monitoring performance. Leslie should be given responsibility for coping with whatever problems occur during the month.

Your Action Guide

Performance improvement is an area of responsibility that every supervisor must address from time to time. It would be great if every employee always performed according to expectations, but that's too much to expect.

Certain key elements should be incorporated into your performance improvement plans in order to help assure their success.

- Broaden your analysis to include *all* of the elements in the performance equation.
- Share the power to decide equally in developing an improvement plan.
- Avoid statements that might evoke face-saving or face restoration behavior.
- Avoid criticism by being problem oriented and helpful.
- Use a goal-setting process to identify specific responses to performance problems.
- Follow up on improvement plans.

The interpersonal dynamics of performance improvement are often neglected. However, whether or not an employee chooses to change often depends upon these issues. When the ideas of power, threat, face-saving, and criticism are considered in light of the chapter 7 discussion on intrinsic and extrinsic feedback, a specific strategy emerges for handling performance improvement planning: don't threaten; don't criticize; don't make anyone appear weak, foolish, or incompetent to others; minimize the distance created by social power and share the power to decide.

The proper role for you in the performance improvement process is that of coach or helper. Be problem oriented. Help the employee examine his or her situation. Use work related, specific information to ferret out problem areas. Then help develop a solution to those problems.

- ✔ Involve the employee in a collaborative problem-solving discussion.

- ✔ Set specific objectives to overcome the roadblocks to performance identified in your analysis.

- ✔ Develop plans to achieve the objectives established.

- ✔ Set specific deadlines for achieving the objectives.

⤸ Set a follow-up date and check with the employee to encourage progress toward agreed upon objectives.

References

Robert R. Blake and Jane S. Mouton, "Power, People and Performance Reviews," *Advanced Management,* July–August 1961.

L. A. Borah, Jr., "The Effects of Threat in Bargaining: Critical and Experimental Analysis," *Journal of Abnormal and Social Psychology,* vol. 66, 1963.

B. R. Brown, "The Effects of Need to Maintain Face on Interpersonal Bargaining," *Journal of Experimental Social Psychology,* vol. 4, 1968.

James C. Conant, "The Performance Appraisal: A Critique and an Alternative," *Business Horizons,* June 1973.

Marion E. Haynes, "Improving Performance Through Employee Discussions," *Personnel Journal,* February 1970.

H. Hornstein, "The Effects of Different Magnitudes of Threat upon Interpersonal Bargaining," *Journal of Experimental Social Psychology,* vol. 1, 1965.

Herbert H. Meyer, Emanuel Kay, and John R. P. French, "Split Roles in Performance Appraisal," *Harvard Business Review,* January–February 1965.

THE PERFORMANCE MANAGEMENT SYSTEM

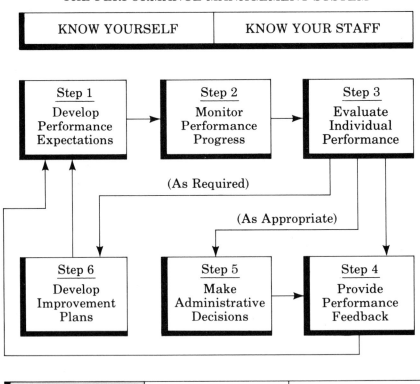

CHAPTER 9

Delegating Responsibility and Authority

As a result of reading this chapter you will

- Identify work you are presently doing that you should delegate
- Understand the process of delegating and how to carry it out successfully
- Recognize which members of your workgroup need more training to prepare them for further delegation
- Understand the benefits of delegation for both you and your staff

$\mathbf{Y}$ou simply can't expect to do everything yourself. To get your job done efficiently you must make effective use of delegation. It's the only way you can broaden your span of influence beyond your ability to personally do the work. It's also the way you can tap the talents, skills, and abilities in your workgroup that otherwise would not be fully utilized. Delegation is the goal of the management philosophy described in chapter 1 around which the Performance Management System is built.

Why Some Supervisors Don't Delegate

Supervisors give many reasons for not fully using delegation within their workgroup. Some of these reasons are temporary situations, such as a staff shortage or lack of adequate staff training, and hopefully will be resolved. But other reasons are less objective and fall more into the excuse category. Some supervisors may feel they're less capable than members of their staff and fear the consequences of being outperformed. This

EXERCISE 9.1

Read the following statements and circle the number that reflects the degree to which each statement describes you.

	Strongly Agree				Strongly Disagree
1. The jobs I delegate never seem to get done the way I want them to be done.	5	4	3	2	1
2. I don't have the time to delegate properly.	5	4	3	2	1
3. I check on work without my staff knowing it so I can correct mistakes before they cause too many problems.	5	4	3	2	1
4. When I give clear instructions and work isn't done properly, I get upset.	5	4	3	2	1
5. My staff lacks the commitment that I have. So work I delegate doesn't get done as well as I'd do it.	5	4	3	2	1

Exercise 9.1   (*continued*)

6.	I can do the work of my section better than my staff can.	5	4	3	2	1
7.	If the person I delegate work to doesn't do it well, I'll be severely criticized.	5	4	3	2	1
8.	If I delegated everything I could, my job wouldn't be nearly as much fun.	5	4	3	2	1
9.	When I delegate work, I often have to do it over.	5	4	3	2	1
10.	I delegate clearly and concisely, explaining just how the job should be done.	5	4	3	2	1
11.	When I delegate I lose control.	5	4	3	2	1
12.	I could delegate more if my staff had more experience.	5	4	3	2	1
13.	I delegate routine tasks but keep the nonroutine work myself.	5	4	3	2	1
14.	My boss expects me to be very close to all details of the work.	5	4	3	2	1
15.	I have not found that delegation saves me time.	5	4	3	2	1

Scoring

75–60	You are failing to fully utilize your staff.
59–45	You can substantially improve your use of delegation.
44–30	You have some room for improvement as a delegator.
29–15	You are an excellent delegator or you fudged your answers.

insecurity makes them carefully guard their jobs so the company will continue to need them. Other supervisors may have another problem—perfectionism. They feel the only way to get something done right is to do it themselves. They automatically assume no one can do a job as well as they can, and no one ever gets a chance to prove them wrong.

But insecurity and perfectionism are only two reasons for not delegating. There are also other more common reasons. For example, some supervisors simply enjoy doing the work of their section so much that they're reluctant to fully let go. This is particularly true when people get promoted to supervise work they previously performed. It's a natural reaction. Just because you're now the supervisor there's no reason to assume you've lost your interest in performing the work. After all, your interest and good performance were probably what got you promoted. Making the transition to a new set of job duties takes hard work.

Occasionally supervisors don't delegate because they do not fully understand their job as supervisor. This usually means they take a short-term perspective on getting the work out rather than a long-term perspective of workgroup effectiveness. Finally, some supervisors may endorse delegation in principle but still not delegate because they mistakenly see delegation as giving up *all* of their authority, responsibility, and control. This, however, is not the case.

It's a bit unfair to assume that the nondelegating supervisor is always the one at fault. The supervisor's superior may expect him or her to know every detail of what's going on in the section. When this happens it's difficult, if not impossible, to delegate. Also, some staff members may resist accepting more responsibility because of their own insecurities or lack of motivation.

Levels of Delegation

The goal in the delegation process is for members of your staff to be self-sufficient and independent of you when carrying out their day-to-day activities. This means that each employee should have the knowledge, skills, responsibilities, and authorities to handle a defined unit of work. Employees should be able to identify the unit of work as their's in terms of inputs used, where these inputs come from, what is done to them, and who they are passed on to in either a completed or intermediate stage of processing. The employee should be expected to make all relevant, routine decisions such as rate of work, quality of work, inventory levels of supplies or materials used, and when others need to be called in—such as maintenance personnel and/or extra help to meet deadlines.

Obviously, you can't bring someone into your section and immediately turn a part of your operation completely over to him or her. It takes time for the individual to acquire the knowledge and skills required to work at that degree of delegation. It also takes time for you to develop confidence in his or her willingness and ability to take on the full range of duties and perform them according to appropriate standards. Full delegation is therefore a target or goal to work toward.

There are two concepts that together help lay out an approach to reach the goal of full delegation. The first is the identification of three distinct levels of delegation. The second is the notion of a "range of task involvement" as presented in chapter 1.

The three levels of delegation are as follows:

- *Level 1.* Delegate by what is to be done and how to do it but leave the employee some degrees of freedom on rate of work and quality control.
- *Level 2.* Delegate by what is to be done but leave the employee free to decide how to do it, at what rate, and within what quality range.
- *Level 3.* Delegate by what is to be achieved but leave the employee free to decide what to do to get there, how and at what rate to do it, and within what quality range.

When the two concepts are merged, it becomes clear that at each level of delegation a supervisor can hold from 100 to 0 percent of the control and influence over what is to be done and how it is to be done. (This is shown in Figure 9.1.) In fact, before delegating at level 1, the supervisor has the opportunity to di-

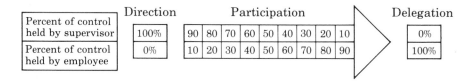

Figure 9.1 Range of control and influence

rect what, how, when, and at what rate *and* inspect each item of work for quality. This degree of supervisory involvement affords absolutely no degree of freedom and judgment to the employee. Let's look at each level of delegation and how authority is delegated at each and how, level by level, you can move towards *full* delegation of authority.

Level 1 Delegation

This is the starting point on the way to achieving full delegation. It is appropriate for employees who are in the moderately low range of maturity as described in chapter 1. The actual delegation is limited to decisions on the rate or pace of work and to decisions regarding acceptable levels of quality—that is, whether or not work measures up to a minimum quality level.

Within this level, you may tell your staff member what is to be done and how to do it. For example, you might say: "Deborah, I've been going over your shift reports and I see that we're losing a lot of production time with machines being down for repairs. Now, what I want you to do is catch as many of these problems as you can before they cause a machine to go down. To do that I want you to review the maintenance log on each of your machines. Those that have gone 750 hours without maintenance are to be checked for proper lubrication and signs of vibration. Those that have gone 1,200 hours or more are to be scheduled for shutdown during the following week for a maintenance check. To do that, call Betty in maintenance and set up a schedule."

Moving toward more delegation, you might tell the staff member what is to be done but allow her or him to offer suggestions on how to do it. As a result, there should be discussion that culminates in an agreement between you and the individual on how the work will be done. The above situation might unfold as follows:

> *Supervisor:* "Deborah, I've been going over your shift reports and I see that we've been losing a lot of production time with machines being down for repairs. Now, what I want you to do is to catch as many of these problems as possible before they cause a machine to go down. What ideas do you have on how we can do that?"
>
> *Deborah:* "Well, I've noticed that failures usually occur on machines that have gone over 1,500 hours without maintenance checks. We could schedule maintenance checks rather than running them 'til they break down."
>
> *Supervisor:* "That should save us some down time. Also, if we shortened it to 1,200 hours, we should catch most of the problems. What else could we do?"
>
> *Deborah:* "We've had several bearing failures lately. I think we should check lubrication and vibration on a 750-hour schedule. You can tell a lot about the condition of bearings just by lubrication color and temperature."
>
> *Supervisor:* "That's a good idea. Work that into your shift routine. Now, how are you going to handle the maintenance shutdowns?"
>
> *Deborah:* "It seems like the first thing to do is phone Betty in the Maintenance Department and work out a schedule based on their work load."

After operating at this level of delegation for a while the employee's level of capability should become clearly established. When the ability and willingness to take on more responsibility have been shown, it's appropriate to move to the next level of delegation.

Level 2 Delegation

Level 2 provides greater freedom and opportunity for employees. It is appropriate for those who in your opinion are in the moderately high range of maturity. Delegation at this level allows employees to decide how things are to be done, at what pace they should work in order to meet deadlines, and whether or not their work meets quality standards.

As with level 1, you have a full range of control and influence available at level 2, but, it is limited to decisions about *what* to do. (Note: A supervisor may operate at different levels of delegation with the same employee in relationship to different portions of the employee's job.) You may *tell* an employee what to do, you may *discuss* with an employee and decide between you what to do, or you may *ask* an employee what to do but reserve the right of approval or confirmation before it becomes an actual course of action.

A discussion at this second level of delegation, where the supervisor exercises a high degree of control and influence, would go something like this:

> *Supervisor:* "Kim, I've been going over your shift reports and see that we're losing a lot of production time with machines being down for repairs. Now, what I want you to do is set up some kind of surveillance program on your machines to catch as many of these problems as you can before they actually cause a machine to go down. After you've given it some thought, let me know what you plan to do."

In this situation the supervisor exercises maximum control and influence available within the parameters of level 2 delegation. The problem is pointed out, what to do about it is specified, and approval of the employee's plan is reserved. Yet the employee still has the opportunity to study the situation, develop a plan to resolve the problem, and sell the supervisor on the merits of the plan.

The supervisor might use a minimum amount of control and influence as follows:

> *Supervisor:* "Kim, I've been going over your shift reports and see that we're losing a lot of production time with machines being down for repairs. What can we do to cut down on this loss?"
>
> *Kim:* "The only time the machines are checked now is when they're due for scheduled service or when they break

down. It seems to me that we could catch some of these problems early if the machines were checked more often."

Supervisor: "That makes sense to me. What would you suggest?"

Kim: "I think we should have a regular surveillance program. Each machine should be visually inspected, checked for vibration, and have a lube sample checked."

Supervisor: "Would that catch the problems we've been experiencing? Is there anything else you would recommend?"

Kim: "That would catch a lot of the bearing problems we've been having, but I also think the machines should be shut down every now and then so a mechanic could go over them. It could be scheduled at a time that would have least impact on our production schedule."

Supervisor: "Kim, that sounds like a good approach to our problem. Go ahead and implement those two ideas and let's see if we can't get this down time under control."

You would operate at level 2 long enough to establish your confidence in the employee's ability and willingness to perform at appropriate standards of performance. After that it's time to move on to level 3 delegation.

Level 3 Delegation

This should be your goal—to get all of your staff members to the point of handling their day-to-day responsibilities without your involvement. This level of delegation is appropriate when employees attain a high level of maturity. However, the high level of employee maturity required for success at level 3 delegation can prevent you from attaining this goal with *all* of your staff for two reasons:

- Turnover within the group may keep you toward the low end of the job maturity range.
- Some individuals will always lack the personal maturity, either in responsibility or self-confidence, to achieve this level of delegation.

At level 3 a staff member is given an area of responsibility and the freedom to make decisions within that area. There is still opportunity for you to discuss and direct or confirm the goals or objectives to be achieved. But, beyond goals or objectives, the employee decides *what* to do and *how* to do it. Furthermore, you must support those decisions after they've been made, whether you believe they are the best ones or not. This means you must be willing to give up some of your authority and be willing to gamble that your staff can do a better job when left alone than when closely supervised.

As you progress through this level to the goal of full delegation, you can vary your degree of control and influence. However, characteristic of this level, is the focus on what is to be achieved. This leaves the staff member free to determine what to do and how to do it in order to achieve the agreed upon results.

The discussion between supervisor and employee at level 3 delegation typically occurs at the beginning of a planning period. At this point the goals for the period might be established in a manner similar to the following.

> *Supervisor:* "Susan, your production for the last quarter was right on target. I appreciate the way you've been able to handle the various problems that come up without losing production."
>
> *Susan:* "Yes, a few things have happened, but I've worked closely with engineering and maintenance to keep little problems from becoming big ones."
>
> *Supervisor:* "What do you think you can do in production next quarter?"
>
> *Susan:* "I'm hoping to increase production by 10 percent over last quarter's figures."
>
> *Supervisor:* "That sounds fine. Let me know if you run into anything you can't handle."

Delegating Effectively

Delegation is both personal and individual. Doing it successfully depends to a large measure on the relationship between you and your staff as well as on each staff member's abilities and interest. Still there are guidelines that must be followed for delegation to be effective.

Communicate Fully

When discussing work assignments, communicate fully the degrees of freedom and judgment you expect the staff member to exercise. Also, share all the relevant information you have about the topic under discussion so that your experience and knowledge can be utilized by the employee. Finally, actively engage the staff member in the conversation in order to confirm his or her understanding of your point of view. Consider how communication or the lack of it plays a role in the following example.

The training manager was organizing a program that was to include a speaker on long-range business planning. He wanted a speaker with a national reputation in the field. He asked his newest staff member to "come up with some names" for him to consider.

The new employee did some research on the experts in the field, telephoned their offices, and asked about their interest, availability, and fees. When he reported back, the training manager was upset that the employee had telephoned the potential speakers.

The employee's position was that this information was required in order to make a final selection. The manager's position was that by letting the experts know of the company's interest and then selecting only one from the group, others who were interested and available could view the fact of their not being selected as rejection. This reaction might cause them to be down on the company—a response that could potentially damage the company's reputation, since the experts operate in very influential circles.

The staff member was introduced in this hypothetical situation as the training manager's "newest" staff member. Therefore, you can infer two things: (1) the manager and staff member have limited experience working together and therefore may not fully understand each other's approach to getting things done and (2) the staff member is probably eager to do a good job to firm up his or her position in the workgroup and therefore may take more initiative than warranted on occasion.

Delegate Authority As Well As Responsibility

Your staff must have the authority to carry out the responsibilities they've been delegated. In most organizations this means authority to spend money and take necessary personnel actions in pursuit of objectives. This authority can be specified within certain limits. For example, you may grant authority to purchase outside goods and services within an approved budget. You may grant authority to authorize overtime to meet production deadlines within some specified limit such as not to exceed 10 percent of scheduled hours.

When you delegate responsibilities *without* authority, you are maintaining control too tightly and, in the process, demonstrating a lack of trust in members of your staff. For example, how would you rate the hypothetical manager who made the following two delegations. The first authorization was issued to professional staff. The second authorization was issued to administrative staff.

- *Authorization 1:* Professional staff are authorized to approve up to $7,500 for the purchase of outside goods and services against approved program and budget.
- *Authorization 2:* All contracts for outside services and all purchase orders are to be approved, in advance, by the department manager.

Although authority was effectively delegated to *professional* staff (in authorization 1), it was immediately taken away by requiring *administrative* staff to obtain the department manager's approval on all contracts written by professional staff members (authorization 2).

Set Performance Standards

Chapter 3 presents ideas on clarifying and specifying performance expectations. This is a significant part of effective delegation. Your staff *must* know the results you expect. They can have an appropriate hand in developing the standards, but should not be given an assignment without agreement from you on relevant standards of performance.

Establish Controls

You can't just cut your staff loose and say, "Okay, you're on your own. Go to it." You must establish controls that let you know progress is being made toward the agreed upon goals and that alert you to problems that may crop up.

Chapter 4 discusses ways to monitor progress, or exercise control over work in progress. Here are a few of the ways you can stay abreast of progress.

- *Personal inspection.* When a tangible product is the output of your group, conduct periodic personal inspections of product quality and operating procedures.
- *Client feedback.* Occasionally ask your clients or customers their opinions on the performance of your group.
- *Visual displays.* Keep charts and graphs comparing actual results and planned results.
- *Computer printouts.* Tie into computer-based financial systems, personnel systems, production systems, and other systems to generate reports that compare actual to planned results.
- *Status reports.* Ask staff members to provide you with periodic reports on progress and problems anticipated. These reports can be either oral or written. Oral reports can be handled privately or in a group setting.

Challenge Your Staff

Some supervisors tend to play it safe and not allow their staff much responsibility or latitude in decision making. Under these conditions people don't develop to their full potential. They need challenge, not restriction.

To fully develop your staff you should tend toward overdelegation rather than underdelegation. This will create some anxiety among your staff as some members will be unsure of their ability to handle the responsibility they've been given. However, most will be able to accept the challenge and will grow in the process.

Most people become frustrated when the level of delegation they experience is substantially out of line with their capabilities. This is the case whether they experience too much or too little delegation. Frustration often leads to irrational behavior, which in the long run will be detrimental to both the individual and the group. To avoid this, match the level of delegation with the employee's capability.

Provide Appropriate Training

Training and coaching are the means available to you for developing your staff to their full capabilities. You can't expect employees to join your group fully trained and ready to assume full responsibility. It takes effort on your part (and theirs) to develop their abilities and experience.

Training provides basic knowledge and skills required to get a job done. It can come from many sources, such as experienced members of your staff, professional instructors, and individual self-study. When handled well, it also bolsters self-confidence and creates an interest in the work. Training is an essential part of the development process.

Unlike training coaching comes only from you, the supervisor. It's the appropriate step following training. Observe the work of the employee, answer questions, correct errors in work performance, and reinforce correct performance. Coaching is most effective when it's handled in a supportive, encouraging way.

Support Your Staff

An essential ingredient of effective delegation is to support and back your staff in the decisions they make. You won't always find this easy. There will be times when you'll honestly believe you could do a job better than your staff member. But to be an effective delegator you must be willing to accept the risk of your employees making errors.

For most supervisors to accept their employees' decisions some realistic limitations must be acknowledged. When the decision represents greater risk than you're willing to accept, obviously you can intervene. But be careful. Don't intervene very often, and when you do, explain the dangers you foresee and involve your staff member in developing an alternative course of action.

When the risk is within an acceptable tolerance, let the decision run its course; then, with the employee, analyze the situation and results. This allows your staff to learn by doing, which is certainly the most effective way. During your analysis, involve the individual employee in looking for and evaluating other possible courses of action so that in future decisions they'll have other options to choose from. Be sure to give staff members second chances.

Delegate . . . Don't Dump

As you consider the work you're presently doing, delegate those things that will result in a more complete job assignment for your staff members. The job should provide meaningful and challenging work that logically fits together. Avoid dumping onto an employee the unpleasant duties associated with *your* job while retaining all the interesting ones. The following kinds of work are good prospects for delegation.

- Work that is reoccurring—save your own time for the unique events
- Work that you are least qualified to handle—use the available talents of your staff
- Work that demands the greatest portion of your time—free up your schedule to be more readily available for problem solving
- Work that narrows your area of specialization—good managers and supervisors don't need to be super technicians

Don't Abdicate Responsibility

You must not abdicate your responsibility as supervisor. You are accountable to your manager for the results of your unit and must exercise prudent judgment in achieving those results. Delegation does not mean letting an aggressive staff member, regardless of how capable he or she may be, take over the operation. You can delegate without fear as long as you stay in charge. Staff members must understand that their authority derives from you, and it can be recalled as quickly as it was delegated, if they begin to overreach the agreed upon limits of their authority.

To be able to exercise full responsibility, you must be genuinely interested in everything in your unit. Don't ignore certain areas because you lack interest in them.

The Benefits of Effective Delegation

Benefits to Employees

One of the most marked effects of delegation is the feeling of self-respect it gives employees. When you assign an area of responsibility and let the employee make the decisions on how it should be handled, it's plain that you consider the individual capable. As a result, the employee gains in importance and self-confidence.

Furthermore, giving employees authority to make decisions establishes their vested interest in the outcome—it's their responsibility, they make the decisions, and they typically want to do well. There's no greater motivational force than to put someone in charge of a portion of your unit's work, delegate the authority to make decisions that spell the difference between success and failure, and then provide rewards commensurate with accomplishment.

Employees working for a supervisor who delegates have an excellent opportunity to grow and develop in their job. Having clear responsibilities provides experience and preparation for taking on jobs at increasing levels of responsibility. In contrast, employees whose supervisor doesn't delegate never have an opportunity to learn by doing. They develop neither the skills nor confidence to move ahead in the organization. As a result, they either lose out when opportunities do come along, or they go elsewhere in search of opportunity.

Benefits to Supervisors

As supervisor, you also benefit from delegating. The most obvious benefit to *you* is the time that's freed up for doing the things that only you can do. When each member of your staff is assigned a significant part of your unit's work and is carrying it out successfully, you should be able to get most of your work done during regular hours rather than take it home with you. Effective ways to spend that time are:

- *Planning* the future of your unit. Rather than operating from crisis to crisis, look further ahead and determine where you want to be and how to get there.

- *Developing* new and better techniques for doing the work of your unit, as well as developing new areas of involvement.

- *Representing* your group and its individual members to higher management. For example, do the appropriate managers know the qualifications and capabilities of your staff?

- *Establishing* better relationships with other groups that you deal with on a regular basis. Effort in this area is frequently required in order to ensure cooperation and support from others.

- *Building and maintaining* relationships with your staff. It takes time to talk to people and develop the depth of relationships that ensure cohesiveness in a group. This time is frequently lost when a supervisor is "too busy."

- *Coordinating* the work of your unit for optimum productivity. You need to avoid duplication of effort as well as make sure certain things aren't neglected. You need to see that those who can contribute to a common task are aware of the potential of others to contribute.

Getting Started

To get started on the path to increased delegation, analyze your personal involvement in the work of your unit. In your analysis, sort all the work you do into three categories:

1. Work that can be delegated immediately.
2. Work that can be delegated as soon as someone is trained to take it over.
3. Work that can only be done by you. This will include your personnel responsibility, such as reviewing performance, coaching immediate subordinates, providing leadership and maintaining morale. It also may include confidential work, projects assigned to you by your manager, and cash-control responsibilities.

Now consider your employees. How ready are they for delegation? Consider two things—their ability to do the work and their interest in doing it well. Have they ever had the opportunity to do these things before? If so, what was the outcome?

Work you are now doing that can be delegated immediately should be assigned to staff members in accordance with the currently appropriate level of delegation. Then, as you acquire confidence in the individual employee's ability, you should increase the delegation until you've accomplished delegation that's as complete as possible.

Now that you've freed up some of your time, you have an opportunity to consider training employees to take over other work you do (the second category). Select the staff members who are to be trained to take on additional responsibilities. These are the ones to be trained either by you, someone else on your staff, or someone from the training department. As soon as they're properly prepared, proceed to delegate by degree until you achieve full delegation.

If a staff member demonstrates lack of interest in an increased level of delegation, first provide work assignments with clear performance expectations then follow up with feedback on performance. Through this process establish a success cycle. Nothing creates interest faster than success—achievement, recognition, reinforcement.

Finally, when increasing the level of delegation to your staff, consider their present workload and level of responsibility. To allow for additional work, it may be necessary to reassign work within the unit, assign work to staff support groups, or discontinue certain work. The benefits of adding an additional staff member to enhance the overall contribution of the group also shouldn't be overlooked.

When Responsibility is Delegated to You

You'll probably sometimes be on the receiving end of delegation from your manager. Therefore consider some of the steps you can take to facilitate delegation to you. Your objective is to become an active, definitive part of the delegation process rather than someone who does only what you're told.

Successful delegation to you (or to your employee) is predicated on willingness

- to accept responsibility for carrying out the assigned duties
- to operate within the limits of the authority delegated
- to do the best possible job on behalf of the workgroup, supervisor, and company
- to accept responsibility for results achieved

In addition to these requirements, the following ground rules will help you fulfill your role in the delegation process.

Take Initiative

Rather than wait passively for your manager to determine the amount and level of delegation, you should take the initiative in these matters. One idea that frequently prevents people from taking such initiative is the notion that delegation always flows downward in the organization chart. While this is true for *authority* and *accountability*, there's nothing wrong with asking for more *responsibility*.

Next you should take initiative in recommending the results for which you will be held accountable. You are one of the best sources of information about what can be achieved in your area of responsibility. Use this information to make your own job rather than have it determined by someone else.

Finally, when discussing delegation with your manager,

take the initiative to see that it's properly handled. You are familiar with the correct methods of effective delegation; your manager may not be. Use your knowledge to see that clear expectations are communicated, that you have sufficient authority to follow through on responsibilities, and that there is an agreed upon progress review scheduled.

Don't Overcommit Yourself

A potential danger faced especially by new supervisors is taking on too much. This is a common hazard because of the desire to do a good job and please the manager. In your eagerness you may accept unrealistic delegations.

To avoid overcommitting yourself, examine the proposed delegation from every possible angle. Are you qualified to do a good job at the proposed level of delegation? Is the time dimension realistic, considering all of the other things you must also handle? Are adequate resources—people, equipment, money, facilities—available to you? Any questions in this area should be fully discussed and resolved before accepting the delegation. To do otherwise will set up a situation doomed to failure.

Decide the Feedback You Need

To ensure successful accomplishment of results, progress must be monitored along the way. And you are in the best position to know what is needed by you to monitor your operations. Don't just take what the system provides. Spend time with the accounting department, and other providers of information, and jointly determine the information needed, its form, and its frequency.

Keep Your Manager Informed

A reporting procedure usually will be part of the agreed upon delegation. However, if it isn't, you should clarify your manager's expectations in this regard. Also, certain events should be brought to your manager's attention as they occur, regardless of the reporting schedule. Generally speaking, the following should be reported:

- Interim status of key responsibility areas, including comparisons of actual versus planned for such critical elements as schedules, income, expenses, and quantity of output

- End results accomplished with appropriate comparisons of actual versus planned

- Recommended action to correct variances when plans do not develop as anticipated

- Unanticipated problems and recommendations for handling them

- Confusion or uncertainty in the extent of delegation or authority needed to carry through with the assigned responsibilities

- Recommendations for improving your job, unit, department, or organization as a whole

Carry Out Your Responsibilities

Within the bounds of the level of delegation afforded you, carry through to completion the responsibilities you've been delegated. Your assessment as a member of your manager's staff will rest heavily on the successful accomplishment of results. Be willing to devote the time and energy necessary to reach your objective.

Avoid any temptation to follow weaker courses, such as making excuses to rationalize the lack of accomplishment, attempting to get the objective modified to make it easier to attain, or passing back to the manager the decision-making responsibility for certain critical issues along the way. It is important to present suggestions in a form that is as complete as possible—spelling out ramifications and implications—rather than merely make tentative suggestions that may or may not be well thought out.

Completed Staff Action

"Completed staff action" is the study of a problem—and a presentation of a solution—by an employee in such a form that the supervisor or department head can simply indicate approval of the "completed action." The following discussion was adapted from the publication *Guide to Administrative Action* (U.S. Air Force, 1952).

The words "completed action" are worth real emphasis. Actually the more difficult the problem is, the more tendency there is to present the problem to the supervisor in piecemeal fashion. It's your responsibility as an employee to work out the details yourself. You shouldn't consult your supervisor in determining these details unless necessary. Instead, if you can't determine these details by yourself, you should consult other persons.

In far too many problem situations the typical impulse of the inexperienced employee is to ask the supervisor what to do. And this recurs more often when the problem is difficult; it's accompanied by a feeling of mental frustration. It seems to be much easier to ask the supervisor what to do, and it appears to be so easy for the supervisor to give the answer. You must resist this impulse.

It is your job to *advise* your supervisor what ought to be done—not to *ask* what should be done. Supervisors require answers—not questions! Your job is to study, analyze, check, restudy, and recheck until you come up with a single proposed action—the best one of all those you've considered. Your supervisor can then approve or disapprove.

The requirements of "completed work" don't eliminate the possibility of a rough draft for some of the problems. But a rough draft mustn't be a half-baked idea. Neither can a rough draft be used as a way of shifting the burden of formulating the action onto the supervisor. It must be as complete as possible but needn't be as neat as a final version.

"Completed work" requirements may result in more work for the employee, but provide more freedom for the supervisor. This accomplishes two things:

- The supervisor is protected from poorly thought-out ideas, voluminous memoranda, and casual oral presentations.
- The person who has a real idea to sell is enabled more readily to find a market.

Test the completeness of your work by asking yourself this question: "If I were supervisor, would I be willing to sign the paper I have presented and stake my professional reputation on its being correct?" If the answer is no, take it back and work it over again, because it is not yet "completed work."

Your Action Guide

In the eyes of some critics of modern business practices, much of the meaning has been taken out of jobs. Employee talents, skills, and abilities lie fallow because of bureaucratic constraints. What can be done to remedy this situation? Delegate! Delegate responsibility, authority, and accountability for a meaningful segment of your department's work to each member of your staff.

Both you and your staff benefit from delegation. You benefit by gaining the time to address the higher order management duties that often get neglected. These include long-range planning, innovation, coordination both within your group and with other units of your organization, and representing your workgroup and its members to higher management. These things just don't get done well when you're heavily involved in the day-to-day work of your group.

Your goal in delegating is to have each member of your staff operating independently of you in routine matters. To attain this goal, you need to delegate by degrees, or levels. This allows both you and your staff members to develop confidence in getting the job done according to your expectations. There are risks involved in delegating, but these are a necessary part of the process and can be kept in bounds by moving slowly toward your goal.

Delegation has been characterized as giving staff members plenty of rope but making sure they don't hang themselves. This means you need to provide the necessary training for them to be able to do the delegated work. It also means that you must provide an environment where they feel at ease coming to you when the going gets tough or a decision has failed. They also need to know that they must keep you informed—because of your mutual interest in what's going on, not because you are the boss peering over their shoulders.

- ✔ Match the level of delegation to the maturity level of the individual.

- ✔ Pass on all the information you have that's pertinent to the assignment being delegated.

- ✔ Agree on appropriate standards of performance for the delegated responsibilities.

- ✔ Grant sufficient authority to achieve the delegated responsibilities.

- ✔ Establish controls to keep you apprised of progress.

- ✔ Provide necessary training and support to move your staff to level 3 delegation.

- ✔ Back your staff when they take action within delegated authority, even though the action taken might not be what you personally would have done.

References

Marion E. Haynes, "Delegation: Key to Involvement," *Personnel Journal,* June 1974.

Marion E. Haynes, "How Do You Score As a Delegator?" *Chemical Engineering,* September 12, 1977.

Marion E. Haynes, "Using the Talent in Your Group," *Texas and Southwest Hotel–Motel Review,* June 1980.

Marion E. Haynes, "Delegation: There's More to It Than Letting Someone Else Do It!" *Supervisory Management,* August 1980.

Theodore J. Krein, "How to Improve Delegation Habits," *Management Review,* May 1982.

Dale D. McConkey, *No-Nonsense Delegation* (New York: AMACOM Division of American Management Associations, 1974).

Lawrence L. Steinmetz, *The Art and Skill of Delegation* (Reading, MA: Addison-Wesley Publishing Co., 1976).

THE PERFORMANCE MANAGEMENT SYSTEM

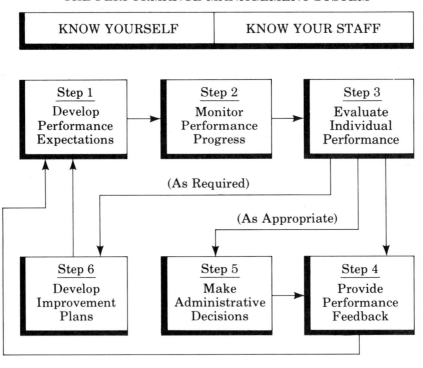

KNOW YOURSELF	KNOW YOUR STAFF

Step 1 — Develop Performance Expectations → **Step 2** — Monitor Performance Progress → **Step 3** — Evaluate Individual Performance

(As Required)

(As Appropriate)

Step 6 — Develop Improvement Plans   **Step 5** — Make Administrative Decisions → **Step 4** — Provide Performance Feedback

DELEGATE RESPONSIBILITY AND AUTHORITY	MANAGE PERFORMANCE PROBLEMS	MANAGE GROUP PERFORMANCE

CHAPTER 10

Managing Performance Problems

As a result of reading this chapter you will

- Be able to diagnose performance problems
- Know how to train members of your workgroup
- Be able to counsel members of your staff
- Know how to handle discipline
- Know how to handle a termination

Most employees want to do a good job. However, once in a while you'll run into a performance problem that can be very frustrating. This chapter lays out a method for diagnosing and dealing with these problems through training, counseling, discipline, and termination. But first let's look at some of the things that motivate your employees and make them behave the way they do.

Diagnosing Performance Problems

As a point of reference for diagnosing performance problems, it's helpful to establish an understanding of employee motivation within the context of a performance system. Then, a procedure for determining what has gone wrong with the system, and what to do about it, can be considered.

What Motivates Your Employees?

It's long been established that unfulfilled wants, needs, and desires motivate people to seek their fulfillment. In the work environment these needs can be divided into two broad categories. First are the basic needs for food, shelter, and rest, both in the present as well as in the future. Everyone who's employed today has the means for satisfying these basic needs, even if at only a minimally acceptable level.

The second category is usually referred to as the higher order needs. These include fair treatment, recognition, achievement, status, and power. These needs do not become significant until the basic ones are fulfilled. But then they are just as powerful as motivators of performance as any of the basic needs. The relationship of needs to performance is shown in Figure 10.1.

This figure illustrates that the unfulfilled needs, wants, and desires cause an employee to exert effort. This effort, cou-

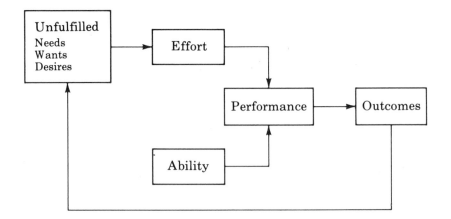

Figure 10.1 A perspective on employee motivation

pled with ability, leads to performance. As a result of the performance, the employee experiences certain outcomes. If the outcomes satisfy a want, need, or desire, the system is *motivational*. If the outcome doesn't satisfy a want, need, or desire, the system is *demotivational*. You can go a long way toward avoiding performance problems by seeing that through job design and equitable administration of sound personnel policies the higher order needs of your staff are satisfied.

Figure 10.1 also provides a framework for diagnosing performance problems, which must be either problems of effort or problems of ability. Problems of effort can be any of three varieties.

1. An employee doesn't see performance leading to the fulfillment of certain needs.
2. Personal problems are diverting the employee's attention and energy away from performance.
3. The employee is pursuing counterproductive objectives.

The starting point for diagnosing performance problems is to be very specific in describing what you observe in the employee's performance and how that varies from what ought to be. Then talk to the employee to assess what's wrong. Following the discussion, any of several strategies may be followed depending upon your diagnosis. Basically, your options are

1. training
2. counseling
3. discipline
4. termination

Figure 10.2 lays out all of the elements involved in managing performance problems.

The Assessment Interview

In a number of cases the staff member will initiate a discussion to diagnose the problem. However, when you observe a

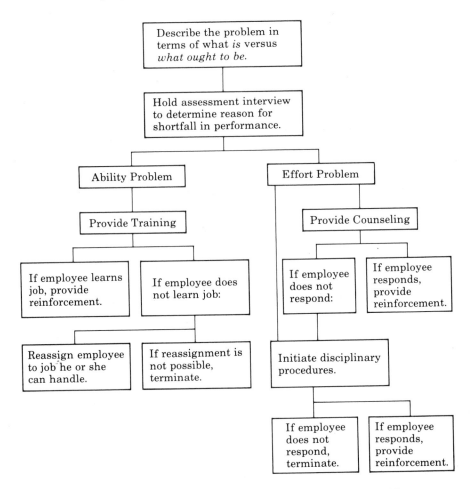

Figure 10.2 A system for managing performance problems

performance problem, don't wait—take the initiative yourself and hold an interview with the employee.

Start the interview with a clear description of the problem as you see it. Stay with the facts—avoid assumptions and inferences. Also, express your concern. For example, you might say, "Murray, I've noticed that your reject rate has gone from 1 to 6 percent this past week. That's $3\frac{1}{2}$ percent over standard. I'm concerned about this. Let's talk about it."

Depending on the nature of Murray's problem, it may take some time for him to feel comfortable enough to level with you.

Don't be too anxious to accept the first explanation offered. There's frequently a vast difference between the *socially acceptable* excuse and the *real* reason. It usually takes a lot of trust for someone to disclose a problem. Sometimes, there isn't enough trust for it to happen. If continued talking doesn't result in a plausible explanation, you may have to take a very direct approach. For example, you might say, "Murray, you have a problem with your reject rate. I'm interested in being of any help I can; but, I can't help you if I don't know what's going on. For your own sake, tell me what you believe is the cause of this increase."

A more difficult problem to diagnose is the one where something inappropriate is happening. In this case, the employee is being motivated to pursue counterproductive objectives or is responding to frustration. This type of problem can include an unending list of behavior including absenteeism, tardiness, too much socializing, horseplay, drug abuse, and fighting. Again, before implementing a response to correct the problem behavior, it's beneficial to try to understand the cause.

Again, the assessment interview can be the vehicle for understanding these problems. With these kinds of problems you should attempt to understand the individual's needs that aren't being satisfied through the regular work experience. What might be causing the frustration that has led to apparently self-destructive behavior? What goals are important to the individual that are incompatible with workplace goals?

Types of Problems

As a result of the assessment interview, supplemented with whatever information you have from direct observation and input from others, you should be able to characterize the individual's problem as one of the following.

Lack of Knowledge or Skill.   This employee is interested but unable to do a good job due to some new equipment or work methods. Key question here is whether the individual has ever done the work before at required performance standards. If not, training is called for.

EXERCISE 10.1

John has been one of your best employees during the three years he's worked for you. You have confidence in his ability and willingness to do a good job. He typically has been easy to get along with and could be expected to be friendly and helpful to other group members.

In the past three weeks there's been a marked change in John's behavior at work. He's frequently late coming in, he's always the first to leave at the end of the day, and he has been withdrawn and irritable. You decide it's time to talk to John. What are the first things you say?

Analysis

Without accusing or blaming, simply present the facts as you see them, express your concern, and ask about the problem and what you can do to help. Your statement might be like this: "John, you've been one of my most reliable employees over the past three years. However, something's changed. You've been 10 to 15 minutes late six times during the past two weeks, you're the first one out each afternoon, and you haven't been your usual friendly, helpful self. I'm concerned about you and want to know what's going on and how I can help."

John's Reaction.   John may try to brush the issue aside by saying it's really nothing, he'll watch it more closely in the future, and he didn't realize things were so obvious to you. But with a little encouragement from you he finally reveals the following: Two weeks ago his wife left him and his two year old son. His mother has been caring for the child, but he has to take the child to his mother's house each morning and pick him up each evening. Sometimes in the morning he has trouble getting the child ready and often the traffic is very congested, causing additional delays. As a result, he arrives to work late. All of this is putting a lot of pressure on him. He hopes to get reconciled with his wife and therefore doesn't want too many people to know about this problem. What do you do now?

Exercise 10.1   (*continued*)

Analysis

Your next course of action depends upon your level of personal interest and your organization's policies and services. You should show concern and understanding and you should get agreement from John to take necessary steps to get to work on time. You might also consider giving some personal leave time and recommend counseling either through community services, John's church, or a private counselor. If your organization provides counseling services, arrange for John to talk to the appropriate person.

Emotional and/or Health Problems.   This employee has done the job well in the past but some outside influence is diverting attention and energy away from the work. In these situations counseling is required to help the employee return to being a contributing member of your staff.

Response to Frustrations.   Occasionally, when an individual's needs, wants, or desires aren't being fulfilled by the outcomes experienced, different forms of frustrated behavior will be observed—either withdrawal or aggression. In these cases counseling is called for. However, if counseling doesn't alleviate the problem behavior, discipline may be appropriate.

Counterproductive Goals or Objectives.   These people choose to march to a different drummer. They ignore appropriate workplace practices in favor of doing their own thing. These cases call for disciplinary action.

✔ **Checklist for Conducting a Performance Problem Assessment Interview**

- State the performance problem and its consequences.
- Be specific as to how actual performance varies from desired performance.

- Listen.
- Follow up on clues offered by the employee to explain the shortfall in performance.
- Don't be too willing to accept superficial excuses.
- Express concern for the individual.
- Avoid drawing untested inferences from what you hear.
- Conclude with an action plan and follow-up date to check on progress.

Training for Improved Performance

Ideally you could bring new members into your group, either by employment or transfer, who would be fully qualified to perform the duties you assign them. However, this ideal is seldom the case. *Some* training is almost always required. Also, procedures and equipment change from time to time, necessitating supplemental training of your staff.

The purpose of training should always be to improve individual performance and thereby improve total workgroup performance. This can be accomplished through either increasing the knowledge or improving the skills of workgroup members.

Knowledge is acquired by reading, listening, and observing. New skills are also learned in several different ways—for example, trial and error or copying how someone else does something. However, the most efficient training is accomplished with the help of a good instructor. You can become a good instructor by understanding and being guided by general principles of learning, preparing for the job of instructor, then following a four-step instruction procedure (described on pages 289–290).

General Learning Principles

The following basic principles apply to all learning experiences. When considering the training of employees, use these principles in the design of the training effort and your expectations of the trainees.

Skills Must Be Used to Be Remembered. One must continue to use a skill in order to stay proficient at it. Therefore, schedule the training close to the time the knowledge or skills you are teaching will be needed.

Learning Is Based on What's Already Known. Begin with some assessment of what your trainee already knows about what you plan to teach. Because learning can be transferred from one situation to another, during this assessment do not limit yourself to just what is known about the precise operation. For example, if you were teaching someone to operate a forklift, you'd want to know of *any* experience your trainee has had, not just with forklifts, but also with tractors, cars, trucks, and so forth.

Learning Progresses. When designing training, break the total job down into fairly simple steps. Then progress through each step until the whole job is learned. This provides opportunity for the trainee to experience success along the way and remain interested and motivated to learn the whole operation. When you don't break the job down, you run the risk of overwhelming and thereby frustrating the trainee.

Everyone Is Different. Some people learn quickly, others take longer. Learning doesn't progress at a steady rate, even for the fast learner. There will be sudden breakthroughs in understanding, but there will also be times when it seems like no progress is being made. Repetition is required to master almost any task. Don't expect anyone to learn something with just one demonstration.

Preparing to Teach

Good instructors are prepared. Most have experience in the operations they teach, therefore they know their material. However, more is required. Other items to prepare include procedures to assure that nothing is left out and support material or training aids that will illustrate and clarify the material being taught.

Task: Refilling a Standard Office Stapler

Important Steps	Key Points
1. Obtain box of standard size staples from supply cabinet in file room.	1. Verify size will work in your particular brand and model of stapler.
2. Visually inspect stapler noting instructions "Lift Cap to Load" with arrows pointing up.	2. There is no catch to be released as in some other models.
3. Open stapler by holding base firmly against desk with left hand and swinging cap up and to the right with right hand.	3. Grasp cap between thumb and index finger near extreme left end.
4. Check channel for loose staples—clear as necessary.	4. Particularly check feed end of channel for lodged staples.
5. Fill channel with new staples.	5. Do not overload—leave $\frac{1}{2}$ inch between last staple and spring driven guide.
6. Close stapler by swinging cap to the left and down with right hand.	6. Keep fingers out of the way.
7. Test by pressing down firmly to lock stapler closed and staple sample material at same time.	7. Be careful to not pinch hand as stapler locks closed.
8. Return box of staples to supply cabinet in file room.	8. If supply is running low, initiate reorder.

Figure 10.3 Example of job-training analysis breakdown

The Job-Training Analysis Breakdown. When an experienced person teaches job details, there's a risk that significant points may be left out. Assumptions are made that "everyone knows that"; or, some particular detail can be so routine and has been done so often, that it is overlooked during the training period. To overcome these potential problems, prepare a job breakdown. In completing a job breakdown, think through and record each step required to complete a job. *Do not assume anything*. Under key points, list the information required to do each step properly, for example, where something is located, how to position something, or safety precautions to prevent injury. (See Figure 10.3.)

Training Aids.   Training is much easier when oral instructions are supplemented with appropriate training aids. Consider these possibilities: training manuals, films, or videotapes that describe the job and show what is to be done. Trainees can study these in advance and be prepared to move ahead more quickly in learning the details of the job. Other training aids that are helpful include pieces of machinery to be operated or repaired that trainees can practice on before actually taking over a job; photographs or slides of products to be produced or equipment to be operated or maintained; samples of products or forms to be completed; and flow diagrams showing where things come from, what is done to them, and where they go.

How to Instruct

With a job breakdown completed and training aids prepared, you're ready to begin instructing. Using the learning principles discussed earlier, the following four-step process will lead to effective and efficient results.

- *Step 1: Prepare the trainee.* During this step, develop interest in learning by pointing out the value of being able to perform the task. Also, find out what is known about the task from prior experience so you do not duplicate anything.
- *Step 2: Present the operation.* Tell, show, and illustrate the operation one step at a time. As you present each step, stress each key point associated with that step.
- *Step 3: Involve the trainee.* Have the trainee perform each step in the operation and explain the key points. Correct any errors you observe and continue the process until you are satisfied the trainee knows the operation. This step must not be omitted. Both demonstration and practice must be provided to verify understanding.

- *Step 4: Follow up.* When you're comfortable with the trainee's ability, turn the operation over to her or him. Then check back frequently to answer questions, correct errors, and praise accomplishments. Taper off this coaching activity as the trainee demonstrates ability to handle the operation.

✔ Checklist for Handling Training

- Prepare a job breakdown for the task to be taught.
- Select or prepare appropriate training aids.
- Schedule the training close to when the knowledge and skill will be required on the job.
- Point out the value to the individual of knowing what you are prepared to instruct.
- Assess the trainee's present level of knowledge.
- Involve the trainee in the learning experience by building in practice with what you are teaching.
- Test the trainee's competency as you progress through each step of your instructions.

Counseling for Improved Performance

It hasn't been many years since the prevailing attitude in the workplace was to separate personal problems from the rest of the person. Employees were told to leave their personal problems at home.

Recently, the significant and direct relationship between personal problems and productivity has been acknowledged. This is shown in Figure 10.4. John's plight in Exercise 10.1 is a perfect example.

In a very broad sense, personal problems experienced by your staff can be classified as either career related or non–career related. Most supervisors are more comfortable dealing with those that are career related, but both need to be addressed.

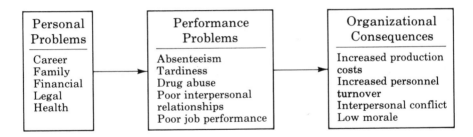

Figure 10.4 Relationship between personal problems
and productivity
Adapted from Meyer & Meyer, "The Supervisor as Counselor—
How to Help the Distressed Employee."

Counseling Career-Related Personal Problems

Many employees experience disappointments and uncertainties with their career. It might be a long-anticipated promotion that goes to someone else, a transfer or reassignment to what appears to be an undesirable position, or an opportunity that's difficult to evaluate completely and objectively. These experiences divert one's attention and energy away from the work at hand. Therefore, career-related problems are not to be overlooked by supervisors.

You can provide a great deal of help to a member of your staff who may be experiencing this type of personal setback. In doing so, keep the following points in mind.

Listen with Understanding. Many times the most help you can provide is listening—letting employees get it "off their chest." To be an effective listener you must display understanding for how the other person feels. And you must avoid being judgmental. These qualities are reflected in responses you make. For example, you might say "I can understand how you feel" or "I can understand why you feel that way." Statements to avoid include "You shouldn't feel that way," or "Don't let things like that bother you."

Share Personal Experiences. As a rule, people don't want to be seen as extremely different. Therefore, when discussing a career-related personal problem, be willing to share any similar setbacks you may have experienced. This lets your staff member know that she or he is not that different—that these experiences have also been encountered and overcome by others.

Don't Accept Excuses. While you may very honestly identify with and understand an employee's reaction to a career setback, you can't allow the experience to justify poor performance. At first glance this may appear brutal. But the best mechanism for recovery is to accept the reality of what has happened and confront present-day living rather than linger in the past.

Focus on the Future. As soon as it's reasonable, but without rushing the discussion, direct the employee's attention to the future. What has this experience taught? How can it be avoided? What can the individual do to increase his or her chances of experiencing what is desired for the future?

Don't Give Advice. Avoid statements like "What you should do is . . ." When you give advice you become responsible for its outcome, at least in the eyes of the one to whom it was given. It's far more helpful to challenge the individual to explore a wide range of alternatives and then select the best from his or her viewpoint.

Refer the Employee to Counselors. Even though most supervisors can become creditable career counselors, your organization may provide counseling by staff or by referral. If they are available, take advantage of these services for members of your workgroup.

Follow Up. All counseling discussions need a follow-up discussion. The purpose of follow up is to determine what next step should be taken. When recovery is being demonstrated, reinforce progress by complimenting and encouraging. When recovery is not being demonstrated, consider whether or not to initiate disciplinary procedures.

Counseling Non—Career-Related Personal Problems

No one is immune to the tragedies of life. There will be family, financial, legal, or health crises in the lives of your staff, or members of their family, that will divert attention and energy away from work and thereby create a performance problem you'll need to deal with.

Here, again, you can provide a great amount of help to a staff member. Keep the following points in mind.

Make Full Use of Personnel Policy. You must know what is available to members of your staff in times of crisis. Is it appropriate to authorize time off with pay for an employee to handle these problems? If drug abuse or alcoholism is a problem, what is your organization's policy on treatment? Obviously, your personnel officer can be a great help in determining what is appropriate in each case. Don't overlook this valuable source of information.

Help Arrange Professional Counseling. Most supervisors aren't qualified to provide adequate counseling in noncareer areas. However most communities have professional services available either on a fee basis or through church and public agencies. Be willing to spend a little time making some phone calls to help establish proper contact for professional help. If your organization has a personal counseling service available, don't overlook it as a valuable referral channel.

Don't Accept Excuses. While you may be willing and able to tolerate a brief decline in performance when a staff member is experiencing a personal problem, these experiences shouldn't be allowed to justify a prolonged period of substandard performance. The mature individual will be able to return to full performance within a reasonable time. Others may have to be pushed in order to get back to their former level of contribution.

Follow Up. Stay in touch with the employee during the period of crisis. Monitor progress in terms of either changing the situation causing the problem or learning to cope with it. Pay particular attention to the impact on performance. Provide support and encouragement when progress is demonstrated in maintaining performance. Provide or encourage further counseling when recovery isn't apparent. Decide how far you are willing to go, and your organization's policies permit, before further action is warranted. There aren't clear-cut guidelines on how much an employer should tolerate. It depends on the type of job, length of service, prior history, policy, and past practices. However, an employee should be clearly advised of the consequences of not returning to full performance within a reasonable time.

✔ Checklist for Counseling

- Recognize the limits of your ability and refer employees to professional care as appropriate.
- Know about and use the policies and services provided by your own organization.
- Do not accept excuses for substandard performance.
- Do not give advice.
- Listen attentively.
- Encourage employees to face up to their problems and work them out.
- Follow up frequently during the period of crisis.

Handling Discipline

You use discipline to help correct behavior that interferes with your workgroup achieving its purpose in an orderly manner when other efforts have been unsuccessful. Discipline is a rational action—not an emotional one.

In handling discipline, nothing takes the place of good judgment. Be objective in viewing the facts, including any extenuating circumstances. Then exercise judgment in your final decision. Keep your goal in mind and take the action that helps you achieve that goal. The point is never to belittle, embarrass, or intimidate an employee.

Types of Disciplinary Action

There are many different types of disciplinary action available to you. Which one is appropriate depends on the severity of the behavior and your history of working with the employee. Clarity of expectations and feedback have been previously discussed in earlier chapters; they're the starting place to correct inappropriate behavior. When they're unsuccessful, the following disciplinary actions are in order:

- Oral reprimand
- Written reprimand
- Probation
- Temporary suspension
- Termination

Oral Reprimand.   When a member of your group makes an abrupt change in behavior, an oral reprimand may be in order. When handling an oral reprimand, be clear and specific about what is to be either stopped or started. Don't argue or debate side issues and don't talk about the person in a demeaning or derogatory way. Essentially, an oral reprimand is handled the same as corrective feedback. The following steps are involved.

1. *Describe what's unacceptable.* Quickly and clearly describe the specific situation or behavior you are concerned about. This is no time to beat around the bush or water down your message just to reduce the chance of an emotional reaction.

2. *Get a reaction.* After you've described your concern, stop talking and get a reaction. Expect the employee to be defensive, to rationalize, and to blame others. During this time, convey empathy and understanding for the employee's feelings but don't discount the importance of the issue. Don't get caught up in arguing or debating any points raised by the employee.

3. *Get agreement.* Convince the employee that the problem or situation can't be allowed to continue. This may

require some selling on your part; but if you don't get agreement, you can't expect the employee to change. (And if you don't get agreement, your only remaining option is to issue an *order* to comply with your request as a condition of continued employment.)

4. *Develop a plan.* With agreement that there is a problem, get the employee involved in developing a plan to overcome it. Don't expect too much too soon. It's better to have a modest plan that *is* carried out than to have a demanding plan that is ignored.

5. *Confirm understanding.* Summarize your discussion in order to ensure understanding. Restate the problem, your expectations for the future, and the plan the two of you have developed to get there.

6. *Follow up.* Set a specific follow-up date to get back with the employee and review progress. Then get together as agreed. At that time, provide appropriate reinforcement of progress made toward the agreed upon goal.

Written Reprimand.   Sometimes it's appropriate to put a reprimand in writing. This typically has more impact on an employee than an oral reprimand. It's appropriately used for more severe problems or after an oral reprimand hasn't resulted in the necessary change in behavior. The written reprimand should include a clear statement of the problem and clear expectations for the future. It usually also includes the statement, "If improvement is not shown, more severe disciplinary action will be taken."

Probation.   Placing an employee on probation, or notice, serves to clarify the gravity of the situation. It clearly points out that the employee's job is in jeopardy and it specifies a time period for improvement. This period may vary from a week to a month depending upon the nature of improvement required.

Many employees will make the desired change in performance and become contributing members of the workgroup. Other employees will seemingly ignore the need for change and continue as though nothing were said. Both are easy to deal with. Where improvement is achieved, compliment the employee, remove the probationary notice, and proceed as with other group members. Where no effort is made to improve, continue with steps to remove the employee from the workgroup.

The difficult case is the employee who makes some effort but doesn't achieve the desired level of performance. There's a tendency to be lenient—to give this person another chance. Equity suggests that you be open to circumstances. Why wasn't the employee able to achieve the desired performance level? How much progress was made? Taking factors such as these into consideration may occasionally justify an extension of probation. However, be careful about accepting excuses. If the terms of the probation were reasonable, failure to fulfill them is sufficient reason for termination. Otherwise, you may have a member of your workgroup who will continually do just enough to get by and have plenty of excuses to support his or her lack of accomplishment.

Temporary Suspension. Violations of rules and minor illegal acts often are treated with a temporary suspension. The time off varies from one day to several weeks according to the severity of the problem. In the vast majority of cases, layoffs are without pay and therefore amount to a monetary fine. Some companies have positive results with a one-day suspension with pay. This clearly emphasizes the gravity of a situation and allows an employee to think through his or her obligation as an employee. The employee can either return to work with renewed commitment or use the day to find other employment.

Demotion. When a workgroup member can't adequately handle the duties of a job assignment, demotion to a job that the employee is qualified for can be an appropriate action. Demotion should never be used as punishment for non–job-related activities. The decision should be based entirely on qualifications to perform the job.

Termination. When it appears that there's little chance of bringing someone's performance up to an acceptable level, termination may be the best course of action. Also, some things are so severe, such as major theft, that termination is appropriate as an example to others who may be tempted to do something similar. Termination also includes requested resignations. When it appears an employee's interests are not being met on a job it may be appropriate to request the employee to seek employment somewhere else.

Progressive Discipline

When working with a problem employee, use the idea of progressive discipline. It's based on the principle that an employee is entitled to an opportunity to improve and at the same time entitled to explicit warning of the consequences of not improving. The normal steps in the progression are:

1. Feedback
2. Oral reprimand
3. Written reprimand
4. Probation
5. Suspension
6. Termination

Sometimes an employee will change before you get to the termination step. If change doesn't occur, however, you'll have a clear record that the person was adequately warned.

General Discipline Guidelines

When handling discipline, a positive reaction by the employee is necessary to reach the goal of improved performance. Sometimes other reactions are experienced. For example, rather than being motivated to improve performance, an employee may be motivated to retaliate or "get even." The following guidelines will help you experience a positive reaction.

- *Be sure of the facts.* Before taking any disciplinary action, dig as deeply as necessary to get all the facts. What happened? What was this employee's part in it?
- *Listen.* Give the employee involved ample opportunity to explain what happened and why. Don't go into the investigation with your mind made up about what you are going to do.

EXERCISE 10.2

Stephanie is a mechanic #2 in your section. She's been in the section just over three years. She was originally hired as a general helper. Although her housekeeping and attendance were poor, she was promoted about a year ago to mechanic trainee because of her time with the section and the lack of other candidates. Stephanie satisfactorily completed the six-month training program and has worked as a mechanic #2 for six months. In this assignment she handles routine maintenance on equipment and assists the mechanic #1 with equipment overhaul.

Shortly after startup today, one of the electric motors caught fire and was destroyed. Although the fire was contained, it represented a severe hazard to the facilities and employees under your supervision. Upon investigation, you find the fire started because Stephanie improperly installed new bearings in it the day before. This installation is work that an employee of her training and experience can be reasonably expected to handle properly. What do you do next?

Analysis

This is a case of poor job performance. Questions you need to answer include, what is Stephanie's work history? was she properly trained? and were there any extenuating circumstances that you should take into account? To answer these questions you need to review Stephanie's personnel file, talk to the mechanic #1 she usually works with, and talk to Stephanie herself.

Investigation

When you carry out your investigation, you obtain the following information.

- *File*. Stephanie's personnel file contains a written reprimand for poor housekeeping dated five months ago. The written reprimand refers to three prior oral reprimands on the same issue. You also find that she has been on probation on two occasions during her three years of employment for excessive absenteeism.

Exercise 10.2   (*continued*)

- *Mechanic #1's statement.* "Stephanie is a below average employee in terms of her interest and ability in mechanical work. On several occasions I've checked her work and found errors that were potentially hazardous. Yesterday, I checked this motor, determined it needed new bearings, and left Stephanie to replace them while I attended to a more complex problem. She's done this same job correctly on two prior occasions. I felt she could handle it because of these experiences."

- *Stephanie's statement.* "It was late in the day when that job came up. I didn't want to stay over because I had plans for the evening. I guess I was just a little careless. I thought I put the bearings in properly although it was hard to make them fit. I figured it was just the way they were supposed to be." Stephanie went on to explain that there's too much work to get done in the time available. Management's always on her back to keep things cleaned up, but there's hardly time to get the work done, let alone clean up as well. From time to time, she just has to take off for a day or two to get away from all the hassle. What do you recommend? How would you proceed from this point?

Analysis

Based on your investigation, either of two recommendations can be made—disciplinary suspension or demotion. In her present approach to her job Stephanie represents a hazard. What are the prospects of her changing? If you believe she should be given a chance, then disciplinary suspension is proper. If not, demotion to general helper would be appropriate. Termination probably crossed your mine as an option, but sufficient groundwork hasn't been laid to justify that severe a penalty. But it is the next appropriate step if improvement doesn't occur. You need your manager's and your personnel officer's approval before proceeding to implement your decision to demote or temporarily suspend.

- *Control your feelings.* Stay calm. Don't do something that will only create new problems, such as name calling.

- *Avoid entrapment.* Don't set out to "get someone." Unless you have sufficient information to suggest that something wrong is taking place, don't get involved. To do otherwise only breeds distrust in the equity and justice of the system.

- *Keep records.* Make notes on what happened and what you did about it. Records may be important later to demonstrate fair and equitable treatment. On the other hand, set a time limit for keeping records. For example, it would be reasonable to destroy records of disciplinary action after two years of good performance.

- *Know your authority.* What action can you take without checking with anyone? What can you only recommend to higher authority? Can you send an employee home, with or without pay, while an investigation is carried out? Know your authority and operate within it.

- *Keep others advised.* In most companies there are other people you should keep advised when you're working with a problem employee. This typically includes your manager and whoever handles personnel. It also might include an equal opportunity officer and/or a labor attorney.

Ensuring Fair Treatment

In general, five criteria are used to evaluate whether or not discipline has been fairly handled. These criteria have been established over the years by labor arbitrators in discipline cases. However, they are appropriate regardless of whether you're operating under a labor contract.

- *Warn in advance.* An employee must be advised of all rules and the penalties for violating them. This can be handled either orally or in writing. You can reasonably expect some conduct to be generally known as unacceptable, such as major theft or coming to work drunk.

- *Relate rules and orders to the business.* Rules and orders can be enforced that contribute to the orderly, efficient, safe operation of the business. Additionally, the rules and orders must not require unreasonable performance such as jeopardizing an employee's safety or violating one's integrity.

- *Investigate the facts.* Before taking disciplinary action, make an effort to find out whether or not the employee actually disobeyed a rule or order and whether there were any possible justifications for a violation. The investigation must be conducted fairly and objectively. This means searching out witnesses and evidence, not just operating on the basis of voluntary information.

- *Be equitable.* Rules, orders, and penalties must be applied to all employees without discrimination. If in the past you've been lax in enforcing a rule, you can overcome this by telling everyone that you intend to start enforcing it from this point forward.

- *Match the discipline to the offense.* A trivial violation doesn't justify harsh and unreasonable discipline. However, an employee's prior record must be considered. A series of minor offenses may accumulate and justify severe discipline that the last act alone would not justify. On the other hand, a long history of good performance may justify a less severe treatment than otherwise might be considered.

✔ Checklist for Handling Discipline

- Be sure everyone knows the rules and the consequences of not adhering to them.
- Keep records of events, dates, discussions held, and commitments made by you and the employee.
- Be fair and objective in assessing the facts and applying the rules.
- Seek out all relevant information.
- Avoid situations where you might be motivated to take a course of action only to demonstrate your authority.
- Keep appropriate company officials advised of the problem and the action you plan to take or have taken.

Handling Employee Terminations

Not every employee will respond to your training, counseling, and discipline. Sometimes it becomes necessary to terminate an employee. Consider the amount of your time and energy required to work with the person, the effect on the workgroup, and the prospects for improvement. When what you must put into the situation exceeds your potential gain, you're probably better off replacing the problem employee.

Terminating or firing an employee is probably the most difficult task you'll face as a supervisor. Many supervisors put off these decisions out of fear of what might happen, both during the discussion and following it. This fear frequently can be overcome by recognizing your obligations to your workgroup and your responsibilities to the individual and by developing an approach to handling the discussion that assures success.

Often, obligations to the group aren't considered. As supervisor you have an obligation to see that all members of your group are capable and willing to do their share. When this is not the case, others have to do more in order to get the work out. When someone is not measuring up, everyone knows it. Your failure to take appropriate action becomes obvious to everyone and, as a result, you may be seen as a weak supervisor.

In addition to the workgroup, you also have responsibilities to the inadequate performer. People frequently get caught up in nonproductive relationships. It often is better to end these relationships and move on to new ones that have a better chance of success. By terminating inadequate performers you can encourage them to seek out opportunity that more closely matches their skills and interests. In the long run, this is certainly more desirable than drifting along, never doing well and never enjoying success on the job, until age makes it difficult to find new employment. More often than not, employees who are terminated go on to quite satisfying careers in other lines of work for which they are better suited.

When You Decide to Fire Someone

The importance of the termination decision is so significant that it must be handled in a way that guarantees fairness and objectivity. These requirements lead to the need for fair warning to the individual and a third-party review of your decision before it is implemented. Fair warning is typically achieved through the progressive discipline described in the preceding discussion. Some terminations are based on non–performance-related activities such as theft of company property, fighting, and bringing weapons or illicit drugs to the workplace. Terminations for these reasons need not be preceded by other disciplinary action.

To verify fairness and objectivity, every proposed termination should be reviewed by someone else prior to the decision being considered final. Usually this review is handled by your own immediate supervisor and/or your personnel officer. It should consider the issues of *fairness, equity,* and *objectivity.* Therefore, you should be sure your proposal can hold up under these tests.

Fairness. Has this employee been expected to do something other employees are not? Has the employee been discriminated against? You shouldn't terminate an employee for either doing or not doing something when other employees are not treated the same in response to similar actions. For example, even though a member of your workgroup has a very poor attendance record, it's not fair to terminate that employee if others have equal or worse records and are not similarly treated.

Equity. Does the employee's behavior or lack of performance justify termination? Or have you overreacted? There are no ironclad guidelines of what constitutes equitable treatment. However, you can look at company history and see how others have been treated under similar circumstances. Also, you can look at what is generally accepted as appropriate or inappropriate workplace behavior.

Objectivity. Is your decision based on facts, or are you letting your emotions rule your actions? This point requires you to have records that verify what has occurred, including dates of discussions, terms of probation, and so forth. Records are particularly important when an employee challenges a termination decision. If you are called to justify your decision to an arbitra-

EXERCISE 10.3

Jerry has been with your department four years. He originally was hired as an accounting clerk, was promoted to accountant after one year, and was promoted to his present position of accounting supervisor one year ago. His performance in the field of accounting has been excellent.

This morning, one of the women in Jerry's section, who has been with your department for three months, asked for an appointment with you. At the meeting, she advised you that she was being sexually harassed by Jerry, and that if you didn't put an end to it she would file a complaint with the Equal Employment Opportunity Commission. Upon questioning by you, she alleged that Jerry made it very clear to her that if she expected to be promoted in his section the price was to entertain him to his liking. Jerry suggested they could start with dinner on Friday evening. What steps would you take next?

Analysis

This a very serious charge. Your investigation should include a check of the files to see that Jerry is aware of your organization's sexual harassment policy and the consequences of violating it. You also need to check the files to see what history may exist in this problem area. You then should talk to Jerry to get his side of the story and to other employees to find whatever evidence may exist to confirm or discount the charge.

Investigation

Upon carrying out your investigation, you obtain the following information.

- *Files.* There is a memo signed by Jerry stating that he has read and understands the organization's sexual harassment policy. Also, there is a letter to Jerry dated three months ago detailing two prior episodes of sexual harassment and management's discussions with him. In this letter Jerry is advised that any further problems in this area will result in more serious disciplinary action including possible discharge.

Exercise 10.3 *(continued)*

- *Jerry's statement.* When you confront Jerry with the allegation, he suggests that you are too uptight about these matters. He acknowledges that he invited the employee to dinner but nothing more was meant by it. If she felt it was a condition for getting ahead with him, she had simply misinterpreted his kidding around. He concluded by observing that, after all, men are men and women are women. When they work together, it is only natural that they will play together.

- *Other employees.* Three other women work in Jerry's section. You talk to each privately and find that all have been invited out on dates by Jerry, including the two that are married. Furthermore, Jerry's general style with women includes the use of words of endearment and words with sexual overtones. He has, on more than one occasion, touched each of them in ways that were inappropriate and embarrassing.

How would you proceed from this point?

Analysis

Based on your investigation, either of two recommendations are possible—temporary suspension or discharge. If suspension is chosen, you must be sensitive to potential negative reactions when Jerry returns to work. Because of a high probability of negative consequences to a suspension, discharge is recommended. You need to obtain the approval of your management and your personnel officer. Be sure you can demonstrate fairness, equity, and objectivity to them. Following appropriate approvals, Jerry should be advised of his discharge late in the day, and be informed to not return to the office.

tor, judge, or Equal Employment Opportunity Commission investigator, you'll need records to prove the objectivity of your decision.

The Termination Notification

The emotional impact of being terminated varies greatly among individuals. Some are relieved that an undesirable situation is finally resolved. Others experience shock, depression, anger, self-pity, confusion, and/or loss of self-confidence. There may be anxiety about finding another job. There may be concern about the reaction of family and friends. There may be financial difficulties to cope with. In fact, for some people, the experience of termination is as severe as the experience of divorce. Anything you can do to minimize the impact on the individual will be remembered.

Principles. To help minimize the impact of the experience keep three principles in mind: dignity, understanding, and a positive outlook.

- *Dignity.* Everyone is entitled to dignity. There's nothing to be gained, and much to be lost, by belittling or berating an employee in the process of termination. Don't blame or accuse. What was done is history, and the natural consequences of that history are now being experienced. Handle termination in a way that allows the person to save face as much as possible.
- *Understanding.* Don't try to depersonalize the experience. Be sensitive to the employee's reactions and try to understand the feelings being experienced. Remember, reactions vary, so stay in tune with this person as an individual. Try to understand and respond accordingly.
- *Positive outlook.* Focus attention on the positive aspects of the experience. Point out, as appropriate, that the employee can now find a job that more closely matches his or her skills and interests. Look at this experience as a learning opportunity. How can the problems experienced here be avoided in future employment? This is an oppor-

tunity to get a fresh start. How can you make the best of it? Rather than seeing this as an ending experience, look at it as a new beginning—a starting over with a clean slate.

Preparing for the Discussion.   You've made the decision to terminate, and it's been reviewed and approved by your manager and personnel department. The only step remaining is to advise the employee. As you prepare for the discussion two sets of information need to be pulled together. First, make a final review of your records so that you're completely familiar with all the details of the case. Second, check with the appropriate authority, usually your personnel officer, about termination policy and benefits. Is it appropriate to terminate the employee immediately and then provide a week or two of additional pay in lieu of notice? How will the final paycheck be handled? How will benefits be handled such as savings plan settlements and insurance plan conversions? Will the employee receive pay in lieu of earned vacation credits? Is there outplacement counseling available? Having completed your homework, it's time to hold the discussion.

Holding the Discussion.   There's no absolute right way to conduct a termination discussion. However there are some guidelines that will increase your odds for success.

- *Timing*. Don't ruin special occasions in the employee's life by terminating someone immediately prior to holidays, birthdays, or wedding anniversaries. Beyond selecting the best day, also consider the appropriate time during the day. If an employee is not expected to return to work, hold the discussion late in the day—the employee won't have to explain leaving early and others won't be available to complain to about the injustice of the experience. On the other hand, if the employee is expected to work a few more days, hold the discussion early in the day. The employee will be better able to deal with the news and move in a positive direction following the discussion.

- *Setting*. The discussion should be held in your office with you seated behind your desk. This provides the privacy the employee is entitled to, and adds formality and authority to your position.

- *Approach*. Be straightforward and direct in your approach. Get immediately to the point. Remember, this probably isn't the first time you've talked about the problem. State the reason for the termination, point out that the decision has been reviewed and confirmed by others, then stop and wait for a reaction before going further. Consider something like "We've talked about your performance record several times. You have been on notice for the past two weeks and, unfortunately, you haven't been able to bring your performance up to the specified level. Therefore, I am terminating your services effective as of the end of the week. This hasn't been an easy decision for me. I've given it a lot of thought and feel it's best for both of us in the long run. I've reviewed my decision with my manager and the personnel officer, and they both agree it is a fair and proper decision."

- *Agenda*. Where you go next will depend on the reaction you get. You may need only to listen to the employee talk a while about what has happened. You may have to agree with the *apparent* injustice of it all. For example, you may find it appropriate to agree that you made a mistake hiring someone not fully qualified to perform the job. Following this reaction stage, move on as soon as you can to a positive outlook for the future and then summarize any appropriate administrative matters, such as
    - last day of work
    - handling of final pay
    - handling of employee benefits
    - references
    - turning in of company property

- *Conclusion*. Conclude the discussion by offering to be of any help you can in the future and referring the employee to any other appropriate person for advice and counsel. For example, the personnel officer may be able to provide more details on benefit plan conversions or settlements and may be qualified to provide personal counseling.

After the Discussion. As soon as the discussion is over, several items need attention. First, write a detailed summary of what happened during the discussion. What did you tell the employee? What were his or her reactions? Next, handle appropriate administrative work to properly remove the employee from the payroll and initiate action to obtain a replacement. Finally, consider whether or not to advise the workgroup about what has happened. Remember, news travels quickly when someone leaves. Often, the news is tainted with rumor, assumptions, and speculations. You might be better off to call your group together and briefly state the facts. This can serve to underscore your willingness to deal with problems and your fairness. This, in turn, may remove some of the threat others may feel as a result of the experience.

Negative reactions to termination can have serious consequences. The employee may go to work for a competitor and divulge valuable information to the new employer. The employee may file a lawsuit. The company's reputation may be tarnished, causing serious effects on recruiting efforts and community image. Remaining employees may experience a decline in morale and loyalty. Therefore, it is certainly in the company's best interests to handle terminations as positively and sensitively as possible.

✔ Checklist for Handling Terminations

- Don't put off facing up to your responsibilities when someone is a disruptive element in the group or is not doing his or her share.
- Provide fair warning, usually in the form of probation.
- Have your decisions reviewed for fairness, objectivity, and equity.
- Check with your personnel officer to see what benefits the employee may be entitled to receive.
- Conduct the termination discussion in a setting, and use an approach, that will contribute to maintaining the employee's dignity.

- End the discussion on as positive a note as possible.
- Handle appropriate administrative responsibilities to remove the employee from the payroll and obtain a replacement.

Your Action Guide

Performance problems represent one of the most frustrating challenges faced by supervisors. Many supervisors put off dealing with problems hoping that things will improve and they can avoid a potentially unpleasant experience. But when problems are not confronted and dealt with, they often become the subject of workgroup gossip. On the other hand, when faced up to and handled with dignity and fairness, the experience can have a positive effect on the group. Group members will respect and admire you for accepting the full responsibility of your position.

Confronting performance problems starts with gathering specific data about performance and then contrasting actual to expected. From this information, an assessment interview is held with the employee whose performance is a problem. In the interview, stay with specific facts about performance—do not accuse or attempt to interpret motives. Get the employee to talk about the reasons for his or her poor performance. Through this interview, attempt to assess whether you're confronted with an ability problem or an effort problem. Do not accept excuses for poor performance but do reflect an understanding for the circumstances the employee may be caught up in.

Depending on what comes out of the assessment interview, you have three potential immediate responses: counseling, training, and discipline. As you continue to work with the individual, two other responses become available to you: reassignment and termination.

Don't expect miracles when dealing with performance problems. There are general approaches that increase your odds of being successful; but remember, everyone decides what they will or will not do. Your efforts to bring an employee's performance up to acceptable standards may fail; not everyone will respond. Sometimes, for the benefit of your workgroup, and often the employee involved, it is necessary and appropriate to terminate the individual with a performance problem.

- ✔ Take time to fully investigate the cause of the performance problems.

- ✔ Be sure you know your company's policies that apply to the type of problem you face.

- ✔ Keep responsibility for the problem clearly in the hands of the affected staff member.

- ✔ Give due consideration to prior service and performance when responding to a performance problem.

- ✔ Have all decisions that reduce the status of staff members, such as temporary layoffs, demotions, and terminations, reviewed by an appropriate third party for fairness, equity, and objectivity.

References

Randolph W. Flynn and William E. Stratton, "Managing Problem Employees," *Human Resource Management,* Summer 1981.

Ferdinand F. Fournies, *Coaching for Improved Work Performance* (New York: Van Nostrand Reinhold Co., 1978).

Robert F. Mager and Peter Pipe, *Analyzing Performance Problems* (Belmont, CA: Fearon Publishers, Inc., 1970).

John J. Meyer and Teresa C. Meyer, "The Supervisor As Counselor—How to Help the Distressed Employee," *Management Review,* April 1982.

George S. Odiorne, "Discipline by Objectives," *Management of Personnel Quarterly,* Summer 1971.

John K. Ross and Ted Halatin, "When Family Stress Affects Worker Productivity," *Supervisory Management,* July 1982.

Geary A. Rummler, "Human Performance Problems and Their Solution," *Human Resource Management,* Winter 1972.

Paul L. Wickens and Joel B. Haynes, "Understanding Frustration—Instigated Behavior," *Personnel Journal,* October 1974.

THE PERFORMANCE MANAGEMENT SYSTEM

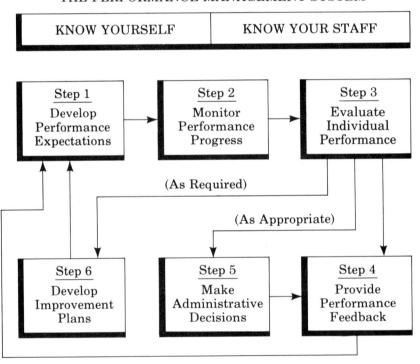

CHAPTER 11

Managing Group Performance

As a result of reading this chapter you will

- Understand the benefits of group-centered management
- Understand your role in building your group into an effective team
- Be able to decide when, to what extent, and how to involve the workgroup in decision making
- Be able to run effective staff meetings
- Know how to involve the group in improving its own effectiveness

U p to this point, attention has been focused on the interaction between you and individual members of your workgroup. In this chapter we'll look at the workgroup as a whole—exactly what it is and how to deal with it.

What Is an Effective Group?

In the workplace there are two different types of groups. One type is called *co-acting,* the other is called *interacting.* In the co-acting group each member works independently, with individual effort adding up to total the overall group effort. In the sports world this is similar to a golf, swimming, or track team. In the interacting group, on the other hand, each member contributes to the achievement of a common objective. This group is comparable to a baseball, basketball, or football team. Regardless of which of these types of groups you supervise, there are some common characteristics that *effective* groups display.

Characteristics of Effective Groups

Effective workgroups display both high productivity and high morale. They do a good job and, at least most of the time, lend individuals a high sense of satisfaction at being members of the group. They tend to develop into their own social system and experience a high level of group loyalty. They occasionally develop elitist attitudes—seeing themselves as better than other groups but, generally, they are known for:

- Sharing information among group members
- Supporting and/or defending members of the group
- Expressing favorable attitudes toward the organization, management, and the work
- Being highly motivated to quality performance
- Exercising self-control and guidance

Role of the Supervisor

Your role as supervisor begins with selecting and training qualified members of your workgroup; then, as they develop, giving individual members the opportunity to have a say in group goals and the freedom to contribute to them. When you've achieved this level of group development, you can concentrate on solving problems that interfere with attaining goals and building workgroup identity. There are four areas to concentrate on: providing support, facilitating interaction, emphasizing goals, and facilitating task accomplishment.

Provide Support. This area of involvement includes the things you do to increase or maintain each group member's sense of personal worth and importance to the group. Included in this area are such things as providing encouragement and recognition for good performance, speaking out on behalf of group members to higher management, and referring others directly to group members to answer questions or solve problems.

Facilitate Interaction. This area of involvement includes the things you do to create or maintain a network of interpersonal relationships among group members. Included in this area are such things as sponsoring or encouraging group socials, holding workgroup meetings, and arranging lunch breaks so that group members can be together.

Emphasize Goals. Workgroups exist to deliver a product or service to their customers. This area of involvement includes the things you do to create a high level of awareness and commitment to that purpose. It includes creating, changing, clarifying, and gaining acceptance of group goals. This typically is best done through the involvement and participation of group members.

Facilitate Task Accomplishment. This area of involvement includes the things you do to provide effective work methods, facilities, equipment, and schedules for the accomplishment of group goals. A large portion of this area is spent solving problems that your group experiences with other groups it interfaces with.

Effect on Group Members

People like to be members of winning teams. They also like to be accepted as an important member of a group. Because of these two characteristics, most people are willing to modify their behavior in order to fit in and make a contribution to goals they recognize as worthwhile. That is the price they're willing to pay to experience the very positive feelings of acceptance. The greater the attraction and loyalty to the group, the more its members are motivated to

- accept goals and decisions of the group
- seek to influence those goals and decisions by actively participating
- communicate openly and fully to group members
- welcome communication and influence from other members of the group
- seek support and recognition from other members of the group

Employees in these highly effective workgroups generally have a positive view of supervision: the supervisor is considered an important part of the total system, and viewed as

- supportive, friendly, and helpful
- having confidence in their ability and integrity
- having high performance expectations
- providing necessary training and coaching
- viewing errors as learning opportunities rather than opportunities to criticize

Decision Making in Groups

One means for providing involvement and participation by group members is to allow them an opportunity to contribute to decisions that affect the group. Decisions are made in the areas of goal setting, planning, and problem solving. Therefore, opportunities exist in each of these areas for group involvement. When considering group involvement in decision making, you must examine two things—the reasons for involving others and what the extent of involvement should be. Then a "rational" approach to making decisions should be used.

Why Involve Others?

There are four good reasons for involving others in a decision. When none of these reasons exist, make the decisions on your own.

Information.   Probably the most important reason for involving others is that you don't have all the information you need to reach a good decision. When this is the case, obtain and use the information you need.

Commitment.   The next most important reason for involving others is to gain their commitment to carry out the decision. This suggests two considerations. First, is the commitment of others required? Occasionally, you'll be the one to carry out the decision, and the commitment of others will be unnecessary. Second, can you count on the commitment of others without their involvement? If you have a track record of making good decisions in the area you're presently concerned with, you probably can count on the support and commitment you need without others being involved in the decision.

Creativity.   Some situations lend themselves to many possible decision alternatives. In these cases, groups can usually come up with more possibilities than a single individual. When you face a decision where there doesn't appear to be any reasonable answer, get a group together and explore the possibilities.

Development.   Occasionally you'll find an opportunity to involve others simply for their own education and development. You have the knowledge and experience to handle the matter, but in the future they will have to handle similar cases on their own. So you get them involved and guide them through a proper analysis and decision.

How Much Should You Involve Employees?

Several degrees of involvement exist. Each can be appropriate under the right set of circumstances. The following ideas will help you choose the best level of involvement for the situation you're concerned with.

Decide Alone.   The least possible involvement is obviously none. Here you make the decision alone. This choice is proper when none of the reasons listed above for involving employees exist. It may also be properly used when time doesn't permit involving others. When this happens, it's a good idea to get with the others later and explain why you found it necessary to act on your own.

Discuss Individually.   This is the least amount of *actual* involvement. It's appropriate when you need information on which to base a good decision. It's also a good choice when circumstances prevent getting together as a group—for example, if people can't leave other duties all at the same time, or when people are spread out over a large geographic area. These discussions can either be in person or by phone.

Discuss in a Meeting.   Meetings allow you to take full advantage of the information and ideas of others. They're particularly appropriate when you need some creative ideas but feel *you* must make the final decision.

Join in the Decision.   When employees are allowed to actually join with you in making a decision, it usually results in the highest feeling of commitment by those involved. Therefore, this is appropriate when a high degree of commitment is required. Letting others help make a decision also takes full advantage of information held by group members and the creative potential of the group. When this choice is selected, follow the "rational decision procedure" (described below) as the agenda for your meeting.

Turn Decisions over to Others.   Occasionally, the best choice will be to turn a situation over to others to decide. Decisions can be turned over either to an individual or a group. Normally, for this to be a successful choice, the employee or employees must be interested in and willing to make the decision, and you must be willing to accept any decision that is made. This requires you to specify any imperatives you have in advance of their making the decision.

A Rational Approach to Decision Making

Good decisions get good results. A good decision must take into account all of the relevant information available and process it through a logical, rational procedure that looks at all possible options or alternatives. After you decide who should be involved in a decision, and to what extent, this approach will help ensure that you properly consider everything in your decision.

1. *Study the situation.* The starting point is to study the situation to be sure you're deciding the proper issue. Time invested in this step will pay off handsomely later on. It's at this point that you make sure you've identified the real problem and that you have all the available facts.

2. *State an objective.* Now state what you want to accomplish. Describe your objective in terms of end results, and avoid any reference to how you plan to get there.

3. *Establish imperatives.* Imperatives are the absolute essentials that must be built into the final decision in order for it to be acceptable, for example, a restriction against increasing the size of the workgroup. The fewer imperatives the better, because they restrict the range of alternatives. On the other hand, if imperatives do exist it's best to get them out in the open early.

4. *Generate alternatives.* Now it's time to make a list of all the possible ways to reach your objective. Don't screen out any possibilities—leave that until later. Jot down even the craziest ideas. Often these will remind you of other, more reasonable possibilities.

5. *Determine evaluation criteria.* After you've come up with all the ideas you can, you need a way to sort through and evaluate them. Select three or four criteria against which each alternative will be measured. For example, feasibility, cost, availability, contribution to objective, and so forth.

6. *Evaluate alternatives.* Take each of the alternatives and evaluate it against each criterion. Where data are available, fill them in, for example, cost and availability figures. Where data aren't available, make a subjective assessment such as high, moderate, or low. This would apply to such criteria as feasibility and contribution to objectives. Exhibit 11.1 is an example of a worksheet for filling in criteria and evaluating alternatives. Exhibit 11.2 is an example of a form for recording each participant's ranking of each alternative. Exhibit 11.3 is a form for comparing alternatives.

EXHIBIT 11.1   Example of Criteria Evaluation Worksheet

Evaluations can be either on a subjective scale such as high, moderate, low; an objective scale such as 1 to 5 or 1 to 10; or actual values can be used, such as price, weight, or delivery time.

Alternatives	Criteria		
	2.		4.
1.			
2.			
3.			
4.			
5.			
6.			
7.			
8.			
9.			
10.			

EXHIBIT 11.2 Example of Consolidated Ranking Worksheet

| Alternative | Participants' Rankings | | | | | | | Consolidated Ranking |
	1.	2.	3.	4.	5.	6.	Total	
1.								
2.								
3.								
4.								
5.								
6.								
7.								
8.								
9.								
10.								

EXHIBIT 11.3 Example of Paired Comparison Worksheet

Yes = X
No = Blank

| | Alternatives | | | | | | | | | | Number of Xs |
	1.	2.	3.	4.	5.	6.	7.	8.	9.	10.	
1.											
2.											
3.											
4.											
5.											
6.											
7.											
8.											
9.											
10.											
Number of blanks:											
Number of Xs											
Total											
Priority											

Alternatives

Exhibit 11.3   *(continued)*

1. Working across, compare the alternative in the left column to each alternative listed across the top. If an alternative listed across the top is better than the one in the left column, place an "X" in the box.

2. When the individual comparisons are complete, count the number of blank boxes in each column and record on the appropriate line at the bottom. Then count the number of Xs across each row and record in the last column to the right. Transfer these data to the appropriate line at the bottom of the matrix.

3. Add the number of blanks and the number of Xs in each column.

4. Assign priorities with the lowest total of blanks and Xs receiving the highest priority. In the event of a tie, look back to where the two alternatives were compared and prioritize according to that prior decision.

7. *Decide among alternatives.* The final step in the decision procedure is to study your evaluation of alternatives and select the best available course of action. Obviously, there's no requirement that you choose the alternative that comes out as best in the evaluation. Consider the consequences of different alternatives and the probability of undesirable consequences occurring. If you do choose a course of action other than the best evaluated alternative, understand your reasons for doing so. For example, the best evaluated alternative may involve more risk than you care to take.

✔ Checklist for Decision Making

- Don't put off making necessary decisions.
- Think problems through before attempting to make a decision.
- Consider several possible alternatives before making a final decision.
- Use a rational, logical means of evaluating alternatives.
- To the extent it is appropriate, involve others in the decision-making process.

Three Additional Techniques

Brainstorming, nominal group technique, and *decisions by group consensus* are three additional techniques that can help you to involve your group in decisions.

Brainstorming Technique

The main value of brainstorming is that, when properly conducted, it can produce far more ideas than conventional discussion—and in less time. There are several reasons for this. For one thing, the power of association is a two-way phenomenon. When a group member voices an idea, this almost automatically steers his or her own imagination toward another idea. At the same time, the idea stimulates the associative power of all other members.

Idea Generation Phase.   The first step is to list as many ideas as you possibly can.

- List *all* ideas offered by group members.
- Do not evaluate or judge ideas at this time.
- Do not discuss ideas except perhaps briefly to clarify understanding.
- Welcome "free wheeling." The wilder the idea the better. It's easier to tame them down than think them up.

- Repetition is okay. Don't waste time sorting out duplication.
- Encourage quantity. The greater the number of ideas, the greater the likelihood of useful ones.
- Don't be too anxious to close out this phase. When a plateau is reached, let things rest awhile then pick up again.

Idea Evaluation Phase.   The second step is to evaluate the ideas.

- Review the list for duplication.
- State or develop evaluation criteria.
- Discuss and evaluate each idea listed.
- Select an idea (or ideas) that best meets the objective.

Nominal Group Technique

The main value of the nominal group technique is that it minimizes group conformity and maximizes participation. This structured process first has group members write individual responses, then report them to the group. Use this technique in addition to other group techniques discussed previously.

Ideas Generation Phase

- Each group member privately lists all ideas he or she can generate in response to the question presented to the group.
- Go around the group taking turns reporting one idea at a time and list the ideas in front of the group.
- Group members may cross off of their lists similar ideas reported out by others. Likewise, they may add ideas that others remind them of.
- The process continues until all ideas are reported.

Ideas Evaluation Phase

- After discussing the ideas listed, each member rates each idea on a 1 to 10 scale for feasibility.

- Ratings are reported by each member, and the ratings for each idea are added together for a total group rating of each idea listed.

- Ideas with low total ratings are dropped from the list (for example, total ratings of less than three times the number of group members).

- The ideas remaining are again discussed, rated, and summarized; those receiving low ratings are dropped from the list.

- This process is repeated three or four times until a clear group choice remains.

Group Decisions by Consensus

In making group decisions, working toward consensus makes full use of available resources and allows conflicts to be resolved creatively. The following discussion is from an article by Jay Hall entitled "Decisions, Decisions, Decisions" that appeared in *Psychology Today,* November 1971, (used with permission).

Consensus is difficult to reach, so not every group decision will meet with everyone's complete approval. Complete unanimity is not the goal—it is rarely achieved. But each individual should be able to accept the group's decision on the basis of logic and feasibility. When all group members feel this way, you have reached consensus, and the judgment may be entered as the group's decision. This means, in effect, that a single person can block the group if he or she thinks it necessary; at the same time, this option should be used in the best sense of reciprocity. Here are some guidelines to use in achieving consensus:

1. Avoid arguing for your own position. Present your position as lucidly and logically as possible, but listen to the other members' reactions and consider them carefully before you press your point.

2. Do not assume that someone must win and someone must lose when discussion reaches a stalemate. Instead, look for the next-most-acceptable alternative for all parties.

3. Do not change your mind simply to avoid conflict and to reach agreement and harmony. When agreement seems to come too quickly and easily, be suspicious. Explore the reasons and be sure everyone accepts the solution for basically similar or complementary reasons. Yield only to positions that have objective and logically sound foundations.

4. Avoid conflict-reducing techniques such as majority vote, averages, coin-flips, and bargaining. When a dissenting member finally agrees, don't feel that he or she must be rewarded by being allowed to "win" on some later point.

5. Differences of opinion are natural and expected. Seek them out and try to involve everyone in the decision process. Disagreements can help the group's decision because with a wide range of information and opinions, there is a greater chance that the group will hit upon more adequate solutions.

Conducting Effective Staff Meetings

Meetings are one of the most efficient ways to include group members in what's going on. However, if not properly handled they can waste time, accomplish nothing worthwhile, and become frustrating experiences. You can avoid this through advance planning and attention to what takes place during the meeting.

What Kind of Meeting Do You Need?

Meetings come in four basic types. Each is designed to accomplish a different purpose and is run quite differently from the others.

Information Meetings. These meetings are used to pass along information to those in attendance. They may be attended by a large number of people who listen to what is said. Little opportunity exists for questions. You must be well prepared in order to hold interest and communicate clearly.

Discussion Meetings.   Use discussion meetings to share ideas, opinions, feelings, and information about a particular topic in order to ensure complete understanding. Discussion meetings do not result in a decision or action plan. They typically have two applications. One application is to clarify something with workgroup members, for example a procedure or policy. The other is when you want to understand others' viewpoints or obtain information prior to making a decision. A positive, supportive climate should exist in order for people to feel comfortable voicing their ideas.

Problem-Solving Meetings.   Problem-solving meetings are used to pool the information and knowledge of those in attendance. When you're unsure of the cause of a problem, or there are several different ways to handle it, a meeting can result in the best solution. You should limit these meetings to the people who can contribute worthwhile information. A positive climate is necessary, and a structured orderly process is required to identify the problem then generate solution alternatives.

Decision-Making Meetings.   When a decision will need the support of the group in order to be successfully carried out, a decision-making meeting should be held. Decision-making meetings vary in size, depending on the number of people whose support is needed. When the group is larger than ten people, voting is probably the best way to reach a decision. The group may set a higher than simple majority vote requirement—for example, two-thirds or three-quarters. With ten people or fewer, discussion and agreement usually form a satisfactory procedure.

Before the Meeting

Much of the success or failure of a meeting is related to the planning done before the meeting is started. One step to assuring success is to see that the following issues are properly dealt with. (See Exhibit 11.4 for an example of a planning worksheet for meetings.)

Be Sure a Meeting Is Necessary.   Many meetings are held that never should have been called. Consider your objec-

EXHIBIT 11.4   Worksheet for Planning a Meeting

1. Objective: What end result do you want to achieve?

   _____

   _____

   _____

2. Type of meeting: Check the appropriate type for your meeting. This tells you the leadership style to use, the communications pattern to foster, how to set up your meeting room, and who should attend.

   ___Information   ___Problem solving
   ___Discussion   ___Decision making

3. Participants: Who should attend? Be sure to include, as appropriate, those with authority to decide, information to be used, whose commitment is needed, or who needs to know.

   _____

   _____

   _____

4. Agenda: Who is responsible for preparing and distributing the agenda? How will participants be included in developing the agenda?

   _____

   _____

   _____

5. Physical arrangements: What facilities and equipment are required? How should the meeting room be set up?

   _____

   _____

   _____

Exhibit 11.4   (*continued*)

6. Evaluation methods: How will the meeting be evaluated in order to improve the next session?

_____

_____

_____

tive. What are you trying to accomplish? Then consider if a meeting is the best way to achieve that objective. There are alternatives to holding a meeting. For example, would it be better to make a few phone calls, write a memorandum, or meet individually with the people involved?

Pick the Best Time.   Some meetings fail because they're too far removed from the event they're concerned with, or because they're called for the wrong day of the week or time during the day. In order to hold participant interest, the subject of your meeting should be very high on everyone's priority list. If your subject has to compete for attention, it may lose. Consider other demands on the participants such as work deadlines, operating problems, and personal issues.

Select Attendees.   As a general rule of thumb, you want to select the *minimum* number of appropriate people. Consider the objective of your meeting. If you want to solve a problem, you need people who can contribute knowledge. If you want to make a decision, you need to involve the people who will be responsible for implementing the decision. If you are passing on information, who needs to know the information? If you are holding a discussion, who is affected and who can contribute? Having decided on the appropriate people to attend, give each a specific and clear invitation to the meeting.

Prepare an Agenda.   All meetings need an agenda. Those in attendance need to know what will be dealt with and approximately how much time to set aside for the meeting. If possible, check ahead of time with participants for their ideas of what should be included on the agenda. If this isn't possible, take a few minutes at the beginning of the meeting and prepare an agenda.

Arrange the Meeting Place.   The meeting room and any needed equipment should be thought of and arranged for well in advance of your meeting. Participants need comfortable seating, adequate space, and proper lighting and ventilation. The room arrangement should support the type of meeting you plan to conduct. As a guideline, you want those who will be talking to each other to be able to maintain eye contact. Auditorium- or classroom-style seating is okay for information or discussion meetings. However, in problem-solving and decision-making meetings, a circular arrangement is preferred.

During the Meeting

Your attitude and activities during the meeting set the tone and either contribute to or detract from its quality. You want to accomplish your objective in a minimum amount of time without anyone feeling railroaded or left out. You want participants to leave the meeting feeling that something worthwhile was achieved. To do this, several issues need your attention.

Manage Time Effectively.   As a standard, use the first 15 minutes of your meeting as effectively as the last 15. Start promptly. Address the purpose of the meeting and adjourn when you've achieved your purpose. Occasionally you may have more to cover than you feel time will allow. In this case, involve the group in prioritizing the items on your agenda. Then address the items in priority order. If time runs out, you'll at least have handled the most important items.

Clearly State the Meeting's Purpose.   Even though you have an agenda, all participants may not agree on the meeting's purpose. To overcome this potential problem, start out with a statement of purpose. Any misunderstandings can then be resolved and won't interfere later on with the meeting's progress.

Exercise Leadership. There's a middle ground between directing a meeting and letting it drift out of control. That middle ground is leadership. Good meetings have leadership. The leadership needs of a meeting depend on the type of meeting it is. Some of the necessary activities of a leader include the following.

- *Keep on topic.* One of the most common complaints about meetings is that they drift off their topic. Keep attention focused on an issue until it is resolved or the group agrees to set it aside. Use your agenda to screen out unrelated conversations.

- *Manage air time.* Some participants may want to do all the talking while others seem to have nothing to say. Make room in the discussion and invite in those who are less participative.

- *Elicit information.* There's a tendency to express conclusions without sharing background information that led to the conclusions. Ask probing questions to bring out the reasons why people feel as they do or want to do as they propose.

- *Compare points of view.* When several ideas are proposed for solving a problem or reaching a decision, compare and contrast the ideas—show where they are alike and where they differ. Then encourage the development of other alternatives that reduce the differences.

- *Integrate and test for decision.* After considerable discussion, a meeting often drifts because no one brings it to a conclusion. This is part of your job. Integrate the various ideas and suggestions you've heard and propose a decision on the issue. It may not be the final decision, but it gets people working toward a final one.

- *Watch for loss of attention.* Pay attention to your group for nonverbal signals that suggest they're losing interest. When you notice these signals, make some changes in the way the meeting is going. For example, you can speak more loudly and more rapidly, ask questions, call a break, or even adjourn the meeting.

- *Exemplify supportive behavior.* Do not embarrass or put down anyone for participating in the meeting. Statements like "That's a dumb idea" will turn off discussion. Even when you feel a suggestion is short on quality, thank the person for speaking up.

- *Manage conflict.* Occasionally two or more people may have strongly held differing views on how something should be done. An effective leader will assist them in working this through by helping them understand each other, identifying the imperatives in their proposals, and using other group members to come up with additional alternatives. Sometimes, discussion may become so heated that it's best to get off the subject for a while. When this seems to be the situation, either table the issue until later in the meeting or call for a brief break.

- *Summarize accomplishments.* End every meeting with a summary of what was accomplished during the meeting. Participants often fail to recognize the benefit of their having been a part of the meeting. Your summary should make this clear. As appropriate, include a review of decisions made, actions planned, and who has agreed to do what by when.

After the Meeting

Your responsibilities don't end when a meeting is adjourned. Three general areas of responsibility still remain: evaluation, summary, and action.

Evaluate the Meeting.   Evaluation is an important part of the growth and development process. All meetings should be examined from the point of view of how they could be run better next time. There are three general ways to accomplish an evaluation: questionnaire, interview, self-critique.

- *Questionnaire.* You can distribute a questionnaire, or evaluation form, to all of the participants. Then study the responses to identify improvement opportunities. Or, you could summarize the questionnaire responses and then, at your next meeting, spend some time discussing ways to improve. Exhibit 11.5 is an example of a meeting evaluation form you might use or adapt for your evaluations.

EXHIBIT 11.5   Example of a Meeting Evaluation Form

Circle one number that best describes how well our group works together.

	Low						High	
Task accomplishment	1	2	3	4	5	6	7	8
Use of time	1	2	3	4	5	6	7	8
Use of people's ideas	1	2	3	4	5	6	7	8
Conflict resolution	1	2	3	4	5	6	7	8
Goal clarity	1	2	3	4	5	6	7	8
Teamwork	1	2	3	4	5	6	7	8
Effective listening	1	2	3	4	5	6	7	8
Leveling	1	2	3	4	5	6	7	8

What can we do to improve our working together?

_____

_____

_____

In our group meetings, what is most helpful for you? Least helpful?

_____

_____

_____

_____

- *Interview.* You may choose to visit with participants in person or by telephone to get their critique of your meeting. Again, summarize the responses and look for improvement opportunities.

- *Self-critique.* The minimum evaluation would be to personally and privately go over the experience. This could lead you to observations of where improvement might be needed. You'll certainly know if the meeting room was adequate or if the time allocation was appropriate. You may *not* know, however, how people react to your leadership or if some important topic was left off the agenda.

Distribute Action Plan Summary.   Write and distribute a list of decisions made and action plans agreed to in the meeting. It's not necessary to provide complete minutes of most meetings in business and industry. However, a memorandum summarizing decisions is an important part of any meeting where agreements were made. It prevents different views of what was agreed upon from emerging as time passes and memories wane.

Take Agreed Upon Action.   If during the meeting you agreed to do anything, get on with carrying out your agreement. Putting things off leads to neglect. It also suggests to others that you lack interest.

✔ Checklist for Conducting Staff Meetings

- Arrange an adequate meeting place.
- Invite the minimum number of appropriate people.
- State the purpose of the meeting.
- Prepare an agenda.
- Keep the discussion on the topic.
- Involve everyone in the discussion.
- Keep the discussion moving—don't waste time.
- Close the meeting with a summary of accomplishments.
- Periodically evaluate your meetings to improve their quality.
- Write and distribute a list of the decisions made and the action plans developed in the meeting.

Improving Group Effectiveness

Since effectiveness has a direct bearing on productivity, every supervisor must be concerned about maintaining the effectiveness of his or her workgroup. You can use group-centered decision making to achieve this objective and, at the same time, contribute to building an effective team.

What Is Productivity?

Productivity, in the context of a workgroup, is essentially a measure of the group's efficiency. Productivity can be calculated by dividing the measurable units of goods or services by the resources used to generate them. This gives an indication of how efficient the group is in converting inputs to outputs. See Figure 11.1.

$$\text{Productivity} = \frac{\text{Output}}{\text{Input}}$$

$$\text{Productivity} = \frac{\text{Quantity} \times \text{Quality}}{\text{Input}}$$

$$\text{where: Quality} = 1 - \left(\frac{\text{Rejects}}{\text{Quantity}}\right)$$

Figure 11.1 Formulas for calculating productivity

Every workgroup processes some form of input into some kind of output, whether in the form of a product or a service. (See Figure 11.2.) The total system of input to output should be examined when you look for ways to increase productivity. In terms of the overall system, productivity can be increased in the following ways:

- By generating more output with the same level of input
- By generating the same level of output with less input
- By generating more output with a proportionately smaller increase in input

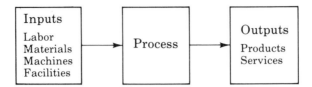

Figure 11.2 A simplified systems model

- By generating less output with a proportionately greater reduction in inputs
- By increasing quality

Group-Centered Change

Change can be initiated by you personally, by a consultant, or by involving the group. Efforts to improve group effectiveness, however, are often more successful when they include group members. This can be either through total group involvement or through a task force made up of group members. In either case, the results are usually improved by assigning a consultant to work with the group who is familiar with both group process and productivity concepts. Your improvement effort needs the full support of upper management before it's begun. Otherwise, group members may become frustrated if they're blocked from implementing the results of their efforts. The following steps should be taken after the approval in principle has been received from management:

1. Evaluate present methods.
2. Select areas with improvement potential.
3. Develop change strategy.
4. Obtain appropriate approvals of strategy.
5. Implement change.
6. Evaluate new methods.

Where and What to Change to Increase Productivity

In addition to input, process, and output, it's usually beneficial to also examine workgroup organization and relationships.

Job enlargement, job enrichment, and work teams have all contributed substantially to increased productivity through more interesting work.

Output. Consider what your group produces. Could you be more effective if your output was modified, packaged differently, or delivered differently? Is everything you produce essential to the operation of the business? Any group that has existed for several years is probably turning out something that's no longer required. If you provide reports, are they all really used, or are they simply received and filed? Consider the form of your output. Can it be redesigned so your customers can utilize it better? When you've identified your essential output and its most effective form, you've identified your group's reason for existing. You can now turn to other areas.

Job Design. Consider the tasks or activities you have grouped together into each job. Is there opportunity for group members to do interesting and varied tasks in order to avoid boredom? Do they turn out an identifiable product or are they doing only a step or two in the total production process? Can efficiency be gained by combining work in close proximity to avoid or reduce travel between tasks? Three basic patterns of operative-level work exists:

- *Serial.* Production moves step by step to completion with each step handled by a different person.
- *Subunit assembly.* Several production steps are combined and handled by one person.
- *Unit assembly.* All the steps required to produce a finished product are handled by the same person.

Job Enlargement. Job enlargement consolidates tasks at the same level of complexity. It is commonly called horizontal job loading. Job enlargement provides variety of task involvement and an opportunity to identify more closely with a finished product. It results in (1) combining steps in a serial production process so there are fewer work stations in the total system or (2) adopting either a subunit or unit assembly process.

Job Enrichment.   Job enrichment moves some of the traditional management functions to lower levels in the organization. It is commonly called "vertical job loading." Job enrichment provides opportunity for planning, decision making, problem solving, and controlling to be added to the doing of the work. As a result, group members experience a greater sense of ownership in their output. This generally leads to increased work quality and personal satisfaction. Key elements in the process are:

- Forming natural work units
- Combining tasks into complete jobs
- Establishing client relationships when appropriate
- Moving decision making down to the lowest possible level
- Opening feedback channels

Work Teams.   Work teams operate as a unit, are self-contained, and include all the skills necessary for performing the work assigned to them. They typically enjoy freedom to organize their own efforts to suit their own unique interests. This form of organization capitalizes on the social dimension of work-centered relationships. Work teams may be an ongoing approach to day-to-day operations or may be ad hoc task teams brought together temporarily to address a particular task.

Goals with Feedback.   Another way to increase productivity is to set production output goals and then let people know how they are doing relative to the goals. To be effective, goals need to be realistic, and it helps if group members have a say in setting them. Without support from the individuals involved, the exercise is doomed to failure. Group goals stimulate cooperation within workgroups and competition between groups. Individual goals, on the other hand, promote competition among workgroup members.

Incentives.   What rewards or acknowledgments do group members experience for good performance? Key areas to include in your examination are the salaries, benefits, and opportunities afforded group members who support and contribute to your improvement efforts. When examining the area of incentives, start with determining what competitive practices exist in your community. You need to be in line with competition in order to attract and hold the manpower you need. Then look at administrative practices. Are incentives equitably administered? Is there a direct relationship between performance and reward? Do those who contribute more receive more in return? Often, well-intended incentive and reward systems cause more dissatisfaction than they do motivation because of administrative practices. Be particularly cautious of any system that restricts the number who can participate—for example, one in which only 10 percent of the group can receive a merit award. Many people respond to these restrictions by giving up rather than competing.

Systems and Procedures. Are members of your group using the most efficient ways to get things done? Can procedures be simplified? This area encourages people to work smarter rather than harder. Again, it's a good idea to get employees involved in looking at how they do things and seek out more efficient ways. Eliminate unnecessary activities and look for the easiest way to do what remains.

Planning and Scheduling. In some workgroups, many potentially productive hours are wasted waiting for materials or the services of others, which are required to move ahead on the work to be done. Recognizing this, some offices schedule mail handling personnel to be at work an hour earlier than others, so that morning mail will already be on everyone's desks when they arrive. How can *you* improve your planning and scheduling to reduce or eliminate waste? Inventories of materials and supplies are another area worth considering. Are things available when needed? And are purchases made in the most economical quantities that balance quantity discounts against storage space and potential loss due to deterioration and obsolescence?

Group Members. The most important input in your production process is the talent and energy of your workgroup members. Do you have the proper number of people with the right mix of talent? For example, you might be able to substantially increase your group's output by adding a person with a special skill. Is there a bottleneck somewhere? Do people have to wait for a particular service or activity? The addition of a typist might increase the output of an office. The addition of a mechanic might increase the output of a machine shop. Check with those involved in the major activity of your group to see if support personnel are needed. Also examine the following areas of personnel administration.

- *Selection.* Consider the qualifications of people being hired into your group. Are new employees interested in the work and able to handle it? The average education in the workforce today is quite high. This frequently leads to hiring overly qualified employees who soon become bored or leave for other jobs. In either case, the effectiveness and efficiency of your group is affected.

- *Orientation.* How are new members brought into the group? They should be made to feel welcome, given a tour of relevant facilities, advised of appropriate rules and regulations, and be introduced to other workgroup members.

- *Training.* Finally, look at the training provided to prepare new employees to take over their jobs. Ideally, you should hire people with the knowledge and experience to immediately become a contributing member of your group. However, you'll seldom enjoy this ideal. Usually some training will be required. See that it's well designed and well presented in order to teach the skills required for effective performance.

Relationships.   A workgroup is a social entity. It provides the setting for the satisfaction of the social needs of its members. This social dimension is vital to the success of the group. What group members do for one another either contributes to or detracts from the achievement of the group's purpose. Through organization, provide opportunity for relationships to develop. Your objective is to build a group characterized by trust, cooperation, and support among group members. Another dimension of relationships exists with interfacing workgroups and members of those groups. Generally, two-way rather than one-way relationships are more satisfying. People enjoy and gain from discussions about issues affecting them personally as well as factors affecting their jobs. Therefore consider establishing contacts between the people doing work and those people for whom it is being done.

Materials.   An analysis of your materials input should include both the form and source. Are there materials available that would be easier to work with, more reliable, or require fewer steps to convert into outputs? Are more reliable, economical sources available? Can contracts be negotiated to reduce unit costs? Would your supplier be willing to customize your materials or their packaging to make handling them easier? Can more economical delivery methods be used?

Machines.   Computer technology has greatly expanded the capabilities of machines. Two significant areas of application are the storage and retrieval of information and computerized control of other machines. What opportunities exist for you to increase your group's effectiveness by replacing existing machines with more reliable, more efficient ones? Also, where can human effort be replaced with machines in routine, repetitive tasks? Frequently, computer-based information systems are both more reliable and faster. When considering the range of opportunities in this area, don't go overboard. Idle machine capacity ordinarily isn't a wise investment. If a typist is able to turn out the work you need on a standard electric typewriter, there's no need to invest in a computer-based word processing system. However, if the computer-based system could turn out the work of *several* typists, it could be a wise move.

Facilities.   In looking at facilities, three areas should be considered. First, is there sufficient space for the activities normally carried out by your workgroup? Second, consider the effect of the facilities on employees. Is there adequate temperature control, ventilation, and lighting? Are the facilities maintained and kept clean? Facilities need to be adequate but not elaborate. Inadequate facilities are inefficient and lead to employee dissatisfaction. However, elaborate facilities do not contribute anything to productivity. Third, consider the layout of work areas, restrooms, central storage facilities, and so on, to minimize confusion and wasted motion. Are these factors contributing to a smooth flow of work or do they create delays and contribute to confusion? Taking the cost into account, would it be feasible to have off-site facilities for such needs as warehouse space and meeting rooms? Based on frequency of use, would it be better to rent such space as needed rather than always have it available but use it infrequently?

Resistance to Change

You should anticipate resistance to your efforts at change by those the change affects. This resistance is fairly common. It can best be handled when you consider its causes and understand how to deal with it. The following ideas will help you identify and overcome resistance to change.

Reasons for Resisting Change

People resist change for many reasons—some of these they recognize and are willing to discuss, others they do not recognize. The reasons generally can be separated into three major categories—economic, personal, and social.

Economic.   These involve pay and employment. In some way or other people often fear that if the proposed change is adopted, their economic benefits of work will be diminished. This can range from actual fear of being terminated, being demoted, or having one's hours of work cut back (including the loss of regular overtime), to fear of having to work harder for the same or less pay.

Personal.   The list of personal reasons for resisting change is limited only by the uniqueness of individual personalities. Some people feel that change implies present methods are inadequate. And they resent this as criticism. Some employees dislike outside interference in their work, or some of the people involved in the change effort. Others resent the lack of participation in setting up the change. Frequently people resist change because they see it as benefiting only the company rather than employees or the public. Sometimes people resist change because they fear their level of skill, and the pride they have in it, will be reduced. Or they expect greater specialization will lead to boredom, monotony, and a decreased sense of personal worth. Some people are simply apprehensive about the unknown, so they resist any change. Others just don't like to have to learn new ways of doing their job.

Social.   Social reasons for resisting change center on the relationships established in the present workgroup. Some people dislike breaking up present social ties and making new social adjustments. Some fear that the new situation will be less satisfying than the present one. Or they may see the change leading to greater social isolation if they enjoy a high level of social contact, or requiring greater contact if they prefer to work alone.

Dealing with Resistance to Change

Overcoming potential resistance to your improvement effort should be one of the first considerations following approval in principle from upper management. If the change effort is well thought out, many of the reasons people resist change can be avoided. The following points should guide your effort:

- *Avoid trivial and unnecessary change.* Since change is unsettling to many employees, make sure what you are trying to achieve is worth the unrest it potentially will cause in the workgroup.
- *Safeguard group members from economic loss.* Since fear of economic loss is so significant, take steps to safeguard group members. This might include help in placing people in other parts of your organization, coordinating placements with other organizations in the community, maintaining existing wages until other opportunities open up, or providing severance pay allowances.
- *Share economic gains with group members.* This isn't as common as safeguarding for loss. However, look for ways

to share the gain. This could include increased wages, a one-time bonus payment, contributions to savings or retirement funds, or improvements in facilities.

• *Keep everyone informed.* When change is contemplated, it is often picked up on the grapevine. People then begin speculating about what will happen and what the impact will be. You can avoid this kind of activity, and the negative consequences of it, by providing open and full communication of all available details of the change effort.

• *Provide opportunity for participation.* The whole principle of group-centered change rests on two issues—information and commitment. Provide as much opportunity as possible for people to participate in determining the need for change and the actual change to be made. By doing so, you develop support for the change effort and thereby minimize potential resistance.

• *Reinforce acceptance.* When the change has been introduced, provide support and reinforcement for adopting the change program. If training is required, see that it's provided. Express your appreciation to those who willingly try to make it work. Counsel those who seem to be resisting your efforts.

✔ Checklist for Improving Group Effectiveness

• Share with your group any information on organization plans and feedback on group performance.

• Through staff meetings, involve the group in setting workgroup goals.

• Utilize small groups to solve problems and make recommendations for improved workgroup operations.

• Look for ways to improve the productivity of your workgroup.

• Involve group members in the search for increased effectiveness and efficiency.

Your Action Guide

The social nature of workgroups is often overlooked in the search for ways to increase group effectiveness. Group-centered supervision touches the group as a social system and utilizes the power of the group to both set and achieve high performance goals. In the process, the talents of group members are freed up to contribute to group objectives.

An effective way to bring the talents of the group to bear on work-related issues is to involve the group in deciding on goals to be attained, courses of action to attain them, and solutions to problems encountered along the way. This allows information held by group members to contribute to the quality of decisions made. At the same time, it allows for the creativity of group interaction to develop effective solutions to problems. As a by-product of involvement, commitment to the goals and plans developed ensures their attainment.

The forum for group involvement is the staff meeting. Many well-intentioned supervisors have added to the frustration and unrest in their workgroups by conducting sloppy, ineffective meetings. You can run effective meetings simply by planning, organizing, leading, and controlling them. Plan your agenda, facilities, and participants. Organize the material to be dealt with in a way that makes it easy to follow the flow of your meeting. Exercise leadership to keep everyone involved and moving toward the final objective. But don't press too hard for your point of view. No one likes to be railroaded! Finally, control the topic of discussion, the amount of air time afforded each participant, and the use of time.

An effective group is a productive group. To maintain group effectiveness, it's necessary from time to time to examine how well the group is carrying out its mission. You can do this quite well by group-centered means. If the nature of your work permits, consider a series of staff meetings to examine and recommend improvement in the group's operation. If you can't get everyone together, consider a task force of qualified group members. In any case, operate with your management's approval, keep everyone informed, and seriously consider augmenting your group with a qualified consultant.

- ↙ Analyze your group's output. Is everything produced of value to the organization?

- ↙ Examine the layout of facilities and change it as necessary to increase efficiency.

- ↙ Examine work schedules and change them as necessary to increase efficiency.

- ↙ Examine administrative procedures and eliminate or modify them as necessary to improve efficiency.

- ↙ Consider updating the technology of your operation to increase efficiency.

- ↙ Examine personnel policies and practices and change them as necessary.

- ↙ Consider modifying job design to increase interest and efficiency.

- ↙ Establish productivity goals and provide feedback on goal attainment.

- ↙ Examine the materials you use and consider ways of improving efficiency through form, volume, and source.

- ↙ Include group members in your productivity improvement effort.

References

Robert Blake and Jane Srygley Mouton, *Productivity: The Human Side* (New York: AMACON, 1981).

Jay Hall, "Decisions, Decisions, Decisions," *Psychology Today,* November 1971.

Marion E. Haynes, "Conduct Meetings That Get Things Done," *Hydrocarbon Processing,* September 1980.

Jay W. Lorsch and Paul R. Lawrence, *Managing Group and Intergroup Relations* (Homewood, Ill.: Richard D. Irwin, 1972).

Francis X. Mahoney, "Team Development," *Personnel* (seven-part series), September-October 1981 through September-October 1982.

Bobby R. Patton and Kim Griffin, *Decision-Making Group Interaction* (New York: Harper & Row, 1978).

Penelope Wond, Michael Doyle, and David Straus, "Problem Solving Through Process Management," *Management Review,* November 1973.

THE PERFORMANCE MANAGEMENT SYSTEM

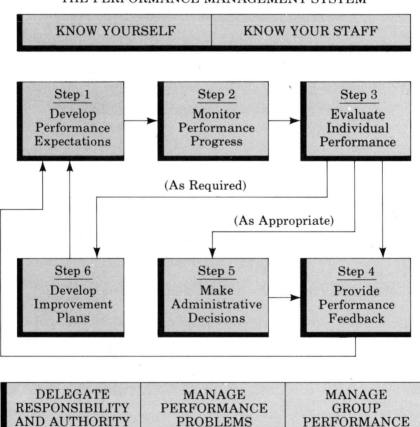

CHAPTER 12

The System
in Action—
A Case Study

As a result of reading this chapter you will

- See how the system and its steps are applied to ten hypothetical management situations and decisions
- Test your own understanding of the system
- Practice applying the principles in the steps

$\mathbf{I}$n this chapter you'll see the entire Performance Management System in action as we discuss Ralph Brown, a hypothetical production manager, and some of the situations he must deal with in his job. Ralph's responsibilities and the decisions he must make are quite typical of many supervisors. You're encouraged to actively consider alternatives and make your own recommendations regarding the decisions Ralph is faced with.

In the chapter you'll see how the steps become integrated into an active system for handling supervisory and management responsibilities and also to see how the way *you* might use the

Performance Management System measures up to an "ideal" application of it.

The hypothetical case of Ralph Brown includes ten decisions that Ralph must make as the new production manager of his company's Bayou Plant in the south-central United States. Ralph must consider several alternatives in each decision, some better than others. If you wish, you can put yourself in Ralph's place, keep score of your decisions, and at the end of the chapter see how well you applied the system.

Ralph Brown and the Bayou Plant

Ralph Brown is the newly appointed production manager at his company's Bayou Plant, which has been in operation for 27 years. As production manager, Ralph supervises three production lines, each operating 24 hours a day, 7 days a week. Each line is staffed by a lead operator and six other operators. Two general helpers work each shift. A production supervisor is in charge of each shift. There are 100 employees in the department, 8 of whom report directly to the production manager. See Figure 12.1 for an organization chart of the Bayou facility.

Ralph started with the company nine years ago upon graduation from a well-regarded state university. He holds a B.S. degree in industrial engineering and an M.B.A. degree in industrial management. To this point in his career he has worked primarily as an engineer in plant modernization and maintenance. He's also had short-term assignments as engineering inspector, maintenance supervisor, and operations supervisor. These assignments were recognized as training opportunities, although Ralph carried the full responsibilities while assigned to each. Ralph is seen by management to have potential beyond the level of plant general manager, and as possibly capable of attaining a corporate vice-presidency by the end of his career. Ralph's current assignment as production manager is intended to challenge his capabilities, develop him further as a manager, and bring new talent into a department that has been having some problems. If he does well in this assignment, he will probably remain in it for three to five years.

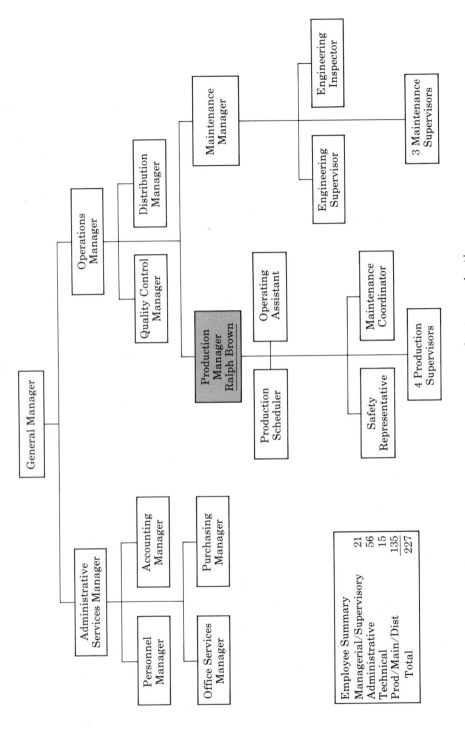

Figure 12.1 Bayou plant organization

Employee Summary	
Managerial/Supervisory	21
Administrative	56
Technical	15
Prod/Main/Dist	135
Total	227

The ten decisions Ralph faces during his first year as production manager at Bayou Plant involve

1. Getting established as manager
2. Holding the first staff meeting
3. Developing performance expectations
4. Providing feedback on performance
5. Handling performance problems
6. Staffing the management team
7. Creating a productivity task force
8. Acting on the task force's report
9. Reviewing a disciplinary recommendation
10. Making salary recommendations

Decision 1—Getting Established As Manager

Ralph recognizes the significance of this assignment to both his career and the company. Therefore, he is anxious to establish himself as manager of the department and be seen as supportive but in control. How should he go about this? Which of the following do you think he should do first? Second? Third?

1. Post a bulletin board notice stating that he is the new manager, effective the first of the month, and summarizing his prior experience and education.
2. Visit each shift and meet everyone in the department. Include in the visit a tour of the facilities to check over the status of the equipment in the department.
3. Meet privately with each of the other managers in the plant to understand their role and the opportunities that exist for them to contribute to the effectiveness of the production department.
4. Hold a staff meeting with the people reporting directly to him and outline his approach to becoming acquainted with the department and its people.

5. Meet privately with each of the people reporting directly to him and discuss their background, qualifications, and the problems and opportunities they see in the department.

6. Spend the first several days going over the records of the department in order to fully assess its current status. This would include production, maintenance and safety records as well as the individual personnel files of his staff.

Analysis

Getting established as a new supervisor or manager is critical to effectiveness. Handled correctly, you can immediately win the support of your staff. Handled incorrectly, you may have to work long and hard to recover. Score your decision as follows.

1. Bulletin board notices are generally seen as cold and impersonal. They should not be used for issues affecting human relations in the workplace. Summarizing Ralph's background will only highlight differences in terms of relatively little service and substantial education. Score 0 points for this choice.

2. Meeting everyone in the department is an important and appropriate gesture. It allows them to see Ralph as interested in them and allows Ralph to see the operation and get a feel for the climate within the group. Care should be exercised to avoid taking commitments on insufficient information. Score 5 points for second, and 3 points for either first or third.

3. An important step in getting established as a new manager is to meet with other managers who will provide support services. Ralph needs to begin establishing these relationships to ensure cooperation between his and other departments. However, Ralph's own department and people must come first. Therefore, based on priorities, score 0 points for first, 1 for second, and 3 for third.

4. Holding a staff meeting with the people reporting directly to Ralph enhances their position as members of his team. Score 5 points for first, 3 for second, and 1 for third.

5. Meeting privately with each member of the management team allows Ralph and his team members to become better acquainted. During these meetings Ralph should be assessing the maturity level of each member of his team and listening for any problems that might be revealed. Score 3 points for third, 1 for second, and 0 for first.

6. Studying the background of the department provides important clues to potential problems as well as information on areas where the department has done well. Being familiar with the history of the department will enhance Ralph's credibility as he meets and talks with others. The question, then, is where this step should fall in the sequence of events. Score 5 points for third, 3 for second, and 1 for first.

The recommended sequence of the five actions would be:

1. Hold staff meeting with management team and lay out your plan.
2. Visit each shift and meet everyone in the department.
3. Go over the records of the department looking for strong and weak performance areas.
4. Meet privately with each member of the management team.
5. Meet with managers of support functions.

Decision 2—Holding the First Staff Meeting

Since it is considered desirable to meet immediately with the management team, thought must be given to planning the meeting. This will be Ralph's first significant contact with these people. Therefore, it must be handled in a way that will begin to win their support and commitment. If you wish, list the things you think Ralph should cover in his meeting and how he might best handle it. In thinking about this decision consider the ideas on how to get to know your staff presented in chapter 2.

Analysis

Some of the things Ralph should cover in this meeting are listed below. Give yourself the points shown in parentheses for each of the items on your agenda.

1. Show confidence in the group to either maintain or develop a high level of performance.   (2)

2. Express commitment to the group and willingness to help in any way necessary to make it a winning team. (3)

3. Detail a plan to meet everyone in the department, tour the facility and review performance records.   (5)

4. Set up private meetings with each of the team members.   (5)

5. Elicit their help and support. Clearly state an interest in their ideas and suggestions for improvement.   (3)

6. Share your management philosophy with the group. (2)

(If you included *all* of these items on your list, add an additional 5 points as a bonus.)

Ralph's Look into the Department

After meeting with his management team, Ralph made an investigation into the status of the department. He toured the facilities and met everyone on the lines, reviewed all the available records, interviewed the members of his management team individually, and talked with each of the managers of support departments. He found the following.

Management Team Members

Generally, the management team is well qualified through experience but is lax in applying modern management techniques. The position of operating assistant has been vacant for two months. Apparently, in anticipation of the change in department managers, the job was left vacant so Ralph himself could select a person to fill the position. Figure 12.2 shows the members of the management team.

Bill Wilson, Production Supervisor.   Bill is the senior production supervisor in the department. He started as a supervisor 27 years ago when the Bayou Plant opened. He is 58 years old. He is a mature employee who enjoys the respect and support of the people on his shift.

John Smith, Production Supervisor.   John is the next oldest production supervisor in the department. He started as an operator when the plant opened, and had considerable prior experience as an operator in a similar plant. He was promoted to supervisor 24 years ago. He is 55 years old. Like Bill Wilson, John appears to be a mature employee who is well regarded by the people on his shift.

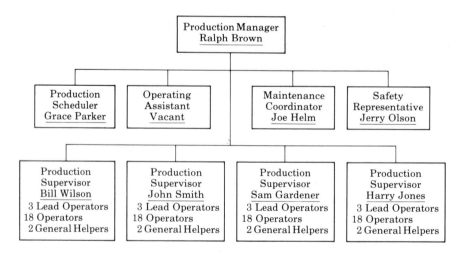

Figure 12.2 Organization of the Bayou Plant's production department

Sam Gardner, Production Supervisor. Sam is the next oldest production supervisor in the department. He too started as an operator when the plant opened. However, he was promoted to supervisor only 3 years ago after 12 years as an operator, 8 years as lead operator and 4 years as an operating assistant. He apparently did an excellent job as the operating assistant but is, at best, a marginal supervisor. He does not have the support and cooperation of the people on his shift. He is low-moderate in both job and personal maturity.

Harry Jones, Production Supervisor. Harry is the junior production supervisor in the department. He was promoted to the position two months ago from the operating assistant position, which he'd held for three years. He has eight years of service as an operator and lead operator. He's 32 years old. Although Harry is new and inexperienced in the production supervisor job, he seems to enjoy good relationships with the people on his shift. Ralph considers him to be low-moderate in job maturity but high-moderate in personal maturity.

Joe Helm, Maintenance Coordinator. Joe has worked at Bayou Plant for 18 years. He was promoted from operator to his present position six years ago. He is 41 years old. He seems to know his job and performs it at a satisfactory level. He has good relationships with the maintenance supervisors.

Jerry Olson, Safety Representative. Jerry has worked at Bayou Plant for 12 years. He was promoted from lead operator to safety representative three years ago. He is 37 years old. Jerry has done a good job of promoting safety programs that are generated at corporate headquarters but has not initiated any local efforts to reduce on-the-job injuries. He is well liked by everyone. Ralph considers him to be high-moderate in both job and personal maturity.

Grace Parker, Production Scheduler. Grace has worked at Bayou Plant eight years. She started as a laboratory technician in the quality control lab and moved to production scheduler five years ago. Before coming to Bayou Plant, she was a science and math teacher at the local high school. She is 37 years old. Ralph considers her to be high in both job and personal maturity. She does an outstanding job of translating sales forecast figures into production rates to maintain a minimum warehouse inventory of the plant's various product lines.

The Status of Significant Areas

Ralph soon discovered that his predecessor was generally uninvolved in the operation of the department. He enjoyed widespread popularity because he left people alone. This resulted in mixed performance from various members of the management team and a significant lack of training for people in new assignments. The following items were particularly noteworthy.

- *Facilities.* Although not the latest technology, the facilities are well maintained. Maintenance costs have been increasing. Some modernization should be considered.
- *Safety Record.* When compared to other company plants, it looks like the time lost due to on-the-job injuries could be improved.
- *Attendance.* Attendance overall needs improving. It is particularly poor on Sam Gardner's shift.
- *Turnover.* The turnover among production workers is reaching a critical level. Over the past four years it has steadily increased to the current level of 15 percent.
- *Production.* The volume of output is adequate but the quality needs improving. Reject rate overall is too high compared to other plants and is particularly high on Sam Gardner's shift.

Ralph's Plan

Ralph discussed his findings with the operations manager and received general agreement to a plan he'd developed to increase operating efficiency by developing an achievement-oriented climate within the production department. He plans to improve both productivity and morale by

- Setting realistic goals
- Providing feedback on performance

- Coaching and training members of his management team as necessary
- Fostering an open communications climate
- Involving as many department members as necessary and appropriate to solve departmental problems
- Setting reasonable rules and enforcing them fairly and equitably

Decision 3—Developing Performance Expectations

While the Bayou Plant has produced at an adequate level to meet sales demand, Ralph believes that there is potential to increase sales and production. Discussions with marketing department personnel turned up an attitude of "We sell all you produce." At the plant, the attitude is "We produce all they sell." Most people in the production department do not know what is expected of them and reflect a feeling that no one really cares what they produce.

Ralph believes the first step toward the goals he envisions for the department is to clarify expectations by setting specific goals and developing plans for their achievement in the following areas:

- Production volume
- Production quality
- Maintenance costs
- Safety
- Absenteeism
- Turnover

How should Ralph go about achieving this first step? Of the six procedures described below, which *three* would you advise Ralph to take? Your choices should reflect the concepts presented in chapter 3, Establishing Performance Expectations, step 1 of the Performance Management System, and the ideas in chapter 9 on delegating responsibility.

1. Meet privately with each team member and jointly set goals and discuss plans for achieving them.

2. Call a team meeting and advise each team member what his or her goals will be for the remainder of the year and ask them to develop plans for your review that will ensure reaching the specified goals.

✓ 3. Call a team meeting and jointly set goals in the six areas of concern and discuss possible ways to reach them.

4. Meet privately and advise each team member what his or her goals are and how they should be achieved.

✓ 5. Have each production supervisor meet with his shift and advise them of the departmental goals and solicit ideas on how to best attain them.

✓ 6. After jointly setting goals as a team, meet privately with each team member to discuss and develop plans for achieving them.

Analysis

Participative goal setting makes full use of the knowledge and experience of staff members, develops commitment to goal attainment, and provides clear direction for the department. Each of the six possible procedures is analyzed below.

1. Meeting privately with each team member to set goals and develop plans is not a bad strategy but has at least two potential drawbacks. It doesn't allow for interaction among team members and the team commitment this interaction can produce. Also, when goals are independently developed, some team members may feel their goals are unfair in comparison to others'. Score yourself 3 points for this choice.

2. Calling a team meeting and advising each member of his or her goals is likely to be seen as arbitrary. Asking everyone to submit plans for approval may demonstrate lack of trust or confidence. The sum of this strategy may be substantial resistance that will require extraordinary effort to counteract. Score yourself 0 points for this choice.

3. Calling a team meeting and jointly setting goals for the department fully utilizes the knowledge and experience of the group, develops it as a team, and develops commitment to goal attainment. Discussing possible ways of attaining the goals causes team members to begin to broaden their perspective on what can be done. Give yourself 10 points if you chose this option.

4. Meeting privately with each team member and advising him of his goals and how they are to be achieved does not stimulate desire for cooperation and commitment. Score 0 points if you chose this action.

5. Having each production supervisor meet with his shift to inform them of the departmental goals and solicit ideas from the group is a good way to begin to involve everyone in the department. Score 5 points if you chose this option.

6. After group goal setting, meeting privately with each team member to jointly discuss and develop plans to achieve goals allows flexibility in the amount of guidance Ralph may have to contribute to each set of plans. Since the level of maturity varies among team members, this would be particularly appropriate. Score 10 points for this choice.

In summary, Ralph should

- Meet with the management team and jointly set goals
- Pass goals on to all production shifts and solicit ideas
- Meet privately with team members and jointly develop plans

Decision 4—Providing Feedback on Performance

After goals for the department were established, Ralph met with the personnel manager, accounting manager, quality control manager, and maintenance manager to develop reporting systems that would keep him advised of progress toward the goals. (Monitoring performance progress, step 2 of the system, is discussed in chapter 4.)

The next decision Ralph faces is to determine the most effective means of passing on the performance data to members of his management team. He realizes there are several ways this can be handled. However, he wants to handle it in a way that will be most effective in motivating team members toward achieving the goals established earlier.

Which three of the following procedures would you advise Ralph to follow? Which of those three do you think will be most valuable to individual team members? (In considering the procedures, think back especially to chapter 6, Providing Performance Feedback, step 4 of the system. Chapter 5, Evaluating Individual Performance (step 3) should also be helpful.

1. Discussion of overall department performance in a monthly staff meeting, followed by postings on bulletin boards throughout the department.
2. Private discussions with individual team members of any deficiencies as they become apparent.
3. Monthly reviews with individual team members.
4. Quarterly reviews with individual team members.
5. Semiannual reviews with individual team members.
6. Annual reviews with individual team members.
7. Immediate discussions with individual team members when honest praise or correction is in order.
8. Immediate discussions with individual team members whenever a positive suggestion for improvement can be offered.

Analysis

Feedback on performance is an important but often neglected part of an effective performance management system. Effective feedback is timely and specific, and it deals with issues under the control of the one receiving the feedback. When group performance is required to achieve a goal, feedback should be to the group. However, discussion of ways to improve on substandard performance should be carefully considered so as not to criticize individuals in the presence of others. Each of the eight procedures is discussed below.

1. Monthly team review of overall performance followed by bulletin board postings keeps employees informed and involved, and it encourages team work. Give yourself 10 points for this choice.

2. Private discussions just of deficiencies never utilizes the motivational power of praise. It focuses only on the negative. Score 0 points for this choice.

3. Monthly reviews with individual team members are too frequent and will consume too much of Ralph's time. Score 3 points for this choice.

4. Quarterly reviews are a better frequency but still may be too time consuming. Score 5 points for this choice.

5. Semiannual reviews with individual team members is about the right frequency in most cases. Score 10 points for this choice.

6. Annual reviews with individual team members is not often enough in most cases. Score 5 points for this choice.

7. Immediate discussion with individual team members when honest praise or correction is in order is the most meaningful form of feedback. Score 15 points for this choice.

8. Immediate discussions with individuals when suggestions for improvement can be offered is not supportive or encouraging of good performance. Score 3 points for this choice.

Now double the points for the choice you selected as most valuable to the individual and add up all the points you scored for this decision.

Here's a summary of Ralph's best course for providing feedback on performance:

● Monthly review with team and posting of information in the department

- Semiannual reviews with individual team members
- Private discussions with team members immediately when honest praise or criticism can be offered

Decision 5—Handling Performance Problems

Of the seven members on the management team, four respond very well to the performance management system Ralph instituted. Grace Parker, Joe Helm, Bill Wilson, and John Smith all are making good progress toward their goals and appear eager to contribute their part to helping improve the production department generally. However, Sam Gardner, Harry Jones, and Jerry Olson are not meeting their goals. As a result of personal discussions with each of these people, Ralph could summarize the situation as follows.

Sam Gardner.   Sam's shift is lowest in goal attainment. Turnover and absenteeism are up; production volume and quality are down. Sam is convinced that the root of his problem is the quality and attitudes of the employees being hired. He maintains that they do not want to do any more than the minimum necessary to keep their jobs. Therefore, believes Sam, they take off work at every opportunity, are inattentive to details when they are on the job, and leave when an easier job comes along. He says he has tried everything he can think of to improve performance, but with no success.

Harry Jones.   Harry's shift is on target in production quality but has not met goals in production volume, absenteeism, or turnover. Trends in these three areas show that performance is holding at the historical rates—things aren't getting worse, but neither have they improved. Harry has achieved his improvement in quality by closer monitoring of his shift's operations and personal inspection of its output. He isn't confident in his role as supervisor and therefore does not make high performance demands of his staff.

Jerry Olson. Jerry has continued to implement safety programs as they are developed, and he conducts well-run safety meetings with each of the shifts. But the on-the-job injury rate continues at the same level. Jerry seems personally committed to safety but is at a loss in how to actually improve the production department's safety record.

Ralph's Strategy

What should be Ralph's basic strategy in working with each of these performance problems? What courses would you advise Ralph to take with Sam, Harry, and Jerry? In thinking about each case, consider some of the principles described in chapter 5, Evaluating Individual Performance (step 3 of the Performance Management System). Also recall the ideas in chapter 6, Developing Performance Improvement Plans.

Analysis

Individual performance is a function of the employee, the job he or she is assigned, and the situation within which the job is performed. There are two basic components to the employee's part in the process—willingness and ability. Willingness can be influenced by incentives, and ability can be influenced by training or coaching. However, there are no guarantees. There are only probabilities. Compare your thoughts to the following analyses.

Sam Gardner. Sam's performance record and his assessment of the situation suggests he is not suited for a supervisory job. He's been unable to win the support of his group and, in the process, he seems to have lost confidence in the members of the group. He did well as an operating assistant, which suggests he probably will perform well in a job that does not require supervision of others. Sam should be removed from his job as a production supervisor. However, because of his age, service, and prior record he is entitled to special treatment. Therefore, a good place for Ralph to start in resolving this problem would be to talk to Sam to see what *he* would like to do. Then Ralph should take Sam's preferences into account as much as possible in working out either a reassignment or early retirement. Score yourself 5 points for the decision to remove Sam as a production supervisor; score 3 points for considering reassignment and retirement; score 2 points if you planned to discuss alternatives with Sam before making a decision; and deduct 5 points if you planned to terminate Sam's services without pursuing other options.

Harry Jones.   Harry has potential to develop into a satisfactory production supervisor. He's hard working and committed. While he is supported by his group, he appears to be reluctant to establish and maintain discipline. Harry needs coaching in how to properly fulfill the requirements of his job. Ralph should meet privately with Harry, reinforce the aspects of his job he is doing well, and jointly develop plans to address the aspects of his job where he falls short. These plans should be specific and detailed; afterwards there should be frequent follow up to reinforce progress. Success will bolster Harry's confidence in handling some of the negative aspects of the job. Score 5 points for the decision to coach Harry; 2 points if you included reinforcement of current good performance in your plan; 3 points for jointly developing an action plan; and 5 points for follow up with Harry on his progress.

Jerry Olson.   Jerry seems to have a very narrow view of his job. He personally identifies with the department's safety record but concentrates on the presentation of programs. He needs to broaden his activities to include safety audits and training in proper work methods. Also, he needs to recognize that he is in a staff position and actual accountability for safety rests with the production supervisors. Ralph needs to meet with Jerry and go over a complete job description with him and then jointly develop action plans to address the areas of his job that are being neglected. Frequent follow up with Jerry is also called for. Additionally, in a team meeting, Ralph should clarify that production supervisors are accountable for safety on their shift and that Jerry is a resource to help them reach their safety goals. Score 5 points for a full review of job responsibilities; 3 points for jointly developing plans to address areas of deficiency;

2 points for follow up; and score 5 points for clarifying roles and accountabilities for safety among the production supervisors and the safety representative.

Decision 6—Staffing the Management Team

As other issues are resolved or come under control, Ralph is able to turn his attention to the vacant position of operating assistant.

Historically, this job has been used as a training assignment for production supervisors. Ralph wants to continue that practice. He does not want to fill the position with someone who does not have the potential to move up to the position of production supervisor. The operating assistant position includes four major areas of responsibility: (1) maintaining departmental records; (2) conducting training for new operators; (3) replacing current production supervisors when they are on vacation, sick leave, or personal leave; and (3) carrying out whatever special assignments might be made by the production manager.

What steps should Ralph follow in filling the operating assistant position? In what order should Ralph follow them?

Analysis

The typical personnel selection decision requires much more administrative time than normally expected. Key elements of the process include gaining appropriate approvals, developing job specifications, generating a candidate list, selecting a candidate, gaining appropriate approvals, advising the candidate, and finally handling the personnel administrative matters to implement the decision. Step 5 of the Performance Management System (chapter 7, Making Administrative Decisions) covers much of the process involved in promoting and hiring. Step 1 of the system (chapter 3) addresses how to develop job descriptions.

The specific steps Ralph should take are listed below. Score 2 points for each of these steps you've included on your own list. Score 5 bonus points if you have all of them, and score an additional 5 bonus points if you included a reason why each step should be taken.

1. Obtain approval to fill position from operations manager to ensure that the position is in fact authorized and budgeted in the department's manpower forecast.

2. Check with personnel manager to obtain whatever assistance is available and to confirm understanding of plant promotion and pay policies.

3. Update or develop a job description and list of specifications so that everyone involved will have a common understanding of what is being sought in candidates and so that each candidate's qualifications can be compared to the same set of listed requirements.

4. Advise the management team of the intent to fill the vacancy, lay out a plan for doing so, and request that possible candidates be identified.

5. Advise maintenance manager, quality control manager, and distribution manager of intent to fill vacancy and request any candidates they may have from their departments.

6. Gather qualifications data on candidates from personnel files, supervisory assessment, and candidate interviews. It is best to not rely only on supervisory recommendations. These recommendations should be augmented with objective data from the files and an assessment of interest level, which often is best obtained through interviews.

7. Select and prioritize the two or three best-qualified candidates by weighing all the data available. A back-up candidate is needed in case the number one choice turns the offer down.

8. Obtain the operations manager's approval of the selected candidate. This allows Ralph's supervisor to ensure that the selection has been equitable and objective.

9. Talk to the candidate selected and offer the promotion. Do not assume acceptance—check it out.

10. Initiate administrative procedures to accomplish the promotion, announce it, and obtain a replacement for the individual being promoted.

Here's a summary of the steps Ralph should take.

- Obtain necessary approvals
- Establish job specifications
- Generate candidates
- Evaluate candidate qualifications
- Make selection
- Implement decision

Decision 7—Productivity Task Force

Ralph becomes interested in the potential of a task force composed of department members that could scrutinize the department's operations. He discussed his idea with the plant's operations manager, who approved the plan but emphasized that the task force would be making recommendations for further management review, not making decisions for automatic implementation.

With this approval, Ralph presented the idea to his management team in one of their regularly scheduled staff meetings. He explained that he wanted three members of his management staff and four operators (one from each shift) to meet weekly. The sessions would continue for as long as necessary to develop recommendations. The task force would be free to invite anyone it chose to meet with it to present information. The task force was free to examine any part of the department's operation and make recommendations to improve productivity and morale.

The team accepted the idea, and Ralph appointed Grace Parker, Joe Helm, and John Smith to the task force. Additionally, he asked each production supervisor to select an operator to become a member. To aid with the selection, the team discussed qualifications and came up with the following list:

- Interested in project
- Open-minded
- Knowledgable/experienced
- Comfortable in group activity
- Diverse in background
- Well-regarded by peers

Ralph met with the task force at its first session. At this time he reviewed the objectives for the group and emphasized his support and confidence that the project would lead to worthwhile improvements in the department. He invited the group to come to him anytime he could be of help.

The task force chose to meet each Tuesday from 8:00 a.m. to 4:30 p.m. At the end of the third meeting Joe Helm reported to Ralph that the task force wasn't making progress. Joe said the group had gotten itself organized during the first session, at which time he was asked to be the group's leader. But the second and third sessions were discussions of what's wrong with the department rather than a search for opportunities for improvement. Right now, Joe feels very frustrated over the group's lack of progress. What do you think Ralph should do? Keep in mind the ideas and principles covered in chapter 12, Managing Group Performance. Six alternatives are described below. Which would be the best for Ralph to take?

1. Call a special meeting of the task force and try to get the project on track.
2. Meet privately with each task force member to assess the extent to which they are experiencing the same frustrations as Joe Helm.
3. Attend the next regularly scheduled session of the group to show an interest, but do not take an active part in the discussion.
4. Encourage Joe to stay with the project and offer suggestions on how to begin to focus the group's attention.
5. Attend the next regularly scheduled session of the group to review the task force's objectives and emphasize the

importance of getting on with looking at improvement opportunities.

6. Tell Joe not to worry, working with groups is always a frustrating experience. Then, leave it to Joe to work things out on his own.

Analysis

It takes time for a group to develop as a productive unit. Part of Joe's frustration may be due to the lack of understanding of this process. At this point, Ralph should not overreact. He has appointed good people to the group, so he should now have confidence in their willingness and ability to get the job done. Score your choice as indicated.

1. Calling a special session of the task force to try to get it on track is an overreaction. Score 0 points for this choice.

2. Meeting privately with each task force member would allow Ralph an opportunity to assess their frustration level and offer appropriate encouragement. However, it's too early in the project for this degree of involvement. Score 10 points for this choice.

3. If Ralph were to attend the next regularly scheduled session as an observer, it would appear that he was checking up on the group. Under the charter the group was given, this would be inappropriate. Score 0 points for this choice.

4. Offering Joe encouragement and discussing possible ways for him to direct the group is the best option at this time. It reinforces Joe's leadership position and does not direct the group's outcome. Score 15 points for this choice.

5. Attending the next regularly scheduled session of the group to review its objective and encourage progress again is an overreaction. If the group had been meeting for 20 weeks and had not made any more progress, this might be appropriate. Score 5 points for this choice.

6. Leaving Joe on his own at this time shows lack of concern for his problems. Joe is not a qualified group leader; he's a maintenance coordinator. He needs help and guidance in fulfilling his role with the group. If Ralph can't provide it, he should refer Joe to a qualified advisor on how to facilitate small group problem solving. Deduct 5 points if you selected this choice.

Decision 8—The Task Force Reports

The task force has worked through its difficulties and in its 15th meeting finalizes its recommendations. Below are highlights of the written report submitted to Ralph.

- In the past, the pay scale for operators was slightly higher than that paid by other companies in the area for similar work. Over the past four or five years, the differential has changed so that now the pay scale has fallen behind some companies in the area. It's recommended that a salary adjustment be authorized that will re-establish the old differential.

- The qualifications of applicants in the community has led to a plant practice of hiring overly qualified new employees. This has contributed to absenteeism, on-the-job injuries, and turnover due to boredom in lower level positions. It's recommended that employment standards be lowered to attract applicants who can find a higher level of personal satisfaction in the jobs available.

- Lead operators, operators, and general helpers all have ideas to contribute to bettering the department and are interested in voicing these ideas. It's recommended that each shift be allowed to participate in setting goals and contributing to the plans for their achievement.

- The technology of the plant is essentially the same as when the plant was built 27 years ago. Much of the cost of maintenance is a few items of equipment that experience the greatest frequency of failure. It's recommended that these items be replaced and that other equipment be studied for possible updating.

- An unreasonable amount of down time is experienced due to lack of response from the maintenance department on high-priority repairs. It's recommended that a mechanic be added to each shift to handle these emergency repairs.

As Ralph contemplates the report, he is satisfied with most of the recommendations and recognizes that considerable work lies ahead in getting them implemented. One recommendation, however, bothers him. The idea of adding a mechanic on each shift may not be the best response to the problem. Perhaps better procedures for classifying and reporting breakdowns would be a better solution.

What steps should Ralph take next? Six possible steps are listed below. Which of them should Ralph take? And in what order should he take them? (As with the previous decision, keep in mind the principles of chapter 12.)

1. Meet with the operations manager and endorse those task force recommendations with which you agree.

2. Meet with the personnel manager and request a wage survey and a study of hiring practices.

3. Meet with the maintenance manager and request that a modernization study of production department equipment be initiated.

4. Meet with Joe Helm and request him to initiate a study of maintenance procedures.

5. Meet with the task force to thank them for their effort and to discuss their recommendations in more detail.

6. Discuss the task force recommendations at a regularly scheduled meeting of the management team and determine which recommendations to endorse.

Analysis

Task force recommendations must be handled carefully. The task force has a high expectation that its recommendations will be implemented, yet the recommendations must receive the approval and support of management before they are carried out. This difference between a recommendation and a decision must constantly be maintained.

1. Meeting with the operations manager is necessary to gain his approval and support before any of the task force recommendations can be pursued. Score 5 points if you listed this as step 3, 3 points for step 2, and 1 point for listing it anywhere else.

2. It is premature to meet with the personnel manager. Ralph needs the operations manager's endorsement before moving ahead. Deduct 2 points if you listed this step in your sequence.

3. It is premature to meet with the maintenance manager. As with the changes in personnel practices, Ralph needs the operations manager's endorsement before moving ahead. Deduct 2 points if you listed this step in your sequence.

4. It is within Ralph's authority to request Joe Helm to initiate a study of maintenance procedures. However, the timing must be handled so as not to indicate rejection of the task force recommendation before it is discussed with the task force. Score 5 points if you listed this as step 4 and score 2 points if you listed it anywhere else in your sequence.

5. A meeting with the task force should be the first step Ralph takes after reading the report. At this time he should thank the members for their efforts, discuss in depth the reasons underlying the recommendations, give his general reaction to each, and outline his procedure for moving forward with the recommendations that the management team endorses. Score 10 points if you listed this as step 1 in your sequence and 5 points if you listed it anywhere else.

6. This is a necessary step in order to include team members in the decision regarding which recommendations to endorse. Score 5 points if you listed this as the second step in your sequence, 3 points if you listed it first, and 2 points if you listed it anywhere else.

The first three steps Ralph should take are

- Meet with the task force and discuss its recommendations
- Discuss the task force report with the management team and decide which recommendations to endorse
- Meet with the operations manager to pass on the report and the management team's endorsements

Decision 9—Reviewing a Disciplinary Recommendation

One evening Ralph is telephoned at home by Bill Wilson. Bill reports that during the meal break six of the employees on his shift were playing poker. It seemed to be a friendly game at first, with only nickels and dimes being bet. However, two of the players got into an argument, tempers flared, and a fight erupted. With the help of a few others, things were quieted down and everyone is now back at work. Bill asks Ralph what he should do.

Gambling on company property has long been against company rules. Likewise, fighting is clearly against the rules. In discussing alternatives with Bill Wilson, the following list of options were developed. Which one should Ralph approve at this time?

1. Send all six employees home immediately to await further investigation and a final decision.
2. Send the two employees who started the fight home immediately to await further investigation and a final decision.
3. Since everyone is back at work, do nothing at this time.
4. Advise the two who started the fight that the incident will be reviewed with management at the earliest opportunity for a final decision. In the meantime, continue to work as scheduled.
5. Advise all six that the incident will be reviewed with management at the earliest opportunity for a final decision. In the meantime, continue to work as scheduled.

6. Post a bulletin board notice restating the company rules against gambling and fighting and emphasize that they will be strictly enforced in the future.

7. Advise all six that the incident will be reviewed with management at the earliest opportunity for a final decision. In the meantime, the four not involved in the fight should continue to work as scheduled; however, the two involved in the fight are not to report for work until advised to do so.

Analysis

A violation of company rules requires an immediate response from management. However, care must be exercised in order to ensure fair treatment. To be fair, an investigation should be made into the extent to which the gambling rule has in the past gone unenforced, both in this department and others. Likewise, extenuating circumstances that may have led up to the fighting incident should be investigated.

1. Since everyone is back at work it doesn't appear reasonable to pull them off their jobs and send them home. Score 0 for this option.

2. As with option 1, it doesn't seem reasonable to take the two employees who were involved in the fight off their jobs and send them home. If there is continued evidence of hostility between them, such as abusive language, they should be sent home immediately since they would become a substantial disruption on the shift. However, there is no evidence of this type of behavior. Score 2 points for this option.

3. Doing nothing at this time is the worst alternative Ralph could take. This type of incident cannot be ignored, and the people involved are entitled to know what course of action will be taken. Deduct 2 points if you chose this option.

4. Advising only the two employees who started the fight that the incident will be reviewed with management for a final decision is a step in the right direction, but it ignores the need for considering discipline for all six of

the employees involved. Allowing them to continue working as scheduled is reasonable if there is no further evidence of hostility. Score 3 points for this option.

5. Advising all six employees that the incident will be reviewed with management for a final decision at the earliest opportunity is a reasonable way to proceed at this time. Allowing them to continue working also seems reasonable under the circumstances. Score 5 points for this option.

6. Posting a bulletin board notice restating the rules against gambling and fighting with notice of intent to enforce the rules may be appropriate after investigation, if the company previously has been lax about enforcing them. However, such action is premature at this time. Score 0 points for this option.

7. Advising all six employees that the incident will be reviewed with management for a final decision and allowing only the four not involved in the fight to continue working as scheduled clearly separates the two rules violations into categories of severity. Score 10 points if you chose this option.

Results of Investigation

The next day Ralph talked with the other three operations supervisors, the personnel manager, and the operations manager. As a result of these discussions, he found that there was no evidence of gambling on company property being overlooked. The rules were well known by all employees and had been diligently enforced by management to the best of everyone's knowledge. During the past five years, two similar incidents had occurred, and the employees involved were all given written reprimands. Fighting was an even less common occurrence. No one could remember any incident of this nature.

Ralph asked Bill Wilson to phone the two employees involved in the fight and get a statement from them about what had happened. After talking to them, Bill reported that one had accused the other of cheating, and they got into an argument. Neither was sure who took the first swing. Later, after work, it was proven that there had been no cheating. Both employees were sorry the incident had occurred. They had been friends for a long time, and each still considered the other to be a friend.

What disciplinary action do you think Ralph should approve for the employees involved in this incident? None of them have any prior record of disciplinary action against them. They all knew the rules.

Analysis

Some disciplinary action is warranted in order to maintain the integrity of the rules. However, the good record of each of the people involved calls for a modest penalty to be imposed.

1. Those not involved in the fight should be given written reprimands for violating the existing rule against gambling on company property. Score 5 points if you recommended this action. Score 3 points if you recommended oral reprimands; score 2 points if you recommended one-day disciplinary suspensions and 0 points for any other recommendations.

2. Those involved in the fight should receive more severe discipline. Score 5 points if you recommended disciplinary suspensions of 1 to 3 days; score 3 points if you recommended written reprimands and 0 points for any other recommendations.

Discipline problems can vary widely depending on the nature of the infraction, its severity, and the records of the employees involved. However, the basic procedure for dealing with them is as follows.

- Move promptly on disciplinary matters.
- Investigate thoroughly to verify knowledge of the rule violated, that enforcement of the rule is not overlooked on occasion, the role each employee played in the infraction, the record of the individuals involved, and any other extenuating circumstances that may exist.
- Be fair and objective in decisions.
- Obtain appropriate approvals before moving ahead.

Decision 10—Making Salary Recommendations

It has been nearly a year since Ralph Brown was promoted to production manager at the Bayou Plant. His management team is working well. The department, as a whole, has met its goals. Morale is high, particularly after several of the recommendations of the productivity task force were implemented. Ralph looks back on his first year as a manager with well-deserved pride and looks forward to his future with confidence.

At this time of year, performance evaluations are completed on all staff and salary recommendations for the next year are prepared. The salary administration guidelines Ralph received from the operations manager set a merit forecast budget of 9 percent with individual merit increases ranging from 5 to 15 percent. Of course not everyone need be forecasted for an increase, if performance during the year does not merit one. An economic adjustment of 5 percent is built into the merit increase budget.

Below are summaries of Ralph's performance evaluations for his staff. What percent salary increase (between 5 and 15 percent) do you think Ralph should give each? Making administrative decisions is covered in chapter 7 (step 5 of the Performance Management System).

1. Bill Wilson.   Bill equalled or exceeded all of the goals set for his shift. Also, his handling of the gambling incident added to the continued respect he enjoys from the people of his shift. Bill's overall performance evaluation is *exceeds job requirements*. Because of Bill's performance history and length of service as a supervisor, his salary is currently at the maximum salary authorized for the classification.

2. John Smith.   John met all the goals set for his shift. In addition, he made a significant contribution as a member of the productivity task force. John's overall performance evaluation is *exceeds job requirements*. Because of his performance history and length of service as a supervisor, he too is currently at the maximum salary authorized for the classification.

3. Harry Jones.   Harry ended the year meeting the goals for his shift. He started off without gains in production volume, absenteeism, or turnover. However, with personal counseling and coaching from Ralph he was able to turn things around and finish the year on target. His overall performance evaluation is *meets all job requirements.*

4. Grace Parker.   Following the completion of her assignment on the productivity task force, Ralph promoted Grace to production supervisor, replacing Sam Gardner. She has only been in the assignment four months but tremendous gains have already been made with the shift. Levels of absenteeism and turnover are on target, production quality is on target, but production volume will not meet its goal primarily because of the deficit she inherited from Sam. Grace's overall performance evaluation is *meets all job requirements.*

5. Sam Gardner.   Sam replaced Grace Parker as production scheduler four months ago. He has learned the duties of the new job in less time than expected and seems to enjoy the administrative nature of the assignment. Sam's overall performance evaluation in his current assignment is *meets all job requirements.* The production supervisor job is one salary grade higher than production scheduler. When Sam was reassigned, his salary was not adjusted downward, so that he currently is earning 15 percent over the established maximum for the production scheduler classification.

6. Joe Helm.   Joe met all the goals set for his part of department operations. In addition, he made a significant contribution as a member of the productivity task force. Joe's overall performance evaluation is *exceeds job requirements.*

7. Jerry Olson.   Following individual counseling and coaching by Ralph, Jerry has shown improvement as a safety representative. He has begun to broaden his range of involvement; however, he has not met some of the goals set at the beginning of the period. Ralph has confidence that Jerry will be able to show significant gains in performance next year. Jerry's overall performance evaluation is *meets most job requirements.*

8. Vern Johnson. Vern is the newest member of Ralph's staff. He was promoted to the position of operating assistant from lead operator six months ago. He has shown a high level of interest in the assignment, has done well on assignments he's been given, but has not been exposed to all of the job demands. Ralph evaluates his overall performance as *meets most job requirements.*

Analysis

Salary recommendations are determined, first of all, by considering performance, placement in the salary range available, and the authorized spending budget. These recommendations are then considered in light of whatever extenuating circumstances are appropriate. For example, did certain circumstances make it particularly easy or difficult to achieve the performance level during the performance period. Compare your recommendations to the following.

1. Bill Wilson is performing at a level that exceeds job requirements. However, he's currently enjoying the maximum salary authorized for his position. Therefore, a 5 percent increase would be in order to pass on to him the economic adjustment built into the merit increase budget.

2. John Smith is also exceeding job requirements. He too is enjoying the maximum salary authorized for his position. A 5 percent increase is in order to pass on to him the economic adjustment built into the merit increase budget.

3. Harry Jones meets all requirements of his job and is thereby recommended for a 10 percent increase in salary. No circumstances were detailed to warrant either an upward or downward adjustment in the basic increase.

4. Grace Parker was promoted to production supervisor four months ago. She meets all requirements of her job and, in addition, has made a substantial improvement in the poor situation she took over. A 15 percent increase is

recommended for her to reinforce and reward the gains she has made on her shift.

5. Sam Gardner is currently meeting all the requirements of his job since his reassignment. However, his salary is above the authorized maximum for his position so no increase is recommended until the authorized maximum salary becomes greater than his current salary.

6. Joe Helm exceeds job requirements and is therefore recommended for a 15 percent increase in salary. No extenuating circumstances were presented to moderate this amount.

7. Jerry Olson only meets most job requirements. Ralph is confident for the future and therefore should continue to coach Jerry on the full duties of his assignment. However, he should not reinforce Jerry's performance with an average or better merit increase. Therefore a 5 percent increase is recommended for Jerry.

8. Vern Johnson is new to the job of operating assistant and currently meets most job requirements. This is the most one could expect after only six months in the position. Therefore a salary increase of 10 percent is recommended to reward performance and reinforce the effort put into learning the job.

Score your recommendations as follows:

- If you set up three levels of recommendations (5, 10, and 15 percent) matched to performance levels, give yourself 10 points.

- If you used the full range of possible increase (5 to 15 percent), score 2 additional points.

- If you gave extra consideration to Grace and Vern, score 3 additional points.

- If you gave Bill and John the 5 percent economic adjustment built into the merit budget, score 5 points.

- If your total recommended increases were within $\frac{1}{2}$ percent of the budget (but did not exceed budget) score 5 points.

Overall Scoring for the Case Study

After adding up all the points you achieved on the ten decisions, compare your total to the table below to see how you did.

201–230	Outstanding
151–200	Excellent
100–150	Satisfactory
0–99	Poor

Career Planning Guide

Now that you have studied the steps involved in effective supervision, consider your own situation. Where do you want to go and what steps must you take to get there. In today's world there is much more career freedom than most realize. Few, however, take advantage of this freedom. Many let their futures be determined by happenstance rather than take an active role in shaping their careers. Assuming you'd like to have some say about your career, the following career planning guide will help you take a look at what is important to you and how you can work toward an objective that will net you the most satisfaction from your career.

Identifying Your Career Objective

Step 1   Look back over your career and list three or four experiences that provided you the greatest satisfaction and briefly describe why you felt good about each one.

Step 2   List three or four career experiences that provided you the greatest dissatisfaction and briefly describe why you felt bad about each one.

Step 3   Examine the information you came up with in steps 1 and 2, and considering other insights about yourself, list the conditions that must be satisfied in order for you to see your career as successful. (Examples: work location, type of work, extent of freedom, etc.).

Step 4   Look into the future. What would you like to do with your career? What type of work would you like to be doing ten years from now?

Step 5   Will achieving the objectives you listed in step 4 satisfy the conditions identified in step 3. If not, what else needs to be considered (i.e., supplementing career with avocational interests, modifying your career objective)?

Inventorying Your Skills

Step 1   List those things you do well.

Step 2   List those things you do poorly.

Step 3   Consider your career objective identified in the previous step 4 (under Identifying Your Career Objective) and list your strengths that can be used in attaining that position.

Step 4   List those things you now do poorly that must be improved in order to attain your career objective.

Action Planning

Good goals are

- *specific.* A good goal says exactly what you want to accomplish.
- *measurable.* Being specific helps make your goal measurable. You need something by which to gauge your progress and tell you when you've reached your goal.
- *action-oriented.* When expressing your goals, use statements that have active-tense verbs and are complete sentences.
- *realistic.* Good goals must be attainable yet should require you to do something that will allow you to grow and improve yourself.
- *time-limited.* You should not direct your goal to some vague future time but select and set a reasonable time limit in which to accomplish it.

Step 1   Identify two goals to work toward in developing strengths or overcoming weaknesses necessary to attaining your career objective.

Step 2   Identify the people whose help you need in order to reach your career objective.

Step 3   Identify the action steps necessary to achieve your career objective—strengths to develop, weaknesses to overcome, relationships to promote. Consider the resources at your disposal and potential barriers you may encounter. Set a target date for completing each action step.

"Career Planning Guide" adapted from Marion E. Haynes, *Stepping Up to Supervisor* (Tulsa, Ok.: PennWell Books, 1983). Used with permission.

Index